"Alfred Tauber offers us a lucid and satisfying presentation and comparison of William James's subjectivism—his study of experience itself—and Sigmund Freud's contrasting objectivism, in which the mind was understood as an entity separate from the observer. But Tauber is not satisfied with a mere comparison: he shows us why and how these differences have *mattered*—in both intellectual and social/political life. The book is an eye-opener; it is downright exciting—perhaps especially for psychoanalysts and psychoanalytic psychotherapists. How is it that this comparative study was not tackled until now?"

Donnel B. Stern, *William Alanson White Institute, New York University Postdoctoral Program in Psychoanalysis and Psychotherapy*

"*William James and Sigmund Freud on the Mind* is a startling original contribution, not only to the debates about human psychology and subjectivity, but also to the role that 'American pragmatism' has had in shaping our understanding of the world about us. If the debate seems to be between Freud and James about whether science can define the essence of the human, it is also about how the claims about individual autonomy, often seen as the hallmark of American pragmatism, has come—for good or for ill—to define our modernity. Alfred I. Tauber's writing is clear and crisp—forcing us to ask how much our understanding of ourselves is embedded in what we define as 'human.'"

Sander L. Gilman, *author of* Freud, Race, and Gender

William James and Sigmund Freud on the Mind

This is the first extended study comparing the philosophies of mind promoted by Sigmund Freud and William James, whose opposing views had profound influences on the development of twentieth-century philosophy, cognitive science, and psychology.

Each asked, can the mind be scientifically characterized? While Freud thought that psychoanalysis had established a science of the mind, James maintained that the subjective could not be objectified, and psychology was left with only "the crumbs" of analysis. Tauber's presentation of a conjured philosophical confrontation occasioned by their first and only meeting in 1909 uncovers the clashing philosophies of mind underlying their respective positions. In comparing their opposing portraits of the psyche, persistent questions about self-knowledge, personal identity, and moral agency are presented at their fin de siècle origin. In this setting, the James-Freud dispute offers a unique perspective about our own contemporary dilemmas swirling around selfhood, consciousness, and the subjectivity of human experience.

This eclectic history of early psychology will interest psychoanalysts, psychologists, and philosophers as well as those interested in the origins of pragmatism, phenomenology, modernism, and twentieth-century positivism.

Alfred I. Tauber, Professor Emeritus of Philosophy and Zoltan Kohn Professor Emeritus of Medicine, Boston University, has extensively published in philosophy and history of science that include philosophical critiques of psychoanalysis and Freud's contemporary significance in *Freud, the Reluctant Philosopher* (2010) and *Requiem for the Ego: Freud and the Origins of Postmodernism* (2013).

Philosophy & Psychoanalysis Book Series
Series Editor
Jon Mills

Philosophy & Psychoanalysis is dedicated to current developments and cutting-edge research in the philosophical sciences, phenomenology, hermeneutics, existentialism, logic, semiotics, cultural studies, social criticism, and the humanities that engage and enrich psychoanalytic thought through philosophical rigor. With the philosophical turn in psychoanalysis comes a new era of theoretical research that revisits past paradigms while invigorating new approaches to theoretical, historical, contemporary, and applied psychoanalysis. No subject or discipline is immune from psychoanalytic reflection within a philosophical context including psychology, sociology, anthropology, politics, the arts, religion, science, culture, physics, and the nature of morality. Philosophical approaches to psychoanalysis may stimulate new areas of knowledge that have conceptual and applied value beyond the consulting room reflective of greater society at large. In the spirit of pluralism, *Philosophy & Psychoanalysis* is open to any theoretical school in philosophy and psychoanalysis that offers novel, scholarly, and important insights in the way we come to understand our world.

William James and Sigmund Freud on the Mind

Saving Subjectivity

Alfred I. Tauber

Routledge
Taylor & Francis Group

LONDON AND NEW YORK

Designed cover image: © Wellcome Collection.

First published 2025
by Routledge
4 Park Square, Milton Park, Abingdon, Oxon OX14 4RN

and by Routledge
605 Third Avenue, New York, NY 10158

Routledge is an imprint of the Taylor & Francis Group, an informa business

© 2025 Alfred I. Tauber

British Library Cataloguing-in-Publication Data
A catalogue record for this book is available from the British Library

ISBN: 978-1-032-93332-0 (hbk)
ISBN: 978-1-032-90036-0 (pbk)
ISBN: 978-1-003-56541-3 (ebk)

DOI: 10.4324/9781003565413

Typeset in Times New Roman
by Apex CoVantage, LLC

To the memory of Hilary Putnam

"I went in search of myself"

—Heraclitus

"The destiny of the soul can never be studied by the reason—for its modes are not extatic—In the wisest calculation or demonstration I but play a game with myself—I am not to be taken captive by myself."

—Henry David Thoreau
(*Journal*, April 3, 1842)

Contents

Acknowledgements

This study of James and Freud owes its germ of inception to Jon Mills, who invited me to contribute to the Routledge series on Freud and philosophy he edits. Through his generous encouragement, Jon reactivated circuits I thought dormant by reminding me that my studies of psychoanalysis were incomplete. Where I had previously argued the philosophical weaknesses of Freud's theory (Tauber 2013a), I still sought a psychology with different philosophical presuppositions. William James offered a notable alternative. I had sporadically thought about James since reading his *Pragmatism* in college and then writing my first philosophy book in which his characterization of cognition (not surprisingly, given his own biological orientation) strongly resonated with my own views about information processing in the immune system (Tauber 1994, 208–15). However, I had not delved into the deeper structure of his thought; Jon offered me the opportunity to do so. And I profess no small satisfaction with having discovered a personal resonance with James's odyssey.

The staff at Routledge were highly professional in launching *James and Freud*. The consideration shown me was evident from the earliest stages of the acquisition process and throughout the efficient production. Beginning with Katie Randall, who shepherded the manuscript through review, and then on to Rachel Cronin, who led the production staff with the able assistance of Kate Fronadel, the Project Manager, a warm partnership developed that I have not taken for granted. To each of them, I extend a heartfelt thank you.

I also thank the following publishers for permission to draw on earlier work: the description of Freud's representational theory of the mind (Chapter 2) is adapted from Tauber, A. I. 2015. "The other within: Freud's representation of the mind." In *Psychology and the Other*, D. Goodman and M. Freeman (eds.). Oxford: Oxford University Press, 71–93; the discussion of Freud's *das Ding* (Chapter 4) is modified from Tauber, A. I. 2013.

Requiem for the Ego: Freud and the Origins of Postmodernism. Stanford: Stanford University Press; the description of *das Ich* (Chapter 5) is based on Tauber, A. I. 2023. "The psychoanalytic *das Ich*: Lost in translation." In *The Routledge Handbook of Psychoanalysis and Philosophy*, A. Govrin and T. Caspi (eds.). New York, NY and Abingdon, Oxon: Routledge, 359–73; and Freud's portrait of moral agency (Chapter 6) draws from Tauber, A. I. 2025. "Freud and the problem of moral agency." In *Sigmund Freud as a Critical Social Theorist: Psychoanalysis and the Neurotic in Contemporary Society*, D. J. Byrd and S. J. Miri (eds.). Chicago, IL: Haymarket, 321–49.

At various stages of writing *James and Freud,* I have discussed its developing ideas with friends and colleagues, most prominently Hilary Putnam. Richard Adler, Lydie Fialova, Menachem Fisch, Snait Gissis, Mark Kaplan, David Kazhdan, Victor Kestenbaum, Jane Kite, Margaret Paternek, Jay Pomrenze, Jonathan Price, Benjamin Tauber, and Ingrid Tauber have listened patiently as I struggled to find the conceptual handles of this study. And in the course of the book's evolution, the critical insights and the support of my wife, Paula Fredriksen, always steadied me as I dealt with the indecisions and doubts that plague any serious project such as this one. Paula is an astute critic and consistently prompts me to reconsider what seems so obvious. Indeed, she is my most cherished interlocutor. To each of these family, friends, and colleagues, I offer my heartfelt thanks. However, my deepest gratitude is reserved for Hilary Putnam, to whom this book is dedicated. His humane vision and ceaseless movement of thought assumed no resting place, and he thus exemplified the pursuit of wisdom. One could ask for no better friend and mentor. May his memory be a blessing.

Preface

When Anna Freud presented her book, *The Ego and Mechanisms of Defense* (1936) to her father, she inscribed a telling dedication: "Writing books as the supreme defense mechanism against all dangers from within and without" (Meyer-Palmedo 2014, 10). If writing is "scholarship as self-knowledge" a defense mechanism, so be it (Tauber 2022, 10ff.). Certainly, my engagement with Freud has been complex enough to warrant that charge. Indeed, to revisit his work with a third monograph suggests that I had left my previous excavations incomplete.

In *Freud, the Reluctant Philosopher* (2010), having discarded the psychic mechanisms Freud had posited and showing that his inference of the Unconscious was viciously circular, I maintained he still held abiding significance by refashioning personal identity and moral agency. However, I remained dissatisfied. Psychoanalytic self-reflection *of* ourselves *to* ourselves could not be sustained by the Cartesian subject-object metaphysics undergirding the theory. I realized Freud had committed "modernity's mistake" by attempting to objectify what is beyond scientific reach. My argument in *Requiem for the Ego* (2013a) built upon the critiques of Freud's most prominent philosophical interlocutors, Theodor Adorno, Ludwig Wittgenstein, and Martin Heidegger (soon followed by Jacques Lacan and several French postmodernists). Their collective assault on Freudianism focused on his representational model of the mind and the conceits of such a model (Tauber 2013a). Freud exhibited the "scar of representation" that these critics regarded as a kind of epistemological imprisonment or, more modestly, veil of obstruction (Colebrook 2005). I explored how their deconstructive critique of the psychoanalytic *ego* rendered the authority of one's own self-knowledge shattered (Tauber 2013a). Freud thus suffered Robespierre's fate. Although he utterly defrocked the Enlightenment (Kantian) ego of its autonomy, that formulation was further undermined by later philosophical attacks, leaving the *ego* to celebrate a second funeral.

Here I return to the origins of what became the conundrum left in the wake of these developments—namely, given the demise of the Cartesian-Kantian ego, how, then, to construe an inner life that resists representation and therefore articulation? While giving up one way of thinking and adopting another may be beneficial, Wittgenstein asked the key question, does that process reveal the *workings* of the mind? "Can we say we have laid bare the essential nature of mind?" (Wittgenstein 1960, 45). The Freudian evidence (at best) attests only to the effectiveness of the analyst to help reconfigure the analysand's life narrative, to create a new "myth" of *me* subject not to Oedipal fate but to psychic determinism (Wittgenstein 1960, 51; Tauber 2013a, 178). Is there another portrayal in which agency might be depicted?

More than a decade had passed since writing *Requiem of the Ego* when I realized that I had left much of the Freud story unaccounted—namely, what would be required to construct an alternate psychology given the philosophical weaknesses of psychoanalytic theory and the distortions that follow? On what basis would a psychology be erected to support *das Ich, the I*? Who had undertaken such an audacious venture? Moreover, what lessons might be applied if a revisionary psychology could be established? In short, from the ruins of a defrocked theory, whose Phoenix would rise from the Freudian ashes?

I cannot fully reconstruct how I focused my renewed inquiry on William James other than to note that my friendship with Hilary Putnam led me to more carefully examine his disputes with Richard Rorty, who in turn directed me to John Dewey, and from there James's importance clearly re-emerged. I had previously seen James as an exemplar of early phenomenology (Tauber 1994, 208–15), but when I again studied his writings, the issue of pragmatic truth dominated my interest. However, I soon realized that pragmatism as such was subordinate to a much deeper revision of metaphysics that spawned his views on consciousness and its eventual replacement with what he called "pure experience." Once I grasped the epic attack on dualism James had launched, his singular contributions to the constellation of questions I had dealt with in my earlier critique of psychoanalytic theory became apparent. Specifically, whereas *Requiem of the Ego* offered an analysis of Freud's philosophy of mind, a constructive alternative awaited further elaboration. James provides that path forward.

Freud and James first (and last) met at a 1909 psychology conference held at Clark University, less than a year before the American died. The psychoanalyst came to receive his only honorary doctorate, and while cordially welcomed, James called him a "*halluciné*." Their respective views of mental life conflicted at any juncture one might want to probe their thought:

philosophy, philosophy of science, metaphysics of free will, consciousness, psychotherapy, emotion, moral agency, the *self*, and religion. Most tellingly, Freud's promotion of *the* unconscious would have quickly led to the substratum of their conflicting philosophies.

James had attacked the very notion of the unconscious as some entity or even a domain subject to study (summarized in *Principles of Psychology*, 1890), and certainly by 1909 he had dismissed characterizing consciousness altogether and thus, even more so, unconsciousness as Freud had depicted it. As James wrote in *Varieties of Religious Experience* in 1902, the "subliminal" is real, but inaccessible to scientific study and objectification (James 1987f, 384, 433–4). James fails to cite Freud, and he actually admonishes the use of "the unconscious" as a "misnomer" to be "better replaced by the vaguer term 'subconscious' or 'subliminal'" (James 1987f, 193). Moreover, he was dismissive of the sexual basis of unconscious mentation (James 1987f, 18)

These obvious differences are but the tips of the iceberg of their philosophical disparities, a divergence that reverberates throughout their respective writings and more widely into the universe of ideas. Their meeting poses a dramatic setting for contrasting two theories of the mind based in radically different philosophies, whose metaphysical systems, the psychologies they generated, and the ethics that they spawned continue to vie in our own era. So, while their most obvious connection concerns their contrasting views of the unconscious (e.g., Myers 1986, 1990; Weinberger 2000; Klein 2020) and perhaps some unacknowledged similarities (E. T. Weber 2012; Colapietro 2022), that issue only points to a deeper chasm separating them and thus comprises a minor element of a much bigger story.

While Eugene Taylor (1999) charted the professional web in which Freud and James worked, and others (e.g., Ellenberger 1970; Koch and Leary 1992) have provided wider historical perspectives on the development of nineteenth-century psychology, few have directly compared and contrasted these pioneers of psychology. In the 1960s, David Shakow and David Rapaport (1964) suggested that James's adoption of Darwinism and his advocacy for a functional dynamic psychology contributed to American receptivity to Freudianism. And Taylor significantly extended this perspective by firmly placing James within the psychological milieu in which he would have shared interests with Freud, i.e., psychopathology and abnormal psychological states (E. Taylor 1983, 1996). However, despite the crossovers Taylor identified, by and large the biographical and, more importantly, the professional intersections between Freud and James were, at best, tangential. And as for their different theories of the mind, only the question of the unconscious draws ready comparison and comment.

Those who have contributed to this comparative scholarship have, by and large, pursued their studies in terms of the conflicting psychological theories adopted by our protagonists, whereas *James and Freud on the Mind* focuses on the divergent metaphysics that directed their respective philosophies of mind. Freud followed the dominant scientific principles of his era and presented an early form of the cognitivist program, while James portrayed the mental phenomenologically. And while Freud believed that he had successfully launched a novel "science of the mind," James held a skeptical view of such approaches, believing that "the mass of our thinking vanishes forever, beyond hope of recovery, and psychology only gathers up a few of the crumbs that fall from the feast" (James 1983, 266). James was referring to the residue of the subjective left by the erstwhile efforts to objectify the psyche, a misappropriation he sought to rectify. In sum, the major theme explored here is that the James-Freud confrontation formed along the battle lines of how the *personal* (and the subjective, more specifically) are to be understood philosophically—either in objective terms as Freud ventured, or as James would allow it to reside *sui generis*. Simply, psychoanalytic theory objectified emotion, while James's crafted a philosophy to save subjectivity.

Here, in my conjured philosophical confrontation, James challenges Freud not only by exposing the conceits of introspection, but by rejecting the determinism embedded in psychoanalytic theory. He did so not by philosophical argument (which Freud would have ignored in any case), but rather by exercising a moral choice. James's "freedom of the will" required revising the underlying metaphysics that drove Freud to his pessimistic conclusions and undergirded his scientific conceits. James's critique goes well beyond pushing Freudianism further into insolvency, for a more profound imperative beckons. He presented a philosophy to contest positivism's infiltration into all the crevices of human self-appraisal. With the ascendancy of a relentless scientism, James elaborated a countermanding response that inflected modern thought both directly through wide dissemination of his ideas and via those who soon followed to further develop his ideas (e.g., Dewey [1931, 1984], Whitehead [1967], and Wittgenstein [Goodman 2007]). And beyond his profound impact on twentieth-century philosophy, James's humanist advocacy of pluralism and pragmatism had broad cultural repercussions as well (e.g., Posnock 1991, 1997; Diggins 1994; Hickman 2007). And in parallel, Freud's impact can hardly be overstated, which (according to the critique presented here) succeeded despite its philosophical failings by providing a compelling modern myth to reconceive personal identity in which "all that is solid melts into air" (Berman 1982, 15).

How one understands the radical break in Western consciousness they inaugurated—Freud by dethroning the autonomous ego, and James by revamping notions of truth and moral agency—begins with the genesis of their ideas. After all, Freud's "hermeneutics of suspicion" launched the deconstruction of the ego (Ricoeur 1970), and as Richard Rorty observed, James (with Dewey) are waiting at the end of the road upon which the postmodernists have been traveling as they answered Freud's provocations (Rorty 1982, xviii; Hickman 2007). Because the "crisis of modernity" they faced remains our own, their story is compelling. So, let us begin, as many good tales do, with the end.

Avaloch Farm
Boscawen, New Hampshire

Introduction

The Conference on Psychology and Pedagogy, held at Clark University in Worcester, Massachusetts, began on Labor Day 1909 and served as Freud's in-person introduction to American psychologists, most notably William James, Edward B. Titchener, and G. Stanley Hall (Koelsch 1970; Evans and Koelsch 1985; Rosenzweig 1994, 171–4).[1] The occasion formally introduced psychoanalysis to America, Freud having quipped to Carl Jung on his arrival in New York harbor, "They don't realize we're bringing them the plague" (Lacan 2006, 336). A therapeutic rebuttal awaited the psychoanalysts, although they had not appreciated how Dr. William James had fully developed a philosophy that would challenge psychoanalysis at its very foundations. Instead of Freud's attempt to construct "a science of the mind," James discarded the effort, altogether. Why is the subject of this essay.

Freud regarded his American visit as an auspicious event. Having been prominently placed amongst leading figures in orthodox experimental psychology, he found a legitimatization Europeans denied him.

> In Europe I felt as though I were despised; but over there [America] I found myself received by the foremost men as an equal. As I stepped onto the platform at Worcester to deliver my *Five Lectures on Psycho-Analysis* it seemed like the realization of some incredible day-dream: psychoanalysis was no longer a product of delusion, it had become a valuable part of reality.
>
> (Freud 1925a, 52)

The honorary Doctorate of Laws and Letters recognized Freud as the "founder of a school of pedagogy already rich in new methods and achievements, leader today among students of the psychology of sex, and of psychotherapy and analysis, doctor of laws" (Hall papers, quoted by Evans and Koelsch 1985, 946). The five lectures Freud delivered in German had been improvised without notes, and later published in similar form and content (Freud 1910).[2]

> Jung had suggested that Freud lecture on the interpretation of dreams, but Freud later accepted Ernest Jones' advice to choose a broader subject. The five lectures were devoted to an account of the development of Freud's own work and to an exploration of such concepts as free association, dream interpretation, repression, hysteria, infantile sexuality, and neurosis. . . . [He] closed the series with a defense of psychoanalysis against the charge that its therapeutic method became socially dangerous by calling repressed material into the realm of consciousness.
>
> (Koelsch 1970)

Historical accounts agree that Freud was well-received but his audience hardly appreciated the significance of his visit.[3] While this would be the only honorary doctorate he ever received, it represents an inflection point in the global expansion of psychoanalysis, the historic origin of what became a predominant model of the mind in Western culture.[4]

Well beyond a theory or a therapeutic modality, the psychoanalytic model has framed fundamental notions of personal identity and moral agency, as well as impacting philosophy of mind, ethics, literary criticism, and social theory. Recognizing the limits of thought and the extent of faulty reasoning, the influence of unrecognized emotion, and the determinism of unconscious motivation, Freud authored a "hermeneutics of suspicion" that has come to dominate Western notions of self-knowledge (Ricoeur 1970; Scott-Bauman 2009). We are Freudians in the sense of how we consider our own motivations, values, and choices with a jaundiced eye. Indeed, Dr. Freud has attained widespread acceptance as a diagnostician of the Western malady (however defined) and thus an authority of doubt that so pervades postmodern culture. Considering such wide influence, can Freud rightly claim to personify the response to Nietzsche's call, "Where are the new physicians of the soul?" (Nietzsche 1982, 33). At least one in that Clark audience, William James, would contest awarding that title and with it the entire Freudian construct.

James attended only the fourth day of lectures (September 10) and commented on the afternoon papers (Freud spoke in the morning [Evans and Koelsch 1985]), and then joined the well-known group photograph. Freud altered the order of the published lectures so that James heard only about free association and the theory of dreams; James departed the next day to attend a funeral (James 1986a, 521; Rosenzweig 1994, 125). Although he apparently spent some time talking with Jung, whom he apparently liked,

Figure 0.1 Hall is in the center of the honorees, who all stand in the front row. To his left, Freud, Jung, Adolph Meyer (psychiatrist, Johns Hopkins Medical School), and Herbert S. Jennings (biologist, Johns Hopkins Medical School); to his right stand honorees Leo Burgerstein (Vienna hygienist), William Stern (psychologist, Breslau), William James (not an honoree), Titchener (Cornell psychologist and coeditor, *American Journal of Psychology*) and Boas (anthropologist, Columbia University) (Harris 2010).

the single private conversation with Freud occurred during their walk to the railway station for James's return to Cambridge. What they discussed is unrecorded. James, already suffering heart disease, died the next year.

Upon returning to Cambridge, James made a few cursory comments that seemingly harbored doubts about the Viennese venture. In a letter to Mary Calkins (Professor at Wellesley College), James wrote,

I strongly suspect Freud, with his dream theory, of being a regular *halluciné* [deluded individual]. But I hope that he and his disciples will push it to its limits as undoubtedly it covers some facts, and will add to our understanding of "functional psychology."

(Rosenzweig 1994, 174)

And to Theodore Flournoy, he wrote similarly:

> I hope that Freud and his pupils will push their ideas to their utmost lim-
> its so that we may learn what they are. They can't fail to throw light on
> human nature, but I confess that he made on me personally the impres-
> sion of a man obsessed with fixed ideas. I can make nothing in my own
> case with his dream theories, and obviously "symbolism" is the most
> dangerous method.
>
> (Rosenzweig 1994, 174)

The interpersonal dynamics were probably strained. Hall insisted that
Freud and James had not been congenial, and that James referred to Freud
as a "dirty fellow" (Hale 1971, 18). Nevertheless, James took Freud's
young protégé, Ernest Jones, aside and declared, "The future of psychology
belongs to your work" (Jones 1955, 57). James was noted for his generos-
ity, but we need not speculate about his motives or sincerity. Fifteen years
before, he had passed judgment on Freud's research, which at that time was
coauthored with Josef Breuer.[5]

James published the first American notice of Breuer and Freud's
work, "Ueber den psychischen Mechanismus hysterischer Phenömene"
(Breuer and Freud 1893) in the inaugural issue of *Psychological Review*
(March 1894). James

> concluded that Janet deserved all the credit for the most sophisticated
> articulation of the psychogenic hypothesis; that all Breuer and Freud did,
> at most, was provide corroboration for Janet's already old findings. Sec-
> ond, James reiterated his belief, but now to professionals in psychology,
> that these French and German sources clearly showed that the American
> mental healers had been practicing sound methods of scientific psycho-
> therapy all along.
>
> (E. Taylor 1996, 52)

Moreover, James observed that

> the two "distinguished Viennese neurologists . . . stumbled accidently on
> cures which enable them not only to give a general formula for the dis-
> ease, but a general method for its treatment." James then alluded to the
> mechanism where shocking memories fall into the subconscious and can
> be discovered only in hypnoid states. The cure, according to Breuer and
> Freud, James said, is to draw out the psychic traumata in hypnotism, and
> "let them produce all their emotional effects, however violent, and *work*

themselves off [James's italics]. They make then (apparently) a new connection with the principal consciousness, whose breach is thus restored, and the sufferer gets well."

(E. Taylor 1996, 54)

Taylor goes on to emphasize James's reservations:

Here, at least, is the germ of Freud's doctrine of abreaction, [but] Breuer and Freud neglected to tell us just how, then, the breach is restored, and this is likely the meaning of James's use of the adverb "apparently," to describe the alleged new connection.

(E. Taylor 1996, 54)

However, James missed a critical aspect of the Breuer-Freud report, namely their insistence that the hysterical symptoms were not "protean" and random but were precipitated by the trauma either directly or symbolically, which then led James's friend, James Francis Putnam, to note that the morbid ideation could be traced back to their original source (Hale 1971, 1983–4). In the 1909 Clark lectures, Freud referred to Breuer and the "talking cure" (so aptly noted by the patient, "Anna O." [Bertha Pappenheim] [Breuer and Freud 1895, 30]) as the fundamental work that launched psychoanalysis.

James's interest in Freud's work grew, and by 1896, in a Lowell Lecture on psychopathology, James offered a more generous appraisal to this early report: "In the relief of certain hysterias by handling the buried idea, whether as in Freud or in Janet, we see a portent of the possible usefulness of these new discoveries. The awful becomes relatively trivial" (Perry 1935, II:123; cited by Hale 1971, 128). And then in the Gifford Lectures (1901–1902), James expressed greater enthusiasm for the vistas opened by hypnosis and, tellingly, the potentials of opening the depth of the psyche:

In the wonderful explorations by Binet, Janet, Breuer, Freud, Mason, Prince, and others, of the subliminal consciousness of patients with hysteria, we have revealed to us whole systems of underground life, in the shape of memories of a painful sort which lead a parasitic existence, buried outside of the primary fields of consciousness, and making irruptions thereinto with hallucinations, pains, convulsions, paralyses of feeling and of motion, and the whole procession of symptoms of hysteric disease of body and of mind. Alter or abolish by suggestion these subconscious memories, and the patient immediately gets well. His symptoms were automatisms, in Mr. Myers's sense of the word. These clinical records sound like fairy-tales when one first reads them, yet it is impossible to

doubt their accuracy; and, the path having been once opened by these
first observers, similar observations have been made elsewhere. They
throw, as I said, a wholly new light upon our natural constitution.

(James 1987f, 217)

And what did Freud think of James? Freud cites James only once in
reference to the James-Lange theory of emotions (see the discussion of the
affects later in Chapter 4), but quickly dismisses it as irrelevant to psychoanalysts (Freud 1916, 396). However, in his *Autobiographical Study*, Freud
wrote fondly of his colleague:

Another event of this time which made a lasting impression on me was
a meeting with William James the *philosopher*. I shall never forget one
little scene that occurred as we were on a walk together. He stopped
suddenly, handed me a bag he was carrying and asked me to walk on,
saying that he would catch me up as soon as he had got through an attack
of angina pectoris which was coming on. He died of that disease a year
later; and I have always wished that I might be as fearless as he was in
the face of approaching death.

(Freud 1925a, 52, emphasis added)

Note, he identified James as a philosopher, not a psychologist, and we have
no record of what he thought of James professionally, since by this time
Freud had discharged philosophers who equated the mind with consciousness. James had clearly stated by 1890 his rejection of the unconscious (discussed later in this Introduction), albeit (as already mentioned) he would
eventually acknowledge what he called subconscious mentation. So, while
Freud must have recognized James as a pioneering psychologist, by the
time they met, James had passed well beyond that orbit of interest. Indeed,
a far deeper gulf separated James and Freud than their respective views of
the psychoanalytic theory of the unconscious.

Outline of a profound dispute

Although James and Freud knew of each other and had more than a passing
knowledge of the other's work, they had little direct exchange. Nevertheless, the parallels between James and Freud are noteworthy: each were at
the nexus of professional associations with rich cross-fertilizations; both
played a major role in the development of the academic fields of abnormal,
social, and personality psychologies, and by virtue of their respective clinical interests, each contributed to the development of modern psychotherapy

(E. Taylor 1999). However, while loosely affiliated professionally, it is difficult to imagine what they might have discussed during their sole short meeting. Nevertheless, we probe how our protagonists would place science and analytics (more generally) in their research programs to ask fundamental questions about the mind: can mental life be objectified? What is consciousness? To what extent do humans possess free will? These are the speculative issues framing this study, the first extended comparative examination of their respective theories. This conjured conversation assumes importance because the issues separating them led to major themes of twentieth-century philosophy, cognitive sciences, and psychology, which then extended well beyond academic discussions into the culture at large.

When Freud and James met, psychology—experimental, phenomenological, and psychoanalytic—had yet to set its disciplinary boundaries and struggled to sort the different philosophies of science competing for dominance. How various aspects of Freudian theory reflected the general scientific culture and attitudes of his intellectual milieu have been well described, and more specifically, the notion of psychic forces defining complex behavior conveys the general tenor of Freud's scientific thinking (Kitcher 1992). Although the neurological basis of consciousness remained well beyond *fin de siècle* science, he nevertheless attempted to extrapolate the neurophysiology of nerves to the global functions of the mind. While only tentative suggestions were made, traces of this unfulfilled ambition to reduce the mental to brain states remained embedded in his thought. From the earliest speculations and throughout his mature period, Freud was passionately committed to a scientific model that would mirror physics, the paragon of the natural sciences. As discussed in later chapters, he modeled psychic force fields on linear Newtonian mechanics governed by push-pull dynamics, again reflecting the extrapolation of physical phenomena to neurophysiology (Freud 1895).

Freud combined (some would say, conflated) two approaches to the mind—scientific and hermeneutical (Draenos 1982). Placing consciousness in a general neurophysiological paradigm invoked his commitments to naturalism; more specifically, he followed Helmholtz's theories of perception (Makari 1994). Accordingly, Freud characterized consciousness as a "sense organ for the perception of psychical qualities," which he trained on the subliminal, i.e., the unconscious (Freud 1900, 615; Laplanche and Pontalis 1973, 84–8; Natsoulas 1984, 1985).[6] Then, following the neuroanatomy lessons of his early laboratory research, he concocted a topography (ego, id, and superego) that metaphorically placed the psychoanalytic stratification of the mind in separate, adjoining spatial domains (Freud 1923a).[7] With the structural model in place, he then applied the same subject-object epistemology for perceiving nature to the assessment of psychic states. Accordingly, his positivism assumed a strict separation of the object scrutinized and the autonomous agent synthesizing, categorizing, and assessing that object. That process required a mediation between the knower and the known, which, in the modality of scientific inquiry, was achieved through the trafficking of abstract signs and symbols. Assuming the veracity of such a system of representations, psycho-*analysis* then required a hermeneutics to decipher the domain that defied logic, had no language, and exhibited no causal or temporal constraints.

Freud's interpretations of an unconscious psychic bedrock of teeming emotions, drives, and instincts sought to discern their clandestine interactions and subsequent effects on thought and behavior that he maintained was "the true psychic reality" (Freud 1900, 613).[8] How, then, are unconscious dynamics translated into a discernable, rational construct? Freud devised a model of unconscious dynamics in which he would discern signs (manifest clues) and track them to their origin to display emotional trauma and consequent repression. He charged the ego to control (and adjudicate) the demands of those inner forces and the strictures imposed by the reality of the social world. On this view, fantasy alienates the subject from full acceptance of external reality, and thus the ego is placed on the battleground over which fantasy and obstacles of fulfillment lay their respective claims. If desire dominates, the primary narcissism of the subject then must struggle in its rejection of the stimuli of the outside world. Alternatively, desire seeks its object, and the world becomes the site for its gratification. So, according to psychoanalytic theory, the subject must meld two frames of reference, in which unconscious fantasy and desire must find resolution within restrictive social realities.

In sum, Freud applied a system of analysis originally devised for the study of nature to the psyche and thereby sought to objectify the subjective *me*. Perhaps new insight (or at least a new narrative) accompanying this redesign is therapeutic, but putting aside (disputed) efficacy, we are left with a bewildering question: where does *the I* reside? Indeed, *who is the subject?*

Freud's project faced unceasing criticism. Despite his underlying aspirations for a scientific description of psychic phenomena, he fully acknowledged that the neurosciences had not advanced sufficiently to support his own hypotheses about psychic function, whether the issue was his proposed topography or the dynamics of the instinctual drives (Freud 1915, 175; 1920, 59). As Freud explained,

We know two things about what we call our psyche (or mental life): firstly, its bodily organ and scene of action, the brain (or nervous system), and on the other hand, our acts of consciousness, which are immediate data and cannot be further explained by any sort of description. Everything that lies between is unknown to us, and so the data do not include any direct relation between these two terminal points of our knowledge. If it existed, it would at most afford an exact localization of the processes of consciousness and would give us no help towards understanding them.

(Freud 1940, 144–5)

James could hardly dispute such a generalization, but he drew radically different conclusions that led him to abdicate his leadership in the nascent field of psychology (James 1987a, 1141–2). Freud, in contrast, despite the lack of objective evidence, attempted to create a science of the mind as he imagined it would function. Thus, the issue that separated them most clearly was not the status of subliminal thought, but rather the attempt to describe the dynamics of such unconscious mentation *scientifically*.

Why James abandoned scientific psychology and the attempt to explain the subjective in objective terms, while Freud held a philosophy that demanded such scrutiny despite recognizing its limitations, guides this study. The hinge of James's turn from the *science* of psychology to an attempt to devise a novel *philosophy* of the mind required him to reject the positivist commitments Freud never relinquished. Having completed his magisterial *The Principles of Psychology* (1890), James acknowledged that he self-consciously sought to remain within the boundaries of science, but intimated some ambivalence:

I have kept to the point of view of natural science throughout the book. Every natural science accepts certain data uncritically, and declines to challenge the elements between which its own "laws" obtain, and from which its own deductions are carried on. Psychology, the science of finite individual minds, assumes as its data (1) *thoughts and feelings*, and (2) *a physical world* in time and space with which they coexist and which (3) *they know*. Of course, these data are themselves discussible; but the discussion of them (as of other elements) is called metaphysics and falls outside the province of this book. This book, assuming that thoughts and feelings exist and are vehicles of knowledge, thereupon contends that psychology when she has ascertained the empirical correlation of the various sorts of thought or feeling with definite conditions of the brain, can go no farther—can go no farther that is, as a natural science. If she goes farther she becomes metaphysical. All attempts to *explain* our phenomenally given thoughts as products of deeper-lying entities (whether the latter be named "Soul," "Transcendental Ego," "Ideas," or "Elementary Units of Consciousness") are metaphysical . . . in this strictly positivistic point of view consists the only feature of it for which I feel tempted to claim originality.

(James 1983, 6, emphasis in original)

James goes on to admit that he is offering but "a mass of descriptive details, running out into queries which only a metaphysics alive to the weight of her task can hope successfully to deal with" (James 1983, 7). And then he closes with an apparent sigh: "that [advance] will perhaps be centuries hence; and meanwhile the best mark of health that a science can show is this unfinished-seeming front" (James 1983).

James was impatient. Over the next two years he summarized the admittedly "descriptive" *Principles of Psychology* and published *Principles* in *Psychology: The Briefer Course* in 1892, which concludes with a condemnation:

When, then, we talk of "psychology as a natural science," we must not assume that that means a sort of psychology that stands at last on solid ground. It means just the reverse; it means a psychology particularly fragile, and into which the waters of metaphysical criticism leak at every joint, a psychology all of whose elementary assumptions and data must be reconsidered in wider connections and translated into other terms. It is, in short, a phrase of diffidence, and not of arrogance; and it is indeed strange to hear people talk triumphantly of "the New Psychology," and write "Histories of Psychology," when into the real elements and forces which the word covers not the first glimpse of clear insight exists. A string of raw facts; a little gossip and wrangle about opinions; a little classification and generalization on the mere descriptive level; a strong prejudice that we have states of mind, and that our brain conditions them: but not a single law in the sense in which physics shows us laws, not a single proposition from which any consequence can causally be deducted. We don't even know the terms between which the elementary laws would obtain if we had them. This is no science, it is only the hope of a science.

(James 1992d, 432–3)

With that appraisal, in 1894 James publicly converted from physician to metaphysician. During a Presidential (!) address to the American Psychological Association (an organization he helped found), he bid farewell to his previous scientific pursuits for heretofore eschewed "metaphysics" (published as "The Knowing of Things Together" [James 1992a]). Why he so radically changed his agenda, and the consequence of that shift, is a major theme of *James and Freud*, for in that story, we have a keen perspective on Freud's own venture and the larger questions pertaining to how the mental might be understood.

In brief, James came to believe that psychology had ironically misconceived mental phenomena by imposing an artifactual dissection on the unity of experience.[9] He emphasized that experience is unified and that by espousing the continuity of consciousness and recognizing the primacy of the unity of parts to form integral wholes, James rejected the "chopping up of 'the mind' into distinct units of composition or function, numbering these off, and labelling them by technical names" (James 1992c, 725). In other words, the science presented a picture of the mind at odds with personal experience, and given the primacy he afforded subjectivity, James sought another route into the mental. As Bruce Wilshire cogently explained,

In *Principles* [James] says his approach to psychology will be natural-scientific and nonphilosophical. He will simply try to discover causal laws of functional covariation between mental states and brain states. He realizes that there are philosophical problems of how mind and brain could interact, and also of how mind could know the world, but he believes that for his purposes he can avoid them.

Of the many valuable insights and results of *Principles*, the most valuable is that James does not succeed in his grand design of avoiding philosophy. He cannot begin to correlate mental states and brain states until he specifies mental states, and he cannot specify mental states until he specifies how they are about their objects in the world. Not only can he not avoid philosophical problems, he sees that the problems are intermeshed and that the "cognitive relation" of mental states to the world is the most basic. (The question of how objects "get known into" mental states he had most wanted to avoid.)

In other words, James sees that he cannot avoid asking where he can stand intellectually if he would begin his natural scientific investigation. He cannot avoid a reflective excavation of the presuppositions of inquiry, cannot avoid turning around, so to speak, from his "main" natural-scientific project. Although he is reluctant to admit it, he is caught up in a transcendental investigation of the conditions of the experience-ability and knowability of the world. His excavation of presupposition is an implicit but extensive and rich phenomenological description of where we always already are in the experienceable world. To go forward scientifically he must also go backward. *Principles* offers the spectacle of a man unable to run backward fast enough to keep up with himself.

(Wilshire 1997, 107–8; see also Wilshire 1979)

So, James eventually fully embraced a philosophical approach that challenged the sciences of the mind and in so doing inflected Western thought.

In the Preface to *Will to Believe*, James announced a new epistemology based on a rejected metaphysical mind-body dualism that he named "radical empiricism" (James 1992h, 447). As detailed in Chapter 2, he intended to redirect psychology from an exclusive study of sensory inputs and attend to pure experience of the immediate moment (Linschoten 1968; Edie 1987; Seigfried 1990; Taylor and Wozniak 1996a). In the search for a psychology more attuned to one's cognitive experience, he joined the early phenomenologists, Franz Brentano (Brentano 1973 [1874]) and Ernst Mach (1914 [1886]) and thereby shed the positivism of his earlier work.[10] Perhaps on their Worcester stroll, James might have suggested to Freud that he should relinquish the conceits of objectification and adopt a phenomenological orientation instead. The suggestion would have fallen on covered ears, although it was hardly a novel option. As a university student, Freud had studied with Brentano, whose views Freud had resisted (Tauber 2010, 16, 29–30, 40).[11] In fact, student and teacher were deeply divided, a division that mirrors the gulf separating James and Freud.

The key characteristic of phenomenological accounts is a demurral on investigating how the mind functions. The experienced self is also left an open question, while inquiries are focused on the interactive process of the subject with the world through discriminant, attendant engagement. On this view, through active attention and then selection, the world assumes order in which intention is enacted. Thus, the acts of perception, recognition, and reaction portray the knowing agent in action, whose intention is key. In other words, human interest parses the plenum of reality into "things," the furniture of the world. From this orientation, James thrusts a dagger into the heart of positivism's basic presumption:

> there is no really inherent order, but it is we who project order into the world by selecting objects and tracing relations so as to gratify our intellectual interests. We carve out order by leaving the disorderly parts out; and the world is conceived thus.
>
> (James 1987d, 634)

Following that tenet, he went on to challenge the status of "things" that become "facts" in the positivist universe, most importantly, the partition of consciousness into "bits" that might then be analyzed. Simply, for James the integrity of "the stream of consciousness" was inviolate and served as the foundation of his characterization of the mind; without segmentation, scientific characterization would be excluded, for there were then no *things* to examine.

James, an apostle of Romanticism

The contentious standing of *objectivity* is a central theme of *James and Freud*. Whereas *facts* in the positivist universe are independent of human values and thus protected from subjective judgment, for James the fact/value distinction is muddled. The argument begins with acknowledging that objectivity itself is a value, subject to evolving standards and dependent on a medley of ancillary norms invoked in different contexts (Megill 1994; Daston and Galison 2011; Daston and Lunbeck 2011). In other words, objectivity serves as a kind of scientific currency whose "valuation" differs among its various "transactions." For James, as for each of the classical pragmatists (Charles Peirce, John Dewey, and Herbert Mead), objectivity cannot assume some ideal insularity, for "value and normativity permeate *all* experience . . . [which includes] normative judgments [that] are essential to the practice of science itself" (Putnam 2002, 30). Thus, the positivist assumptions about neutrality and objectivity belie how facts are comingled with the values and theories in which they are "entangled" (Putnam 2002, 27). Such supportive elements (or what Hilary Putnam [1982] called "action-guiding terms") hardly remain stable, further undermining positivist suppositions. Indeed, to unravel the relative roles of these supports becomes a highly convoluted, and sometimes irresolvable, endeavor. The issue then becomes *how* those values are arrayed in the generation of knowledge, for various forms of judgment must coalesce to construct facts and then incorporate them into models and theory.[12] Interpretation is *always* at work.

Since no formal method exists to define fact/value relationships, James (if he were so inclined) would have pummeled psychoanalysis for its pretensions of objectivity and sneered at its scientific affectations. After all, what could be more value-driven than the interpretive methods Freud employed?

With his later philosophical development, James turned his back on positivism. His understanding of mental life closely adhered to the romantic sense of human being that centered on the primacy—and legitimacy—of the subjective. Freud assumed an opposing orientation, the positivist stance of objective analysis. As mentioned, he believed the subjective realm could be examined with the same scientific principles that had been so spectacularly applied by nineteenth-century natural scientists. By appropriately applying those principles to the introspective ego, Freud maintained that access to the unconscious would be achieved and the mechanics of the mental revealed. Their conflicting views of objectivity applied to the personal puts our protagonists into widely divergent philosophical pathways that would lead them to their respective psychologies.[13]

These contrasts between James and Freud also led to divergent ways of thinking about moral agency and self-knowledge. While both of our protagonists held humanist sentiments, the profound issue separating them was how to understand freedom in a world increasingly disenchanted. By placing the mind in the natural world of cause and effect, Freud's theory was entrapped in a deterministic metaphysics, whereas James asserted freedom of choice. The roots of that view originate in his romantic quest for a unitary metaphysics and his "artistic" description of human experience (Barzun 1992).

The Romantics replaced the Enlightenment ideal of a universal Reason with the inviolability of individual judgment, imagination, and emotional experience free of objectification. Rationality has different meanings in different domains; no steadfast method is comprehensively applicable. Thus the world and the modes by which it may be understood and governed become more pliable, require more tolerance, allow for plasticity, and must be understood as amenable to acts of will and free choice. On this view, there are no abiding structures of things or thought or morality. Indeed, Romanticism initiated a break in Western consciousness that shifted *everything* and led to Marx's observation that "all that is solid melts into air" (Berlin 1999, 14; Berman 1982, 15). The philosophical portrait of James presented here places him within this Romantic Zeitgeist, a pluralistic universe in which sundry values construe facts by diverse rules and in which *experience* organizes reality.[14] That world encompasses divergent and even contradictory characteristics: harmony and turbulence, unity and multiplicity, integration and fragmentation (Berlin 1999). Then, one might well ask, what is the normative? Which values govern? And then, how does one find bearings without foundational values? These questions outline an ethics without ontology characterizing our own times (Putnam 2004). In this sense, the Romantics forecast our own moral agenda, not as they originally posed their challenges, but as similar anxieties reappeared in the context of our own era (Tauber 2022, 223–4).

Ironically perhaps, James's philosophy frees psychoanalysis from its own strictures and suggests justifications for alternative ways of conceiving human psychology and thereby liberating the soul from distorting impositions of a Reason mediating one reality, but not necessarily that defined by personal experience. As James wrote late in life, "We add, both to the subject and to the predicate part of reality. The world stands malleable, waiting to receive its final touches at our hand" (James 1987c, 599). He thus asserts a constellation of human-centered, human-derived, human-constructed, and human-intended values to guide "a person-centered science."[15] James followed Romantic aspirations to "save" subjectivity, to believe in the freedom of the will, and to valorize individual experience as the resource of creativity. His radical empiricism displaced Cartesian dualism and offered a stark alternative to the fragmentation of experience resulting from that dualist metaphysics. Indeed, he readily admitted that his critics might find his "system too *bottomless* and romantic," but asserted that "it is essential to the evolution of clearness in philosophic thought that *someone* should defend a pluralistic empiricism radically" (James 1920, II:203–4, emphasis in original; quoted by McDermott 1976, xxvii).[16]

This excursion into Romanticism's response to a dualist subject-object metaphysics introduces a critique of Freud's psychology that assumes the inner division of self-consciousness and attempts to objectify it. While James wore the scientific mantle early in his career, he eventually shed it and devised a way of registering subjective experience *sui generis*. In detailing the contrasting James-Freud philosophies, we gain insight into how underlying metaphysical commitments drive epistemologies that, in turn, frame moral philosophy (see Chapter 6). The Romantic crusade opposing the imperative for objectification and concretization (instantiated by science) required a philosophy to challenge positivism's infiltration into all the crevices of human self-appraisal. Answering that challenge, James elaborated an alternative philosophy and in doing so, upturned psychology.

Concerning the subject

James, as already mentioned, took early note of Freud. In 1894, he published an abstract of the Freud-Breuer paper on hysteria and continued to cite their work in academic and public lectures (E. Taylor 1999, 466). Such recognition is hardly surprising, inasmuch as both Freud and James shared interests in psychopathology, hypnosis, and psychotherapy. However, their respective psychologies were based upon very different lines of inquiry that began with their divergent views of the unconscious. For James, and most philosophers of the period, *mental* and *consciousness* were interchangeable. Thus, the unconscious was but a

> "transmarginal field of consciousness" operating in a numinous fashion "like a 'magnet field,' inside of which our centre of energy turns like a compass-needle, as the present phase of consciousness alters to its successor. Our whole past store of memories floats beyond this margin, ready as a touch to come in; and the entire mass of residual powers, impulses, and knowledge that constitute our empirical self stretches continually beyond it." The transmarginal field is the whole fabric of our potential being—in James' schema, an infinite element. . . . James did not explain why in such a perfect, if intricate, contiguity there was any division between the realm at all, or what that division really consisted in.
>
> (Prochnik 2006, 150–1, citing James 1996, 437)

That position, hardly unusual at the time, drew Freud's ire, repeatedly. For instance, in 1925, he penned "The Resistances to Psycho-analysis," in which he forgives physicians (encumbered with their mechanical, material-ist orientation) for misconstruing the authority of psychoanalysis, but to the philosophers he offers no respite. He accused them of narrowly perceiving "mind" only in its conscious functions, and thus failing to recognize that "what is mental is in itself unconscious and that being conscious is only a quality, which may or may not accrue to a particular mental act" (Freud 1925b, 213–22, 216). Further, Freud simply asserts that because philoso-phers have no experience with hypnosis or dream analysis, they are locked into self-observation and thus, consciousness.

Freud's defense of psychoanalysis draws a distinction between the "sci-ence" of his methods and the "speculation" of philosophers. This polemical position belies the complexity of the influences on psychoanalytic theory by ignoring the difficulties of drawing bridging concepts between Freud's own clinical empiricism and neuroscientific modeling, on the one hand and, on the other hand, the philosophical construction of a new discipline that heavily depended (albeit without acknowledgement) on the antecedents of previous characterizations of unconsciousness, for example, Hegel (Mills 2002), Schopenhauer, Eduard von Hartmann, and Nietzsche (Ellenberger 1970). Freud's accusations hardly applied to James given their shared psy-chiatric interests. Moreover, Freud could not include James in his discipli-nary squabble when he laments that psychoanalysis resided in some middle position between medicine and philosophy, deriving no benefits from any kinship with either discipline on either flank. James, of course, straddled that boundary as well.

To the extent that the contrasts between Freud and James rest in discipli-nary affiliations is superficial to the main issue at hand, namely, the status of the unconscious, which quickly becomes a dispute about the nature of psychic causation. Freud was a determinist; James was not. For Freud, the psyche was the unconscious that followed its own laws; consciousness is a veneer, subject to the whims and fancies of unconscious desire; for James, free will is the exercise of *conscious* choice. Upon that platform, he devel-oped a liberatory vision of agency.

In many respects, Freud and James refract the pertinent questions about agency in ways still highly relevant to how we think of the inner dialogue that comprises a sense of self; the expression of feeling and intuitions; the ineffability of aesthetic and spiritual wonder; the "no-voice" articulation of intimate love, all of which resides in an inner sanctum of subjectivity—the deepest sense of *me*, the indefinable core that Freud dubbed *das Ding* ("the thing") and that James called *the vague*. Each intuited some inner source of being that remained just beyond articulation and in the attempt to better characterize that essence, they witnessed the retreating sense of an ineffable subjectivity, one Freud attempted to represent, while James left it lying well beyond scientific reports.

So where does the James-Freud dispute leave the subject—the knowing, feeling *me* in terms of both moral and epistemological agency? What is the character of that inner presence that resides in the pre-linguistic domain? How to define the "space" between the feeling and its expression? These are the fundamental questions underlying cognitive psychology and cognitive linguistics, and while those sciences have generated a vast library of information and opinion, we have yet to finalize the relationship between language and thought, especially at the juncture of how emotions emerge in thought and then in speech (Bucci 1997). While these questions are central to psychoanalysis, by and large, little comment has been made about the basis of that transition, which, as discussed in Chapter 4, underscores the theoretical and methodological limits of Freudian "science."

However, Freud's abiding influence does not derive from his particular psycho-mechanics or his psychic-architecture, which have been largely discarded even by his most ardent supporters.[17] So, when the psychobabble has been silenced, unadorned by dramatic case studies and apparent cures, Freud's profound claims about the stranger within may be viewed more clearly. We may easily discard psychoanalytic theoretical and therapeutic claims, but because of the power of a narrative fashioned by our own subjectivity—memories, feelings, and fears—lying well beyond analytics, the deeper truths Freud discovered remain ensconced in the modern imagination. After all, self-appraisals constitute the beginning of moral cognizance that ends with choices and the responsibility assumed for those decisions. Accordingly, we must recognize his pre-eminent influence in architecting contemporary notions of identity and thus re-casting ancient insights about the skepticism of self-knowledge and its conceits.[18] On this basis, his advocacy for self-reflection stands and cannot be relinquished despite its tenuous standing as offering objective accounts of emotional trauma and subsequent psychic conflicts.

Freud's accomplishment is not that psychoanalysis is based on a putative scientific explanation, but rather how he redrew moral agency (Tauber 2010). He concluded that while humans are subject to deterministic psychic forces, they must still exercise freedom of choice despite lacking such capacity. And here we insert a Jamesian perspective: To the extent one deliberates, the exercise of self-reflection, limited and inescapably biased, comprises the wellspring from which the "right" is determined, oriented by the pragmatism of collective flourishing and the pluralism required for interpretive latitude. That ethical source lies within the subjectivity James sought to save from a distorting science and the indenture to psychic determinism. Note, our protagonists held a humanist ethos in common, but Freud could not resolve the logic of the philosophy he had adopted: humans are determined yet free—determined by psychic forces they neither know nor control, yet free to the extent they exercise rational insight in the face of compromised self-knowledge. In short, James provided a philosophy of liberation. How and why is the story narrated here, framed by the clash of opposing metaphysics. In detailing the James-Freud confrontation, we clearly see how underlying philosophical commitments drive epistemologies that, in turn, lead to ways of thinking about self-knowledge, personal identity, and ethics. In exploring the philosophical sources of Freud's venture juxtaposed to James's alternate philosophy of mind, we will see how their respective metaphysics radically differed and from that vantage unravel the philosophical commitments and corresponding weaknesses of psychoanalytic theory that obstructed Freud's larger humane purposes.

Plan of the book

Offering a historical and philosophical perspective of an idea—namely, that the mind may be regarded as an object in the same objective ways the world is known—has required balancing its specialized aspects while accounting for the broader contexts in which that conception was developed. *James and Freud* presents the philosophical positions of our protagonists with a minimum of technical language, while assuming that the reader is conversant with the major ideas of Freudian psychology and philosophy of mind, more generally. As a descriptive exposition, I have not attempted to evaluate James's philosophical complexity in the context of the idealism argued by others, nor to unwind the aporias embedded in his formulations of *experience*. I have endeavored to describe enough to juxtapose his thinking with Freud's and highlight the significance of those differences (representative appraisals of James's philosophy include McDermott 1976; Myers 1986, 242–71, 307ff.; Skrupskelis 1988; Putnam 1990a, 1990b, 1990c; Sprigge 1993; Gale 1999, 303–32; Campbell 2017, 180–99).

The discussion follows the development of our protagonists' respective thought within the major categories of consciousness, psychic causation, notions of personal identity, metaphysics, and philosophy of science. Chapter 1 describes how Freud presented psychoanalysis as a science in which the Cartesian ego surveying the world through an idealized autonomous rationality would turn that same gaze upon the psyche and then, holding to this naturalist stance, positing psychodynamics governed by the same laws of causation governing the physical world. He designed psychoanaly-sis to interpret the putative representations (e.g., dream symbols, parapraxis, associations) of unconscious psychic dynamics and thereby establish what he called "a science of the mind." In contrast, James moved from a scien-tific psychology to a metaphysical revamping of the subject-object dualism underlying Freud's own venture. Chapter 2 recounts why James disavowed the positivist examination of the mind for a phenomenological account. In the process he sought to free subjectivity's entrapment by a science that would organize experience solely in its own terms. This overview high-lights their different approaches to psychology that in turn reflect their divergent philosophies.

With the conclusion of the synopsis of their respective philosophies of mind, we commence with more detailed topical discussions. In Chapter 3, the place of emotions in their respective writings highlights the stark contrast of James's romanticism against Freud's positivism, a theme that reappears throughout the narrative but no more clearly in how they dealt with the subjective. Chapter 4 then considers our protagonists' views of that mental domain resisting articulation, namely, Freud's unconscious *das Ding* and James's creative reservoir, "the vague." Those differences fore-cast their respective conceptions of the ego in Chapter 5, a discussion set in its historical context and analyzed in terms of their respective underlying philosophies, namely, James's phenomenological account and then Freud's surprising avoidance of the entire matter. With this background, Chapter 6 portrays their very different versions of moral agency, and while our pro-tagonists shared a humanist orientation, how their respective epistemolo-gies, prefigured by conflicting metaphysics, drove them to very different conclusions: Freud's irresolvable conundrum arising from the strictures of psychic determinism against the moral necessity of free will contra James's emergent, dynamic psychological model that embraces freedom as a philo-sophical conclusion and enactment.

The Conclusion summarizes their respective general views about phi-losophy and how their divergent attitudes underwrote the paths upon which they trekked to radically different psychologies. Their opposing metaphys-ics were, in a sense, the sequalae of the critical attitudes each exercised and the temperaments that framed their intellectual commitments. Placing our protagonists in the context of modernism situates the broader implications of their thought, and a comment on what they might have discussed as Freud accompanied James to the Worcester train station on September 11, 1909, concludes this dual intellectual portrait of two major architects of late modernity, whose influence can hardly be exaggerated.

Notes

1 Other speakers and attendees included Freud's proteges, A. A. Brill, Ernest Jones, Sandor Ferenczi, and Jung, who also received a doctorate for his research on word associations and reaction times, not for his work in psychoanalysis (Harris 2010). Other attendees: the anthropologist Franz Boas; psychiatrists Adolph Meyer and William Alanson White; neuropathologist James Jackson Putnam, founder of the American Neurology Association; Mary Whiton Calkins, the first woman President of the American Psychological Association, Solomon Carter Fuller, recognized today as the first African American psychiatrist, and Emma Goldman, the well-known and "widely feared anarchist" (Levin 2009). Hall, the President of Clark University, had initiated the invitation to Freud and had kindred interests in the role of sexuality in personality. Although he once was a student of James, he had become estranged (Bjork 1983; Rosenzweig 1994; Lepore 2011). Titchener, a key adversary of James, "was a rigorous Wundtian a 'structuralist' in the sense that he emphasized the analysis of states of mind into their elementary parts. His strict adherence to introspection and Wundtian experimentalism distinguished him and at the same time isolated him" (Perry 1935, II:123). There was no affection lost between Titchener and James. "James's influence in philosophy and psychology appears . . . to be getting positively unwholesome: His credulity and his appeals to emotion are surely the reverse of scientific" (Titchener letter to James McKeen Cattell 1898) and "The function of Titchener's 'scientific' psychology . . . is to keep laboratory instruments going, and to provide platforms for certain professors. Apart from that it seems to me more unreal than any scholasticism" (letter from James to Calkins in 1909 cited by Bjork 1983, 73).
2 The lectures do not exactly follow their later publication that are ordered, as: (1) symptoms have psychological meaning; (2) repression and symptom formation; (3) psychic determinism, dreams, and parapraxes; (4) infantile sexuality and neurosis; and (5) transference and resistance (Freud 1910).
3 "Newspaper accounts of the 1909 celebration made relatively little of Freud's lectures, all of which were open to the public. They devoted most of their space to other speakers, for the most part referring rather *proforma* to the fact that Freud was a distinguished scientist, and had worked with sexuality, and that these were his first talks in America. The Worcester Telegram reported . . . that his first lecture was 'greeted with much applause' . . . [and] The Boston Transcript, conservative house organ of Boston's 'best families,' gave Freud's visit excellent coverage and even sent out a reporter to interview him at Dr. Hall's home; the result was a sympathetic explanation of Freud's ideas for the educated Boston public. None of the clippings from Worcester, Boston, New York, or other papers now preserved in two big scrapbooks in the Clark Archives contains a word of criticism or opposition to Freud's ideas or his presence at Clark; several contain praise of both" (Koelsch 1970).
4 Freud did not receive other academic or scientific accolades, but was awarded the Goethe Prize in 1930, joining other literary figures (Gay 1988, 571).
5 Freud visited Paris in 1885 to observe Charcot's study of hysteria. Early ruminations on the relationship of sexual practices leading to "neurosis" in the late 1880s led Freud to collaborate with Breuer to create the "talking cure" during

the early 1890s (Breuer and Freud 1895). *Interpretation of Dreams* was published in 1900, and by 1905, his *annus mirabilis*, Freud had established his
theory of psychodynamics with the publication of *Jokes and Relation to the
Unconscious, Three Essays on Theory of Sexuality*, and *A Case of Hysteria*
[Dora]. In 1908, about 40 disciples convened in Salzburg, Austria, for the first
International Psychoanalytic Congress, signifying the establishment of a new
discipline.

6 That orientation was elaborated in Freud's early *Project for a Scientific Psychology* (1895), which may be interpreted as a "connectionist" theory of the
mind (Freud 1895; D. Smith 1999). He posited the ebb and flow of incessant
processing of neurophysiological events in a hierarchy of neurons (D. Smith
1999, 2004). In such a schema, simple processors are arranged in an intercon-
nected network, which Freud postulated as three integrated functional systems:
(1) perceptual input, (2) cognitive processing, and (3) consciousness generat-
ing. According to this model, all conscious items are ultimately sensations or
associated with sensations and thoughts enter consciousness by "parasitizing
sensation" (D. Smith 1999, 417). See Greenberg (1997, 165ff.) for a full discussion of Freud's pre-psychoanalytic writings on the relationship of neurology
and psychology, and more particularly, the development of his philosophy of
mind based on Kantian representationalism.

7 The model thus closely follows the pattern of distinctive neuro-anatomic areas,
where conscious processes like sight and speech are localized to the more
superficial layers of the brain, while vegetative functions such as breathing and
sleep controls reside in the lower portions of the brain stem (Freud 1923a, 24).
In 1923, Georg Groddeck coined *das Es* ("the It") to capture the radical limits
of characterizing the unconscious,

> that man is animated by the Unknown, that there is within him an "Es," an
> "It," some wonderous force that directs both what he himself does, and what
> happens to him. The affirmation "I live," is only conditionally correct, it
> expresses on a small and superficial part of the fundamental principle, "Man
> is lived by the It."
>
> (Groddeck 1976, Letter II)

8 For Freud, the primordial mental, "the Unconscious," reaches back in phy-
logeny to include instincts, drives, elemental cognition, and emotional states
(Ben Jacob, Shapira and Tauber 2005, 2011; Feinberg and Mallatt 2016;
Lenharo 2024). From this substratum, higher cognitive functions evolve
to ascend and metamorphose into self-consciousness and more developed
forms of rationality (Sulloway 1979).

9 In 1902, James succinctly defined *experience* in an entry for Baldwin's *Dictionary of Philosophy and Psychology*: "Psychic or mental: the entire process of
phenomena, of present data in their raw immediacy, before reflective thought
has analyzed them into subjective and objective aspects or ingredients. It is the
summum genus of which everything must have been a part before we can speak
of it at all. In this neutrality of signification it is exactly correlative to the word
PHENOMENON . . . If philosophy insists on keeping the term indeterminate,
she can refer to her subject-matter without committing herself as to certain

questions in dispute. But if experience be used with either an objective or a subjective shade of meaning, then their question-begging occurs, and discussion grows impossible" (James 1978, 95). Note that the entry was written after James was well on his way to fully developing his non-dualist radical empiricism that leaves experience undivided by subjective and objective aspects. For a comprehensive review of the concept's complex history and meanings, as well as James's understanding of religious experience, see Jay 2005, 102–10, 272ff.

10 Phenomenology literally means the description of appearances; the word "appearances," like "phenomena," attempts to describe what actually happens in human consciousness in connection with the "objective" world. The phenomenological psychologists began with the premise that the mind does not see the object "as is," but rather through a complex integration of related perceptions. A total experience is thus constructed from imperfect and piecemeal data. A correcting mind formed the conscious image, for perception was based on an "interactive relationship between subject and object: the object was, in effect, partially 'created' by the act of seeing it" (Ryan 1991, 11). Brentano went further: The object did not exist except with reference to the act of seeing, and conversely perception existed only in reference to its object. He called this relationship "intentional," and it served as the origin of twentieth-century phenomenology as expounded by Edmund Husserl and his followers. This constructivist orientation began with Kant, but with the newfound optimism of a scientific approach, a strong empirical element entered the philosophical discussion.

11 How "mental" was defined swirled around the standing of the unconscious at the end of the nineteenth century as Freud invented psychoanalysis. Brentano maintained that unconscious thought was an oxymoron and thus regaled against those (e.g., von Hartmann and Maudsley) who regarded the mind as possessing both conscious and unconscious domains (Tauber 2010, 48–53). Freud thus directly opposed his teacher and asserted the primacy of unconsciousness, while adopting his mentor's notion of intentionality as the key characteristic of mental function (Tauber 2009c, 2010, 40–8).

12 A key tenet of post-Kuhnian science studies maintains that despite the claims of acquiring *positive* knowledge, *facts* do not simply derive from objective, neutral standards of observation, but are created from the choice of values and theories in which they are embedded (Crosby 1997; Poovey 1998; Zammito 2004). A set of varying epistemic and non-epistemic values determine what is chosen as evidence and how it is interpreted (Putnam 1982, 2002). Epistemic values pertain to cognitive success, i.e., true knowledge or justified belief, e.g., parsimony, coherence, predictability; non-epistemic values, so-called "contextual values," are derived from personal judgment, aesthetic bias, as well as social, historical, linguistic, ideological, and philosophical determinants (Tauber 2009a, 52–4; 2022, 8, 173). Knowledge acquisition is thus *constructed* by a medley of values that inform the production of facts that are then interpreted and integrated into models and theories.

13 "Personal" appears throughout James's writings and differs from "subjective" as largely determined by the context in which the two words appear—*subjective*, referring primarily to the emotional, and *personal*, encompassing that which

pertains to individual significance more generally. The connotations of personal as meaningful build on Jamesian tenets that "loosen" the strictures of objectivity in understanding how humans acquire and process useful knowledge. Michael Polanyi (in reaction to mid-twentieth-century positivism) renewed and extended James's views by arguing that humans see the world through different cognitive lenses, each of which has a part to play in scientific discovery and interpretation (Polanyi 1962; Zammito 2004; Tauber 2009a). Polanyi was wary of becoming ensnared in the confines of restricted theory and, more importantly perhaps, limiting scientific method to only a narrow wedge of experience and modes of knowing. On his view, objectivity, although a critical component, is a late tool in cognitive assessments. Instead of denying the selective process of observation and the interpretative character of scientific investigation, he embraced them. Thus "personal knowledge" (the partially articulated conditions, frameworks, and subjective elements of tacit knowledge and preconscious thinking) became his catch-all for the necessary, creative elements that cannot be accounted for in the positivist rendition of science. Accordingly, *understanding* entails many layers of interpretation that draw from science's supporting culture, the values that govern its use, and, ultimately, the sense of meaning and significance ascribed to the scientific portrait of the world. And the necessary correlate then follows: Scientific findings transcend the individual investigator, because facts and their interpretation belong to the communal group and are adjudicated collectively. On this view, objectivity is a derivative of collective judgment. Thus, in his use of "personal," Polanyi broadened the cognitive category of "objectivity" to include those mental faculties that are invoked in discovery and cannot in any formal fashion be finalized in a logical format—i.e., aesthetic sensibility, probabilistic judgment, intuition, metaphoric extension, and the like. Polanyi apparently had read James carefully when he studied *The Principles of Psychology* at age 16 (Scott and Moleski 2005, 16).

14 Among others who have cited James's Romanticism (e.g., Goodman 1990; Reed 1997; Schulenberg 2015, 2022), John McDermott introduced his overview of James's writings by citing Thoreau's poem "Our Country" as encapsulating James's own vision of a human creative life:

> All things invite this earth's inhabitants
> To rear their lives to an unheard of height
> And meet the expectations of the land . . . (Thoreau 1962, 135)

James echoed that credo by his own assertion that "the inmost nature of the reality is congenial to *powers* which you possess" (James 1992e, 521), by which he meant "the powers of the 'energies of men' in human creativity" (McDermott 1967, 7), the romantic *poesis*. The phrase "congenial to *powers* which you possess" may be construed as a motto for James's character, governing his assertion of the freedom of the will and the potentials of human creativity in a pluralistic universe. The phrase first appeared in the 1889 paper "The Psychology of Belief" (1992g, 1052) and then was incorporated in *Principles of Psychology* as "The Perception of Reality" (James 1983, 913), and again reprinted in *Will to Believe* in the 1896 revised essay "The Sentiment of Rationality" (James 1992e, 521).

15 The phrase is appropriated by Eugene Taylor from the writings of Gordon All-port and Carl Rogers (E. Taylor 1996, xiii). Taylor's study outlines a "uniquely American Jamesian tradition [that] influenced the personality-social psychologists of the 1930s and 1940s and the humanistic psychologists who followed them into the 1960s" (E. Taylor 1996).

16 The "radical" of "radical empiricism" was James's rhetorical signal that Hume had not gone far enough in his own empirical philosophy, his offering being "too thin" and giving rise to "problems of skepticism and its equally trouble-some purported solutions" (Janack 2012, 7).

17 Although Freud claimed that psychoanalysis is "the starting point of a new and deeper science of the mind" (Freud 1925a, 47), as a scientific enterprise, psychoanalysis failed the standards of his own era, and even more so the gauntlet of later critics (Grünbaum 1984; Eysenck 1985; Webster 1995; Macmillan 1997; Cioffi 1998; Crews 2017). Given Freud's own prediction, we are left with an ironic verdict: "Psycho-analysis makes a basic assumption, the discussion of which is reserved to philosophical thought but the justification for which lies in its results" (Freud 1940, 144). And that has proven, unfortunately for those seeking scientific justification for psychoanalysis, prescient. However, as discussed in Chapter 6, the long tenure of Freudianism attests to its contribution to Western ideas of personal identity and self-knowledge rather than its verification as a scientific depiction of the mind (Tauber 2010).

18 Stanley Cavell complained that self-knowledge is a topic remarkably neglected by philosophers. "Classical epistemology has concentrated on the knowledge objects (and, of course, of mathematics), not on the knowledge of persons. That is surely one of the striking facts of modern philosophy as a whole, and its history will not be understood until some accounting of that fact is rendered" (Cavell 1976, 68). Perhaps as a response to Cavell's admonishment, within ten years the philosophical literature on self-knowledge significantly expanded (e.g., Shoemake 1984; Cassam 1994; Carruthers 2011; Gertler 2011) with important repercussions in the literatures on self-deception, moral philosophy, and philosophy of psychology, more generally.

Chapter 1

Freud's philosophy of mind

At the end of the nineteenth century, nascent Psychology appeared as the self-assured daughter of Philosophy. Unlike Psyche's unknown parentage, we know how the science emerged in a fraught birth, when the umbilical cord was abruptly cut to set the new science of the mind on its own trajectory, albeit with contentious debate (Koch and Leary 1992; Bordogna 2008). The boundaries between the parent discipline and its child were disputed, but the science, legitimated by its empiricism, enjoyed impressive growth. In the early 1890s, the American Psychological Association and several specialty journals were founded. By 1903, in the United States alone, more than 40 psychology laboratories had been established, and the new discipline had awarded more doctorates than other sciences except chemistry, physics, and zoology (R. Smith 1997a, 493).

This revolution was based on a positivist philosophy of science newly applied to human behavior. First presented by August Comte in 1825, nineteenth-century positivism followed two general precepts: (1) human thought and social life are continuous with the natural world and therefore susceptible to the same modes of investigation; and (2) knowledge may be regarded as falling into three grand stages where progression from a theological to a metaphysical stage culminates finally in a "positive" stage in which the world is explained in terms of scientific truth (Tauber 2001, 106–9). Positivism's guiding ethos sought a collection of rules and evaluative criteria by which to distinguish *true* knowledge as opposed to opinion or interpretation. Thus, positivism in its various guises was conceived as a normative attitude that would regulate how such terms as "knowledge," "science," "cognition," and "information" are used. Most pertinent to our theme, positivism contrasted sharply with the Romantic view of the world, by denying any cognitive value to value judgments. Such positivist neutrality would be based upon the Cartesian dualism underlying the tenets of objectivity. Indeed, the radical separation of the observing/knowing subject

DOI: 10.4324/9781003565413-1

and her object of scrutiny assured dispassionate observation. The more careful the design of the experimental conditions, the more precise the characterization of phenomena, and the more likely the diminution of subjective contaminants. Thus, the strict positivist confined himself to phenomena and their ascertainable relationships through a vigorous mechanical objectivity (Megill 1994; Daston and Galison 2011; Daston and Lunbeck 2011).

Positivists presumed that all of nature was of one piece and that the study of life was potentially no different in kind from the study of chemical reactions, the movement of heavenly bodies, or the evolution of mountains.[1] Thus, if all of nature was unified—constituted of the same elements and governed by the same fundamental laws—then the life processes were simply on a continuum with the inorganic. Because there was no essential difference between animate and inanimate physics and chemistry, the organic world was therefore subject to the same kinds of study so successfully applied in physics. This approach allowed newly adopted physical and chemical laboratory techniques to establish the disciplines of physiology and biochemistry. These sciences were based on the belief that organic and inorganic chemistries shared the same fundamental principles, differing only insofar as the molecular constituents of living organisms were governed by complex constraints of metabolism.

The new problem was both to reduce the organic to the inorganic, that is, to exhibit the continuity of substance and operation, and concomitantly to understand the distinct character of life processes (Galaty 1974). The reductionists did not argue that certain organic phenomena were not unique, only that all causes must have certain elements in common, and thus they connected physics and biology by equating the ultimate basis of their respective explanations.[2] And with that general consilience, why not also establish the pathways of brain states to their expression as mental phenomena?[3] Thus, the experimental science of the mind was launched upon a platform comprised of the philosophical union of positivism and reductionism that drew together philosophical materialists (from opponents of theology to speculative metaphysics).

Early psychology took its bearings from this form of naturalism that had captured all the sciences in a philosophical alliance against a defunct idealism. So instead of the speculative exercise of propounding schemas to describe the transcendental conditions from which knowledge would be derived, objective criteria would establish Truth and the Reality based upon austere positivist principles (Tauber 2001, 2009a). Various strands of empirical, reductionist, materialist, and positivist philosophies placed sensory experience as the basis of all knowledge that would be understood in terms either of some kind of introspection of conscious experience or by some naturalistic extrapolation of neuro-physiological processes. Philosophy took notice and debate about idealist versus empirical basis of the mind assumed new vigor.[4] That is the academic arena James entered—stage left. While he began as a physician scientist, later, as a philosopher, he set philosophical boundaries on the new science that he had helped to launch. James regarded the new discipline from a unique position, because as a philosophically informed scientist, he straddled the academic divide.

In 1840, William Whewell highlighted the distinctions wrought by professionalization of the empirical disciplines with a new name for its practitioners: "scientist" (Whewell 1840, cxiii).[5] He thereby designated an individual engaged in an endeavor separated from the rest of philosophy. Prior to this new terminology, "natural philosopher" reflected a continuity of the sciences and other branches of philosophy. For instance, Charles Darwin referred to himself as a "natural philosopher," which for him meant that the line separating science from broader philosophical questions could not be definitively drawn. (Note that "science" derives from *scientia*, knowledge of the world, and *sciens*, "knowing," originally meant "to separate one thing from another, to distinguish.") Whewell thus defined a profession that dissected nature to hopefully put it back together, but now for human enrichment. However, with this practical aspect, "scientist," carried a pejorative connotation of someone more interested in applying knowledge than in discovery for its own sake, a veiled indictment suggesting for-profit motivations and possible corruption of sanctified knowledge for knowledge's sake. This compromised image of a searcher for truth clearly corrupted the earlier designation of "philosopher," namely, one who sought "wisdom" as a noble pursuit for its own sake. And conversely, scientists, Freud included, disparaged philosophy as only speculative, without an empirical basis. In any case, James was comfortable in both domains and dealt with the philosophical issues underlying the new science, while Freud was not. After outlining the approaches adopted by Freud and Wilhelm Wundt, we will consider James's own course through the thickets of early mind science.

Freud's representational theory of the mind

The birth of experimental psychology, marked by the establishment of laboratories by James (in Boston in 1875) and Wundt (in Leipzig in 1879; Harper 1950), coincides with the beginning of Freud's student research in neuroanatomy in 1877. He was influenced, as were all physiologists of his era, by the German reductionists, Ernst Brücke (his immediate mentor), and earlier proponents (Emil du Bois-Reymond and Hermann von Helmholtz). As mentioned, they sought to establish all biological phenomena on a common chemical-physical basis that would characterize organic phenomena on the basis of those same forces identified in the physical sciences. The mechanical character of forces in opposition, or at least in some kind of linkage, underlay Freud's own conception of neurological function, which was then readily extended to his early model of mental dynamics (Freud 1895; Decker 1977; Kitcher 1992; Sacks 2000).

Freud fully embraced the naturalistic stance. It was the arena in which he believed his new "science of the mind" would establish its legitimacy. After all, his earliest ambitions were formed as a physician and scientist, and just as a physicist must infer the character and placement of a particle, so would the psychoanalyst infer the character and expression of the psychical apparatus. So, as Newton discovered $F = ma$ and Einstein derived $E = mc^2$, Freud sought to create a science of the psyche based on a system that would represent unconscious dynamics. To discern this uncharted territory, he invented a "language of our perceptions," by which he meant a system of representations to describe the flow of psychic energies (Freud 1895). Because consciousness establishes conditions that preclude direct "observation" of the unconscious and, correspondingly, because the unconscious has no "language" (as normally construed) and functions with a "logic" alien to conscious thought, a new representational scheme was required for its discernment.

Here we find the philosophical genesis of Freud's psychoanalytic theory, namely, a version of a representational conception of mind that (at least philosophically) is an idiosyncratic precursor of later twentieth-century sciences of the mind comprising the so-called "cognitive revolution" (Lycan and Prinz 2008). The entire enterprise rests on a fundamental Cartesian separation of the knowing self from the world in which we live, so that the basic epistemological issue is, how does the subject *know* that world? Kant authored the basic cognitive conception by positing that the human mental structure *actively* organizes reality with an innate mental faculty organized by embedded *a priori* forms of reason (space, time, causality, number, and so forth). Nature then, at least from the human point of view, is comprised of what we know through this cognitive faculty, *phenomena*, and an underlying unprocessed domain, the *noumenon*. The *noumenon*, the thing-in-itself, cannot be known as such, that is, unmediated by mental processing. And because Kant's epistemology asserts that the thing-in-itself cannot be known directly, reality is *constructed* with architectonics that process *representations* of that reality to generate the phenomena required to depict the reality humans know. Simply, *what* is known requires a *re*-presentation to a subject. Accordingly, because all mental activity is mediated as representations, there is no immediate knowledge of the world. In short, passive reception is replaced by an active mental faculty whose modes of knowing present a particularized picture of the world and oneself in it.

Freud inherited this philosophical understanding and built upon its basic postulates (Tauber 2009b, 2010, 2013a, 26–34).[6] Assuming this scientific posture, he posited the same subject-object relationship adopted for perceiving nature to the challenge of accessing the psyche. For him, an autonomous epistemological agent (the ego) synthesizes, categorizes, and assesses the object of scrutiny and brings it to consciousness as mediated by representations. For example, just as the word "knife" has a universal meaning and reference in English, so too would a knife in a dream carry meanings, albeit not necessarily conforming to those definitions used in the everyday world. Given that "phenomena" are not the thing-in-itself, Freud thus makes the intimacy of psychic experience a special case, i.e., the immediacy of personal feeling provides more direct epistemological knowledge and thus a lesser problem than faced with perception of the exterior world.[7]

Two different meanings of the unconscious underwrite Freud's theory. When regarded from the representational perspective of consciousness, the unconscious becomes an object susceptible to scrutiny and thus attains meaning as it is deciphered to a conscious understanding. A second meaning refers to a deeper ontology, where the primordial psyche lies opaque or even hidden and consequently utterly inaccessible to representation. Only conscious constructions drawn from *interpretations* of psychic clues translate affections (emotions, feelings, moods) into public language. When the second meaning is subordinated to the first, the unconscious, originally the ego's radical Other (not representable), has, through the imposition of representation, lost its thorough alterity. In other words, once *represented*, the Unconscious is no longer *unconscious*. Freud's representation of the mind thus carries a double meaning and, more to the point, a theoretical weakness directly related to the epistemological uncertainties of psychoanalytic theory, namely, on what basis might an interpretation of a putative representation be objectively evaluated and verified? Simply, can psycho-*analysis* claim scientific legitimacy? Although failing positivist standards, Freud rejected the skeptical indictments and applied a hermeneutics of his invention—for better and for worse.

Freud recognized that the drives themselves are never represented as such but appear in the psyche as *ideas* to which the drives attach themselves. He posited that *ideas* were seemingly attached to drives; these ideas are "promiscuous" and move from one drive to another. Despite their shifting associations (resulting from repressive effects that disguised their true source), psychoanalysis would purportedly place the correct (i.e., original) idea with the drive. This would be accomplished through a process of insight (led by an inferential strategy) to account for trauma, repression, conflict, and, ultimately, anxiety. Accordingly, effective therapies would depend on shifting the misplaced (and misconstrued) false (repressed or defensive) idea to its truer source, and thereby identify the drive (or its desire) more accurately. Note that the ideas were repressed, not the drives themselves that had no representational standing. Then, through a representational model (i.e., the ideas were the representatives of the drives), Freud presumed to identify the forces at work as expressed by free associations, dreams, and parapraxis of everyday life (e.g., jokes, slips of the tongue, and other disguised display of unconscious fantasy).[8] And then according to psychoanalytic theory, following such insight and subsequent emotional release, neurotic resolution would commence.

In sum, since *ideas* postulated or inferred unconscious drives, Freud required a language in which those ideas were given meaning within a narrative of psychic trauma. Accordingly, dream images assumed symbolic meaning as derived from both a larger symbolic universe (the words of psychoanalytic language) and the emotional constellation in which the dream is interpreted (the interpretive context). These ideas become the métier of psycho-*analysis*, that is, representations serve as purveyors of the drives' associated ideas, which have been repressed and when deciphered point to an intrapsychic Other. Note that the idea is repressed, not the drive per se, whose expression through desire continues its own quest in defiance of repressive effects. The entire psychoanalytic enterprise of studying unconscious dynamics rested on these (putative) tell-tale signs of psychic trauma and tension, which then served as the material for interpretation of unrequited desire and fantasy. The overall scheme from desire to neurosis was modeled on a posited physics of forces that required conduction and ultimately release, either in untoward emotional effects or more successfully in sublimation that achieves some resolution of psychic conflict.

Freud's "associative" formulation dates to his pre-psychoanalytic writings on aphasia (Freud 1953 [1891]). Framed by the neurological discourse of the time, he joined attempts to model the relationship of brain localization studies to speech, namely, how to balance the contributions made by areas with localized language competence (i.e., Broca's area) and the complex processing that must occur as sensory data ascend to higher cortical regions. Very much in the same spirit of his later hypothesis presented in the *Project for a Scientific Psychology* (1895), where he postulated that different types of neurons fulfill different neurological functions, Freud assumed that a nerve on its way to the cerebral cortex changed its functional significance or meaning (1895, 52).

Making the case for a more global integration, Freud relied on some modality by which "a word sound image" associates with an "impression of word innervation" (Freud 1895, 73), and he suggested that the word concept appears as a "closed" complex of images of visual and auditory perceptions that processes the object through both specialized and more general anatomic locales. Then Freud makes the representational move: "In light of observations in speech disorders we have formed the view that the word concept (the idea of the word) is linked with its sensory part, in particular through its sound impressions, to the object concept" (Freud 1895, 77–78) that is then processed through the ascendant and integrative functions of various specialized anatomic centers.[9]

Freud invoked this essential *symbolic* function of language, one independent of the sensory domain, to the psychoanalytic scenario for deciphering the unconscious in three modalities: the *source* of the drives (somatic process), their *aim* (tension reduction), and the *object* (person or thing through which the drive is satisfied) that operate according to simple mechanics in which the mind was "to take its place among the inhabitants of the 'billiard-ball' universe of Newtonian mechanics" (MacIntyre 1958, 17). As described in the next chapter, James had utterly discharged these metaphysics underlying Freudian psychoanalysis and, in the process, discarded a scientific approach to mental life.

A science of the mind?

By 1909, when James and Freud met in Worcester, the intellectual gulf between them could not have been wider. Even though James attended a conference of psychologists, he had long since moved his principal interests to philosophy. Indeed, Freud in his memoir identified James as a "philosopher" (Freud 1925a; see also the Introduction to this book), which probably would have doomed any serious discussion between them, given Freud's unrepentant bias against philosophy. Once choosing medicine over philosophy after extensive studies with Brentano, Freud explicitly rejected philosophy because of its "speculative" character.[10] He struggled with balancing the intellectual appeal of philosophy with the "certainty" he hoped to find in science. Like many of his generation, he swam in the turbulent crosscurrents of an imperialistic positivism opposing the lingering influences of Hegel and his followers.[11] However, Freud did not engage in the philosophical debates of his era. He complained that if not "philosophy," certainly "speculation" served as the condemnatory judgment, and to suffer indictment as practicing simple conjecture, or worse, moved psychoanalysis beyond a scientific argument to speculative opinion. Of course, he strenuously objected to being aligned in any way with a critical inquiry so alien to his own.[12]

Ironically, given this biographical history, Freud, in many respects, built psychoanalysis on a philosophy of mind firmly grounded in a model he uncritically accepted: reality was constructed on a subject-object, self-other dichotomy and governed by its well-rehearsed logic. He thus remained a committed Cartesian-inspired dualist by depicting the ego as responsible for surveying the world and, most saliently, the inner cosmos of its own psyche. Rational and observant, the analysand was empowered to analytically describe the underlying natural forces of psychic life. The unconscious became "the other," and the entire psychoanalytic process developed from the Lockean conceit of the ego as the punctual source of objectification (C. Taylor 1989). Simply put, the Freudian schema turned the ego from objectifying the world to objectifying the alien depths of its own psyche. In the process, subjectivity, the innermost sense of self, would be objectified.

To be fair, Freud as an erstwhile scientist made no effort at philosophically examining his assumptions and presuppositions.[13] Although he had a working knowledge of Kant and phenomenology, he repeatedly disparaged philosophy after his student studies with Brentano at the University of Vienna (Tauber 2010, 29–30, 35–6). Freud assumed that consciousness and the ego's representing function were given as self-evident constructs and required no further examination or definition: "There is no need to discuss what is to be called conscious: it is removed from all doubt" (Freud 1933, 70). He had long considered the ego equivalent to consciousness, and given the primacy of the unconscious in his "meta-psychological view of mental life, the more we must learn to emancipate ourselves from the importance of the symptom of 'being conscious'" (1915b, 193). Note that he didn't demote consciousness for philosophical reasons, as did James, but rather because he had trained his sights on the subterranean reaches of the mind as the true site of the psyche. He therefore consistently contrasted this view with those philosophers committed to the mind as coincident with consciousness, and he tirelessly defended his "incompleteness theorem": the mind consists of conscious and unconscious domains, and while conscious mental function may be readily plotted, such depictions can only partially describe thought (e.g., Wilson 2002; Reber and Allen 2022).

As discussed, in the psychoanalytic scenario, psychic experiences are *re*-presented with a novel vocabulary and grammar that attempts to render "ideas" that may then be interpreted by Freudian "categories of understanding." The analysand is encouraged to freely associate and through that exercise reveal the movement of "ideas" that will be the target of interpretation and, hopefully, therapeutic insight. So, associative pairing not only characterizes the dynamics of drives connected to ideas, but the analysis "works" because it parallels (or reflects) the psychic phenomena of coupling.

The foundation of the entire enterprise rests on accepting that the unconscious cannot be directly known, inasmuch as it follows its own "laws" of causation and temporality. But with symbolic representation, access is achieved through an indirect correspondence of an *idea* (*Vorstellung*) attached to the drive, *Trieb*.[14] Once the *idea* is identified and confirmed as forming a "true" relationship with the underlying unconscious drive, then an inferential interpretation is exercised.[15] Freud thereby claimed to *objectify* unconscious mental states (see Searle 1992, 151–73). Two striking omissions appear in this formulation. For all of his efforts to capture the unconscious, Freud's assumptions about rationality and, more generally, the "laws" of consciousness escaped his purview (Tauber 2010, 2013b). Consequently, the basis of the objectivity Freud sought and the modes of representation he concocted were not critically regarded. So, the key question looms: can mental states, *in fact*, be treated as physical sciences deal with their objects of scrutiny as he claimed? Let us examine this model of the mind more carefully.

Freud relied on the commonplace linguistic understanding that words represent the world to the cognizing agent. So, just as words represent things, ideas, and emotions, so too would he interpret symbols that he saw as reflecting the dynamics of unconscious forces. He remained entrenched in this representational modality, which in the psychoanalytic context plays out in a drama between the reasoning (rational) ego and the *representation* of its "other"—the unconscious. As the *other* of the *conscious* mind, and most evidently as deciphered by psychoanalytic interpretation, the unconscious mirrors the semantic structure of consciousness, which, in turn, reflects the ego's rationality. "Thus we shall not hesitate to treat them [unconscious latent states] as *objects* of psychological research, and to deal with them in the most intimate connection with conscious mental acts" (Freud 1915b, 168, emphasis added). To do so, he posited that the drive (*Treib*), which characterizes the unconscious, escapes the laws of consciousness and functions as an "other," which, however, may be represented to consciousness as an *idea*:

> The antithesis of conscious and unconscious is not applicable to instincts. An instinct can never become an object of consciousness—*only the idea that represents the instinct can*. Even in the unconscious, moreover, an instinct cannot be represented otherwise than by an idea.
>
> (Freud 1915b, 177, emphasis added)

And with that assumption, Freud proceeded to analyze the idea so garnered.

The problematic relationship between an "idea" and its unconscious association was recognized at the beginning of psychoanalytic theorizing and was commented upon by Josef Breuer in the jointly authored *Studies in Hysteria*:

> The objections that are raised against "unconscious ideas" existing and being operative seem for the most part to be juggling with words. No doubt "idea" is a word belonging to the terminology of conscious thinking, and "unconscious idea" is therefore a self-contradictory expression. But the physical process that underlies an idea is the same in content and form (though not in quantity) whether the idea rises above the threshold of consciousness or remains beneath it. It would only be necessary to construct some such term as "ideational substratum" in order to avoid the contradiction and to counter the objection.
>
> (Breuer and Freud 1895, 223)[16]

Note that Breuer directly links the mental state to the physical brain state to justify his nomenclature, and in that easy translation of categories, he echoed Freud's own efforts (in the "Project for a Scientific Psychology" [Freud 1895]) to correlate a hypothetical neurological system with the psychology they were describing at the same time.

Through this scheme, Freud taps into a version of *knowledge* derived from a subject-object epistemology. Indeed, using representation as the mediator between the two psychic domains—conscious and unconscious—psychoanalysis proceeds by processing such information:

> [Because] *we know for certain* that they [unconscious processes] have abundant points of contact with conscious mental processes, with the help of a certain amount of work they can be transformed into, or replaced by, conscious mental processes, and all the categories which we employ to describe conscious mental acts, such as ideas, purposes, resolutions, and so

on, can be applied to them. Indeed, we are obliged to say of some of these latent states that the only respect in which they differ from conscious ones is precisely in the absence of consciousness.

(Freud 1915b, 168, emphasis added)

Thus, Freud devised a system to identify what he thought were epiphenomena of unconscious processes (via language, symbols, secondary manifestations) that would be suitable for interpretation. Simply, through word-presentations, "internal thought-processes are made into perceptions" (Freud 1923a, 23; see also Cavell 1993, 47).

In the posthumously published *Outline of Psycho-analysis* (1940), Freud clearly reiterated how psychoanalytic theory adopted the basic Kantian division between *phenomenon* and *noumenon*. *Phenomena* are cognitive products of perception and conscious thought processed through the "psychical apparatus," and the *noumenon*—"the thing-in-itself"—could not be known directly, i.e., it is that which exists independent of human cognition. Accordingly, humans *know* the world through phenomena, while primary (or ultimate) noumenal reality remains veiled. Adopting this basic scheme, Freud regarded the unconscious as a *noumenon* (Tauber 2010, 117–22), and just as reality emerges only through *re*-presentational processing, so would the unconscious be similarly revealed to disclose its hidden nature:

In our science as in the others the problem is the same: behind the attributes (qualities) of the object under examination [the Unconscious] which are presented directly to our perception, we have to discover something else which is more independent of the particular receptive capacity of our sense organs and which approximates more closely to what may be supposed to be the real state of affairs. *We have no hope of being able to reach the latter itself,* since it is evident that everything new that we have inferred must nevertheless be translated back into the language of our perceptions, from which it is simply impossible for us to free ourselves. But herein lies the very nature and limitation of our science . . . *Reality will always remain "unknowable."*

(Freud 1940, 196, emphasis added)

Freud goes on to draw parallels between psychoanalysis and physics, since he regarded each discipline as following the same basic scientific strategy: perceptive abilities are constantly improved; sense perceptions permit connections and dependent relations to be made, which are "somehow" reliably reproduced or reflected in our internal thought; "understanding" follows, which in turn permits prediction and control (Freud 1940, 196).

He concludes his primer on scientific method with another parallel to physics:

> We have discovered technical methods of filling up the gaps in the phenomena of our consciousness, and we make use of those methods just as a physicist makes use of experiment. In this manner we infer a number of processes which are themselves "unknowable" and interpolate them in those that are conscious to us.
>
> (Freud 1940, 196–7)

In this respect, Freud proceeded as a scientist—or at least so he thought, albeit without considering the philosophical assumptions underlying his theory and the status of the hermeneutics to discern the psychology of his clients. As discussed in the next chapter, James's philosophy of mind would be constructed upon utterly different principles.

Comment

From Descartes to Locke to Kant, and then adopted by Freud, the fundamental characteristic of their shared "cognitivist" program is a reasoning, intellectual system built upon a causal theory of perception: objects are perceived as sensory data, which then follow a trajectory that ends in a mental percept that corresponds to that object. Freud fully accepted this model and applied it to mental states he sought to describe. He did so by invoking a cognitivist account (envisaged in terms of rules and representations defined in symbolic or propositional form [Newell, Shaw, and Simon 1958; Fodor 1980, 1981]) that strikingly contrasts with non-cognitivist conceptions (e.g., Still and Costall 1991; Shanon 1993; Ramsey 2007). As we draw out those differences, the weaknesses of a host of concepts central to psychoanalysis and, for that matter, introspection writ large will emerge. The most important conundrum arises from Freud's positivist commitments, namely, can subjective states be *represented*?[17]

Freud remained a positivist in the reductionist modality throughout his career, and his psychic models were built on premises drawn from the physical sciences. In that endeavor, he adopted a subject-object epistemology that held his psychoanalytic theory in the grips of aspired objectified accounts that, in turn, were based on the metaphysics of Cartesian dualism coupled to a reductive methodology. Adherent to the scientific orthodoxy of the era, Freud modeled the psyche on unobservable brain dynamics that he sought to infer by interpretive means. The assumptions embedded in this approach seem crippling: the effort to *represent* the unconscious, the putative source of the affects, introduces a philosophical obstacle that arose from a dependence on the veracity of the relationship between words and the world they describe (Tauber 2010, 2013a). He had no objective way of establishing that relationship, no basis for public consensus, no standard of measurement, and certainly no option for prediction. Simply put, Freud assumed an "internalist view according to which the role of language [consciousness] is to give expression to 'ideas' that are prior to and logically independent of it, ideas that are entirely subjective and internal" (Cavell 1993, 47); or, to quote Freud, through "interposition [of word-presentations] internal thought-processes are made into perceptions" [Freud 1923a, 23]).[18] For him, as for Kant, "it is not the thing itself, but a representation of it, that is being interpreted" (Rieff 1959, 105), and so, "the object of either conscious or unconscious mental processes is not the world itself but a mental representation of it, outer world or inner as the case may be" (Cavell 1993, 14). The presumptions he adopted are staggering.

What Freud immodestly called a "new science of the mind" required defining the deterministic causation of natural phenomena, namely the dynamics of psychic forces by applying the same principles that had characterized instinctual drives (Sulloway 1979). Irrespective of the overdetermination (multiple causes) of psychic phenomena and the inaccessibility of the unconscious that defies the ordinary reality of everyday life (having "no organization, produces no collective will . . . [nor] logical laws of thought"; Freud 1933, 73). Because Freud hoped he could reconstruct a causal chain of mental events, psychoanalysis, following the basic premise that mechanical effects have definable causes, would attempt to discern the "strict determination of mental events" (Freud 1923b, 238) and expose "the illusion of Free Will" (Freud 1919, 236).

However, when the criteria of evidence are subject to the interpretive faculties of "entities" that exclude public review, negotiated acceptance must be conferred. In the psychoanalytic setting, that arbitration rests solely between the analysand and the analyst. If successful, a narrative is formulated. There is no communal objectivity that seeks to minimize idiosyncratic observation with standardized methods and instruments organized into large observational systems. In the public setting, all parties point to a shared view that corresponds to objective evidence. If controversy arises, then the evidence and its interpretation are debated. However, even scientific facts (and their interpretation) do not reside in some insular objective haven protected from non-epistemic values and thus immune from subjective judgment. Recall that objectivity based on shared consensus is an idealized standard with a history of varying parameters and applications (Megill 1994; Daston and Galison 2011; Daston and Lunbeck 2011). Indeed, the history of science is the history of controversy arising from interpretations of what fulfills the objective ideal in consideration of ineliminable bias, disputed philosophical commitments, social interests, economic consequences, etc. Obviously, this public adjudication is inapplicable in the psychoanalytic setting, both because there is no public judgment and because each case is unique. And science is about the universal.

On what basis might the idea identified as representing a drive be accepted as establishing a direct correspondence between the mind and the world? In other words, how does the individual *know* that the object of her intentionality is mediated by a putative representation? In everyday life, communal language and evolved concepts allow consensus about shared reality. The chair I see is, by consensus, the chair you see. But that folk psychology does not mitigate that the individual remains inescapably bound up in her world of representations that, in terms of a universally shared reality, is attested by others. More to the point, how does a representation convey the experience of inner feelings, memories, and other primary experiences? Responding to this query, James would launch a very different psychology, one based on a radically different philosophy of the mind.

To his credit, Freud acknowledged the tentative status of his explanation of psychodynamics, an uncertainty originating with his earliest recognition that inferential evidence did not hold the epistemological power he would have preferred (Tauber 2010, 60–9). Despite repeated avowals of the scientific character of his work, Freud was clearly aware that his stance within positivism was problematic (Reeder 2008). From his earliest publications, an uneasiness about the scientific status of the "talking cure" is evident:

> It still strikes me myself as strange that the case histories I write should read like short stories and that, as one might say, they lack the serious stamp of science. I must console myself with the reflection that the nature of the subject is evidently responsible for this, rather than any preference of my own.
> (Breuer and Freud 1895, 160)

Indeed, how could such a model built from his assumptions be tested and verified? And regarding the therapeutic aspects of his theory, again Freud himself recognized that he had provided little theoretical understanding of transference and its consequences. But these clinical issues, originating with the battles about the sexual basis of unconscious motivations, remained superficial to the deeper philosophical imbroglio of capturing inner mental states through some objectifying means to fulfill the requirements of a scientific model. In that regard, he required a system of causation, in which natural psychic forces would follow the same principles governing the physics of apples falling from trees. And then, true to his model, human psychology would be governed by the same determinism observed in all of nature. That series of extrapolations proved to be unsupportable by the very scientific criteria Freud himself endorsed (see the Introduction, note #17). As James might have advised, the ways of the mind need not follow from the presuppositions Freud selected.

Wundt

In conclusion, to briefly place Freud and James in the nascent field of psychology, we consider a representative experimentalist, Wilhelm Wundt, who opened his research institute (1879) during Freud's own medical studies (Kusch 2005). Instead of venturing into this newly created discipline, Freud studied neuroanatomy, then turned to neurology, and eventually practiced psychiatry. He thus never engaged in the new empiricism. Wundt's early investigations focused on the physiology of muscles and nerves. Recognizing the limits of positivist scrutiny of mental functions, his experimental research was circumscribed by following firm demarcations between the psychology that could be studied through physical manifestations and functions inaccessible to objective measurement. He thus acknowledged that quantitative findings only secured access to one dimension of psychological knowledge, namely, perception, psychophysics, and reaction times (as well as more general physiological aspects of mentation). Wundt denied that this approach was introspection, for in minimizing the self-consciousness of the subject, he only sought to correlate reports of changes in conscious awareness with recorded physical conditions. In other words, these quantitative studies were stripped to the extent possible of any subjective element. Note that only correlations were obtained, so causality could not be established.

Wundt maintained that the mind and the body are aspects of the same reality, though each dimension has its own form of causation. In this important respect he differed from Freud, who sought to define the unconscious pathways determining behavior. Wundt also diverged from James, who freely admitted that he did not have the patience for the German experimentalist efforts, which were focused upon sensation and perception (primarily vision), e.g., reaction time, attention, feelings, and associations, by measuring the quality, intensity, or duration of responses. James believed that a scientific psychology based upon such data (despite statistics and application of quantitative scales) was misconstrued, a vain attempt to reassemble the mind from *measurement* (James 1983, 191–3).[19]

In regard to associationist theory that Freud endorsed, and James rejected, Wundt aligned with the American. The theory had originated with John Locke, who conceived *ideas* as "thing-like" (something akin to entities) that could be shuffled about and linked in various ways with each other.

Such entities consequently existed in time and space and putatively were linked to other ideas by "association." A kind of Newtonian billiards placed ideas into play by rules that might be discovered just as the laws of chemical association might be discerned. Indeed, associationists saw unity in the physical and psychic world on this basis, which is why Freud accepted the associative idea while Wundt and James rejected it. For them, mental processes are an *activity* of the brain, and neither material nor analogous to entities. Thus, following Spinoza's metaphysics of parallelism of mental and material, they held that consciousness could not be fit within the paradigms of physical science and therefore could not be deciphered by a reductionist strategy. For Wundt and James, the psychic emerges from biology, chemistry, and physics, and this *emergence* became a catch-all for acknowledging the unknown principles by which a phenomenon arises from a materialist universe (Bedau and Humphreys 2008; Humphreys 2019). So, the mind, as *experienced* by a subject, evades reductionist characterizations; the psychic resides within its own domain (Boeree 2000). Wundt accepted a unique causal reality for the mental, one without a known script or choreographer, and thus released ideas from some set interactive relationship (Toulmin and Leary 1992; Goldsmith and Laks 2019, 195).

Wundt's *apperception psychology* sought to capture a more free-flowing, active dynamic and emergent process that puts him into alignment with James's own description of the mental. This construction contrasts with the passive (or preexisting) linkage of associated ideas predetermined by a mechanical mentality extrapolated from Newtonian physics. Upon this basic postulate, Freud and Wundt diverge. For Wundt (and James), the mind does not shuttle ideas as if they were behaving as *entities* and thus amenable to representation. Indeed, mental "ideas" are not *represented* as such, for if they exist as a kind of fluid, they cannot be objectified as a *thing*. In sum, for Wundt, thoughts are not discrete impressions or ideas; they are activities, or what we would today call *processes* (Nicholson and Dupré 2018). This was James's view as well.

Yet, in terms of establishing the science of psychology, Wundt, like Freud (and in contrast to James), was an ardent positivist, and heralded what he called a "new domain of science" by insisting that "all accurate observation implies . . . that the observed object is independent of the observer" (quoted by Mandler 2006, 60). The difference lay in how the mind was conceived: Freud assumed a physicalist model; Wundt insisted on a science of the mental on its own terms. So, Wundt was a positivist in terms of methodology but diverged from positivist-reductionist principles that would establish physical laws for all biological phenomena.

While Freud and Wundt were both positivists, the former directed his attention to dynamics of pathologies and the complex responses to emotional trauma, while the latter restricted his experimental science to a strictly quantitative analysis of cognitive functions. Despite these vast differences in the goals of their respective research, they both understood that the mental in some sense emanates from physical brain states, but from that point they diverged: Wundt remained steadfastly within the objectivity of the data he possessed and made no attempt to extrapolate those findings to a model of the mind. For him, the brain remained a "black box." Freud was far less cautious. Because of his own philosophical and scientific commitments (and, some would say, a result of an irresistible search for professional respectability [Gay 1988]), he was guided by the ultimate desire to reduce the unconscious to a *physical* reality (i.e., a product of brain states) and thereby claim that he was, in fact, doing *science*, science as a "psycho-physicist." If he had examined his philosophical assumptions more carefully, he might well have reconsidered his formulation. James suffered no such myopia and was acutely aware of the philosophical problems underlying psychology, and as discussed in the next chapter, he eventually discarded positivism altogether. To complete this triangulation, Wundt and James shared an intellectual kinship in agreeing that the mental is fundamentally *emergent*, and thus they rejected the implicit reductionism embedded in Freud's theory. Thus, Wundt philosophically resides between our protagonists, in that he rejected any notion of mental atomism, while Freud stood at the other end of the positivist spectrum in his full endorsement of the natural science research program that required an atomism he would apply to the putative objectification of the unconscious. James would have none of it and put a pox on both houses.

Notes

1 The romantic/positivist polarization must be balanced with the aims of scientific investigation shared with the Romantics, namely, the goals of science must be distinguished from its methods (Tauber 2009a). While positivism argued for a radical shift in investigative practices, its basic objectives were similar to Romantic holism, i.e., discerning the unity of nature that undergirded all its variegated manifestations, including the apparent unique standing of humans (Smocovitis 1996). Thus, despite its contrasting methods, positivists also pursued the same metaphysical aims of defining that coherence which characterized Romanticism, albeit with different emphases on the subjective aspects. And as to emotional "contamination," key scientists and philosophers of science throughout the latter half of the nineteenth century explicitly attempted to integrate a Romantic sense of imagination and beauty as important factors

in the appreciation of the scientific worldview (see various essays in Tauber 1996). In other words, they saw no inconsistency in gleaning objective facts by a radical separation of subject and object, and then synthesizing and interpreting those data with human sensibilities.

2 Ontological (metaphysical) reductionism holds that reality is the sum of its parts; methodological reductionism seeks to provide explanation in terms of an object or a phenomenon's parts. In the modern context, holism is understood in terms of emergent properties, i.e., those properties which cannot be explained from the sum of parts, e.g., swarming phenomena among fishes, birds, insects; the stock market; and mental states (Bedau and Humphreys 2008; Humphreys 2019).

3 Some would argue that consilience could not be achieved, in principle, because: (1) two kinds of Reason were required (one for the natural world and the other for the "moral," per Kant), and thus the so-called "unity of Reason" problem could not be solved (Neiman 1994; Beiser 2014); or (2) science, by employing a restrictive form of Reason in which its limits remained unacknowledged, simply ignores the matter as irrelevant to its concerns (Tauber 1993, 2009a); or (3) as James argued, diverse forms of knowledge have legitimacy and thus pluralism, not some underlying unity, should govern the discussion. Despite lingering complaints, the Unity of Reason problem sputtered along in the first half of the last century and then largely abandoned after World War II (M. Weber 1946; Husserl 1970; Toulmin 2001; Tauber 2009a; Heidegger 2017), while the dream of consilience remains (e.g., Wilson 1998). Those who discard the very possibility of some enveloping philosophy basically ignore the unification project or dismiss it as misconceived. For those in that rejecting camp, "multifocal" reason characterizes human life, and to pursue integration smacks of eclipsed metaphysics. This was James's basic position in his advocacy of pluralism.

4 Parallel to the debates about the philosophy of science that would guide the newly hatched discipline of psychology, a vigorous polemic among philosophers commenced over *psychologism*, a debate about the extent rationality is a matter for *psychological* study (Kusch 2011; summary in Tauber 2013a, 95–7). That discussion reflected a much deeper philosophical problem, namely the relation of mind and nature. The original dispute centered on the question of whether logic (and epistemology) is a subject of psychology and to what extent philosophy's own analytics were subject to the cognitive structures embedded in the mind's workings. Thus, arose this newly minted dispute over psychologism that drew from both the ebb of idealism (and a renewed materialism) and the birth of the scientific discipline, psychology. The pragmatists, James included, could not evade that debate and generally sided with the advocates of psychologism. They maintained that logic and psychology could not be separated and thus conflated criteria of truth with the use and practical consequences of rational thought (Bordogna 2008, 163–81). The controversy reflected the larger struggle over the boundaries of a newly emergent psychology against philosophy that sought to protect its traditional jurisdictions (Bordogna 2008; see Chapter 2). Note that in 1900, the American Philosophical Association was founded and thus splintered the American Psychological Association that had been established in 1892, with G. Stanley Hall as President.

5 *Scientist* and *artist* each first appeared in English about the same time. "Artist" was coined from the French, *artiste*, in 1823, to signify a specialization of those who practiced the creative arts requiring differentiation.

6 In his steadfast adherence to a positivist theory of knowledge, Freud failed to appreciate that Kant himself understood the limitations of a representational schema that would be misapplied to all categories of experience. Freud clearly knew the first *Critique* and closely applied epistemological parallels between the *noumenon* and the unconscious (albeit with glaring errors) (Kant 1998 [1787]; Tauber 2013a, 219). In that construction, a subject-object relationship is established by an ego that serves as a faculty to represent the mind to itself (see Tauber 2010, 179ff.). However, Freud apparently did not know or appreciate Kant's third *Critique, The Critique of Judgment* (1987 [1790]). There, Kant attempted to establish how scientific thinking, as objective knowledge, might be reconciled with subjective ways of knowing.

7 Note that Reason's capacity to fulfill its role in psychoanalysis rests on an astonishing claim, one that truly indebts Freud to Kant. At the end of his 1915 acknowledgement to Kant, Freud writes, "like the physical, the psychical is not necessarily in reality what it appears to us to be. We shall be glad to learn, however, that *the correction of internal perception will turn out not to offer such great difficulties as the correction of external perception*—that internal objects are less unknowable than the external world" (Freud 1915b, 171; emphasis added). Apparently, the smaller space separating the subject (the conscious ego) and object (the unconscious) changes the epistemological relationship normally separating the knowing agent from nature (i.e., the unconscious). On what basis could Freud make such an assertion? Justification is not offered.

In following Kantian transcendental philosophy, Freud took no account of Kant's own view of introspection. As I have previously observed (Tauber 2010, 255–6), in his *Anthropology from a Pragmatic Point of View* of 1798, Kant clarified his notions of "inner sense" and "apperception": "This difficulty [the objectification of inner states] rests entirely on the confusion of inner sense with apperception (intellectual self-consciousness), which are usually taken to be one and the same [but are not]" (Kant 2006, 31). Interestingly, the "inner state" Kant refers to apparently only possesses a one-way vector in the healthy mind, for those states that seemingly arise spontaneously, that is, appear independently of self-conscious scrutiny or intelligible self-awareness, and then are brought to self-consciousness (namely to "spy upon one's self" [Kant 1996, 17]), are of a dangerous sort. Thus, the entire métier of psychoanalysis—free association and unbidden thoughts and emotions—repelled Kant's sense of mental propriety (Stone 1983)—and this difference from Freud's psychiatric pursuits cautions to be cognizant of the vast differences in their theories of psychology while observing their deeper philosophical affinities.

8 In "The unconscious" (1915b), Freud explicitly addressed the relationship of language (representations) with the unconscious object, where he asserted that the "thing-presentation" cannot become conscious until associated with words, and this step occurs in the preconscious (not the unconscious, which knows no language as such). He posited that at the interface of conscious and unconscious mental life, this associative locale (where unconscious objects or drives become associated with language) provides the key link between the sectors of the psyche to offer the coherence required for normal mentation.

9 The semantic basis of the process is critical: Freud employed a symbolic function of language, one independent of the sensory domain. While "verbal aphasia, in which only the associations between the single elements of the word

concept [word-presentation] are disturbed," a second *asymbolic aphasia* is defined as occurring when "the association between word concept and object concept are disturbed" (Freud 1953 [1891], 78). He goes on to explain that he uses *asymbolic* as a designation for the relationship between the word and the idea of the object, as opposed to the relationship of the object and its idea. In other words, the *word* represents the idea of the object, not the object itself: *symbolic* captures the relation between word presentation [*Vorstellung*] and object presentation, rather than that between object and object presentation (Freud 1915b, 214). As Greenberg observes, "[T]he word is not a symbol of the object—which would imply a nonarbitrary or necessary connection—but rather the relationship is between the idea (*Vorstellung*) of the word and the idea of the object" (1997, 171). Freud's use of *Vorstellung* (presentation) is complex with differing uses and translations employed during the 1895–1915 period (see Tauber 2013a, 221). The concept originates in Mill's philosophical construction, which in turn relies on Kant, that "a Sensation is to be carefully distinguished from the object which causes the sensation" (J. S. Mill, *A System of Logic* [1873, 34], quoted by Greenberg 1997, 165).

10 In establishing their respective psychologies, Brentano and Freud presented radically opposed philosophies of mind: Brentano assigned the unconscious to metaphysics, while Freud claimed to have studied the unconscious as an object of scientific scrutiny. The key element in their divergent views hinged on the notion of psychic causality. Brentano set the criteria that Freud later would attempt to fulfill in his own theory, and, in this sense, Freud remained committed to Brentano's original project, one guided by empiricism and strict observational standards. That Freud failed to fulfill Brentano's challenge for establishing unconscious causation is discussed in Tauber (2010, 40–53).

11 The rejection of idealism as a philosophy does not mean that Freud was immune to its wider influence. As Rudnytsky so richly illustrates (1987, 193–8), Freud's adoption of the Oedipus myth and the constellation of ideas swirling around mythic depictions of human nature and the metaphysics of freedom and fate cannot divorce Freud from the romantic philosophers he took such efforts to reject.

12 Note, Freud exhibited some inconsistency (and perhaps revealed some ambivalence) as he played to the philosopher's band by imagining that instead of rejection, the new theory "would be all the more likely to meet with applause from philosophers" as he hoped to direct them towards a new understanding (Freud 1925b, 216). By and large he failed, and in frustration he ranted throughout his career against the consciousness-oriented philosophies of mind as a misdirected basis for their inquiries. A comprehensive overview of Freud's ambivalent attitude towards philosophy is given by Richard Askay and Jensen Farquhar (2006, 16ff.), who cite the key remarks Freud made about philosophy throughout his career and then show the various philosophical influences on him from the ancients to Nietzsche. Having demonstrated that Freud was well educated in philosophy, they then offer a critique of psychoanalysis in the context of existential phenomenology (i.e., emphasis on Husserl, Heidegger, Sartre, and Merleau-Ponty).

13   While this is true of his clinical writings, late in his career Freud became, in a manner of speaking, philosophical through his metapsychology writings and extrapolations of psychoanalytic insights to social concerns. He transformed "his science of the unconscious into the mythology of Eros and death instincts [Freud 1920]" (Draenos 1982, 147) and applied psychoanalytic theory to social theory and human culture from *Totem and Taboo* (1913a) to *Moses and Monotheism* (1939).

14   *Vorstellung* functions as a signifier (Laplanche and Pontalis 1973, 200; see note #9), but the precise meanings of *Trieb* and *instinkt* remain unsettled in the psychoanalytic literature, given Freud's own ambiguous uses. Generally, *instinkt* is used to convey the reflex arc, an inherited neurological pathway with designated sequence of behavior or physiological response. *Trieb* connotes the more general drive, urge, and pressure towards a goal (Laplanche and Pontalis 1973, 214). In this general sense, the English, "drive," captures unconscious forces of desire. "The concept of *Trieb* is one of the most obscure notions that psychoanalysis retains in its theoretical baggage, precisely because it is, as it were, a 'mythological' entity" (Sinatora and Mezzalira 2021, 57).

15   Freud based his interpretations on "inference to the best explanation" (Lipton 1991) that bypasses syllogistic proof for a rational interpretation driven and framed by a particular *telos*, i.e., the analyst reconstructs the unconscious dynamics exhibited through the analysand's associations, dreams, parapraxis, etc. (Freud 1937; Rubovits-Seitz 1998). Of course, the interpretation must hold together as a whole; one piece supports the others, so a hermeneutic circle is established. Note that an inference is a mode of reasoning from a premise to a conclusion; however, the logical structure of Freud's argument shows that he drew his inference from a premise that already contains the conclusion. What he hoped to derive along a causal chain of reasoning from empirical data is in fact an inference drawn directly from his *definitions* of the mental (constituted by conscious and unconscious activities), which he did not establish. Thus, his reasoning is circular, and the entire argument for the unconscious collapses as an exercise in deductive logic, which does not gainsay other interpretive strategies (see Tauber 2010, 63–6; 2013a, 213).

16   Later, Freud clarified that while he thought intra-psychic divisions were maintained, he allowed for some exchange, both through repression from "above" and unconscious "derivatives" (e.g., "instinctual impulses") thrust into preconsciousness, and then potentially making their way to consciousness. Especially regarding the latter dynamic, Freud disavowed any clear-cut distinction between unconscious (Ucs.) and preconscious (Pcs.)/conscious (Cs.) and, furthermore, he had a most circumspect view of consciousness:

> Consciousness stands in no simple relation either to the different systems [Ucs. and Pcs.] or to repression. The truth is that it is not only the psychically repressed that remains alien to consciousness, but also some of the impulses which dominate our ego—something, therefore, that forms the strongest functional antithesis to the repressed.
>
> (Freud 1915b, 192–3)

17 Freud most directly followed those who regarded "representations" as serving as the currency of the psychic apparatus from the first generation of scientific psychologists, e.g., Johann Herbart (1776–1841) (De Kesel 2009, 295). Herbart posited that

> all mental phenomena result from the actions and interactions of "ideas" (presentations [representations]); that ideas are of different kinds, stronger and weaker; that arrested (inhibited) ideas are obscured and disappear from consciousness, leaving the field to others; that such inhibited, unconscious ideas constitute a mass and continue to exert their pressure against those in consciousness; and that there is a continual conflict between conscious and unconscious ideas at the threshold of consciousness.
>
> (Whyte 1978, 143)

Thus, Herbart, who assumed Kant's Königsberg philosophy chair in 1809, was heavily influenced by his predecessor's representationalism. Although Herbart's associationist psychology had an important influence on early psychoanalytic theorizing, that genealogy is more immediately tracked to Gustav Fechner (1801–1887), whose Herbartian theorizing directly influenced Freud's own Newtonian psychodynamic postulates (Ellenberger 1970, 478–9, 489).

18 The representationalism embedded in modern cognitive science models of the mind are inspired by cybernetic-inspired theories, in which representations are phrased in terms of a defined code—symbolic and static—that comprises a vocabulary governed by syntax. Criticism argues that contextual factors and synthetic modalities of thought cannot be constructed from such a limited conception of language (Shanon 1993; Ramsey 2007).

19 James opined that these efforts have "borne little theoretic fruit commensurate with the great labor expended in their acquisition. But facts are facts, and if we only get enough of them, they are sure to combine. New ground will from year to year be broken, and theoretic results will grow." But he had little hope that such efforts would yield a valid picture of the mental (James 1983, 193). James divided experimental psychology into

> 1) the connection of conscious states with their physical conditions, including the whole of brain-physiology, . . . physiology of the sense-organs, [and correlations] between sensations and the outward stimuli by which they are aroused; 2) the analysis of space-perception into its sensational elements; 3) the measurement of the duration of the simplest mental processes; 4) the accuracy of reproduction in the memory of sensible experiences and of intervals of space and time; 5) [how] simple mental states influence each other, call each other up, or inhibit each other's reproduction; 6) the number of facts which consciousness can simultaneously discern; finally, 7) the elementary laws of oblivescence and retention.
>
> (James 1983, 192)

Chapter 2

James's assault on metaphysical dualism

James's career falls into two overlapping stages. From his first scientific studies in the early 1870s until the publication of *The Principles of Psychology* in 1890, he was considered a pioneering psychologist committed to scientific principles. After 1892 he discarded the robes of the laboratory and focused on the philosophy that had interested him since adolescence (with C. S. Peirce), read Kant and Renouvier at Harvard, and continued intense philosophical discussions in the Metaphysical Club shortly after graduating from medical school (Perry 1935, 285–90; Bjork 1988, 42–7; Menand 2001; Richardson 2006, 128–38).[1] By 1885, James was appointed a full professor of philosophy at Harvard, and then inaugurated as the first Alford Professor of Psychology in 1889. Simply put, the two disciplines were not fully separated during this period, and the two stages might better be labeled dominantly "physician" (researcher) and "metaphysician" (in a very particular sense James would redefine), respectively.

Acknowledging the parallel course of his interests, James, like Freud and Wundt, initially accepted the framework of physiology as offering the "template" for psychology. As a research physician, this was his professional starting point and would guide his early investigations. However, the character of that science can only be described as tentative. For example, consider his "physiological" description of memory storage and retrieval: "The condition which makes [recall] possible at all . . . is neither more nor less than the brain-paths which *associate* the experience with the occasion and cue of recall" (James 1983, 616, emphasis in original). No evidence is provided; the statement is simply given without direct evidence and skips from a descriptive observation about recall to a cloaked "quasi" fact. The ready acceptance of such a deduction as an "explanation" illustrates the state of both the psychology and the physiology of the era (Mandler 2006, 68). We must look elsewhere to contrast the philosophical divergence of the American from his European experimentalist colleagues.

DOI: 10.4324/9781003565413-2

To tease out these differences, consider how James's own conception of the mind challenges Freudianism in ways that had even deeper implications than Wundt's own cognitive approach. As mentioned, they both shared a deep skepticism about the associationist strategy stemming from their similar opposition to reductionist analyses. James built an entire philosophy on his steadfast argument that consciousness could not be broken into parts, and if continuous, then associations of one element with another could not take place. I quote at length from his 1884 essay, "On Some Omissions of Introspective Psychology," for within its critique of associationist psychology lies the kernel of his radical reformulation of the mental:

> From the continuously flowing thing it is, it is changed into a "manifold," broken into bits, called discrete; and in this condition, approved as its authentic and natural shape by the most opposite schools, it becomes the topic of one of the most tedious and interminable quarrels that philosophy has to show. I do not mean to say that the "Associationist" manner of representing the life of the mind as an agglutination in various shapes of separate entities called ideas, and the Herbartian way of representing it as resulting from the mutual repugnancies of separate entities called *Vorstellungen*, are not convenient formulas for roughly symbolizing the facts . . . But, if taken as literal truth . . . [they] lead to pernicious results . . . for one and the same reason, that what God has joined together they resolutely and wantonly put asunder. . . . For the stream of our feeling is sensibly continuous, like time's stream. This is surely the natural way of viewing it in the first instance, and as an empirical fact. It presents itself as a continuum.
>
> (James 1992b [1884], 991–2)

Here is the core of James's insight, the established credo of his psychology, whether called "the stream of thought" (*Principles of Psychology*, 1890) or the "stream of consciousness" (*Briefer Course*, 1892).

The key to James's thought is through his characterization of consciousness as a "selecting agency" (James 1983, 142), "the very keel on which our mental ship is built" (James 1983, 640), and thus forming the "nucleus of our inner self" (James 1983, 423). This is the central motif of *The Principles of Psychology* and constitutes the basis of viewing the mind as active and selective, whose volition is dictated by attention: "[E]ach of us literally chooses, by his ways of attending to things, what sort of a universe he shall appear to himself to inhabit" (James 1983, 401). James regarded the selective attending of consciousness an extension of the cognitive expression of an active organism in its environment, and it is manifest from the simplest responses to the most complex interactions. Human action—volition, thought, reorganization, and manipulation of the environment—can be understood in light of the Darwinian position that individual variation is the basis for adaptive change and adjustment. Given that context, James asserts an ideal of freedom of action and the unique value of the individual (Seigfried 1984).

Because the world must then be organized from "one great blooming, buzzing confusion" (James 1983, 462), the selective focus must be exercised in two respects: (1) immediate attention driven by (2) underlying interests. Attention is thus regarded as an active response to external stimuli. In that dynamic, objects of attention and inquiry are never viewed twice in the same context or from the same perspective. The experiencing subject continuously shifts attention, resulting in adaptations. This epistemology demands an organizational, dynamic psychology and thereby asserts freedom of action in which the stimulus-response reflex of simple nerve circuits is modified by choice. James thereby rejected linear mechanical models of the mind. The how was a mystery, but the why was grounded in a conception of the individual and the authority of pragmatic utility (Pawelski 2007). The animal seeks its own flourishing in a world of change and opportunity.

James built this philosophical construct from the bottom up with his insistence on the primacy and integrity of the "stream of consciousness" that (when active) suffers no disruption. Indeed, the continuity of "experience" becomes the *sine qua non* of subjectivity; when "arrested" and processed into segments or "bits," the continuous flow undergoes a distortion in its *retroactive re*-presentation. Note that, in this epistemological schema, the subjective has been objectified by converting immediate experience into an object of conscious scrutiny, which in turn generates the romantic challenge: how to recapture the immediacy of the original subjectivity with its full vibrancy, its *life*, given that the pre-articulated experience transmutes into "something else" upon self-conscious reflection. The first-order experience (without self-reflection) has no such subject-object configuration.

James decried positivism not as a philosophy of science, but, more generally, as a philosophy of knowing, whose objectivity was inadequate for navigating the world as *experienced* subjectively and thus making it meaningful. Thomas Nagel (1986) observed that "absolute objectivity"— or all-embracing knowledge—is deeply paradoxical because such knowledge cannot adopt a particular view—that is, be inclusive of reality as one knows it (the subjective)—and is thus always partial and incomplete. Ideally, the subjective and the objective should be joined, but because of the limits imposed on absolute objectivity, science can offer only "a view from nowhere"—that is, a knowledge which cannot be situated. And with no perspective, there is no significance, no meaning, and no human-oriented order. Simply put, radical objectivity distorts experience because the view from nowhere subtracts the human vantage. James sought a more comprehensive view of reality and thereby fully affiliated with Romanticism.

For Romantics, the key issue is the relation between *me* and the world. As Henry David Thoreau opined:

> I think that the man of science makes this mistake, and the mass of mankind along with him: that you should coolly give your chief attention to the phenomenon which excites you as something independent on you, and not as it is related to you. *The important fact is its effect on me.* He thinks that I have no business to see anything else but just what he defines the rainbow to be, but I do not care whether my vision of truth is a waking thought or dream remembered, whether it is seen in the light or in the dark. It is the subject of the vision, the truth alone, that concerns me. The philosopher for whom rainbows, etc., can be explained away never saw them. With regard to such objects, I find that it is not they themselves (with which the men of science deal) that concern me; the point of interest is somewhere *between* me and them (i.e. the objects).
>
> (Thoreau 1962, 10:164–5 [November 5, 1857], emphasis added)

Thoreau's artistry exemplifies how subjective experience becomes conscious, and that consciousness is both the means for re-creating the moment of encounter and at the same time reflects the attempt to capture the immediacy of his original feelings. In other words, he celebrated the Romantic's reconfiguration of his primary experience—the artistic rendering, the crafted report of a subjective moment (Tauber 2001, 2012a). And James would concur in drawing the larger conclusion: "Our judgments concerning the worth of things, big or little, depend on the *feelings* the things arouse in us" (James 1992i, 841, emphasis in original).

However, James went radically further. In the cognitive rendering, such "feeling" is captured as "content," which is a second-order processing of the primary experience. And as a *re*-presentation it is never complete. Indeed, whenever *any* experience is translated into an articulation (written, spoken, codified), the *re*-presentation leaves behind "an excess" that remains unsaid and, in a sense, unthought yet "present."[2] One's feelings or intuitions, that which may escape self-consciousness itself, resists expression and, in this sense, remains beyond the enunciation of other kinds of knowledge. On this view, the conscious, expressed version of the primary experience is a second-order *re*-presentation, irretrievably incomplete and thus distorting the primary unprocessed experience.[3] And then the critical philosophical issue appears: *What* is primary experience if the pronounced distillation or translation of that experience is the product of one's consciousness? Or, simply, what is consciousness? That is the question James addressed, and he did so fully acknowledging the subjectivity in which such experience resided. His was a philosophical psychology fully embracing the Romantic attempt to recapture experience and with it the subjectivity underwriting all that escaped analytics. Indeed, viewing the psyche from James's perspective highlights the *sui generis* of subjectivity and the limits of objectivity.

James's philosophy of mind

Given the partition between unprocessed experience and consciousness, James focused his philosophical lens on *experience* in its primordial state, before the stage of consciousness. He called that domain "pure experience"—"the immediate flux of life which furnishes the material to our later reflections with its conceptual categories" (James 1987g, 782). He thereby forsook *consciousness*, and the *science* of consciousness for a non-dualist metaphysics (detailed in this section). As James testified, he became dissatisfied with his earlier *Principles of Psychology*, and shortly after its publication, he began a reformulation based on his own observations concerning the mind's unity and the pragmatism by which it connects to the world and constructs meaning. In that rendering, he attacked the dualism that spawned what he called, "the psychologist's fallacy," and with that transfiguration he left the science of the mind to others.

James fiercely protected subjectivity from encroachments by the scientific ethos. For him, inner states do not adhere to the demands of objectivity and thus required a mode of understanding that dispensed with a misapplied scientism. That mature position followed from a more orthodox preamble. His early psychological career rested firmly within the physiological framework of an ascendant positivist biology. This was James's starting point, given his training as a physician, and that attitude guided his early research, one that would, however, eventually evolve into what may be fairly described (as he himself dubbed his philosophy) a "radical empiricism." While psychology as a science required the subject-object dualist schema, he would eventually substitute a view of the mind that displaced that basic configuration of investigation. In an early essay, "The Sentiment of Rationality" (1879), James explicitly set his agenda that took another 25 years to fully articulate:

Metaphysics of some sort there must be. The only alternative is between the good metaphysics of clear-headed Philosophy and the trashy metaphysics of vulgar Positivism. Metaphysics, the quest of the last clear elements of things, is but another name for thought which seeks thorough self-consistency; and so long as men must think of all, some will be found willing to forsake all else to follow that ideal.

(James 1992f, 977)

Indeed, even as he established the first American psychology laboratory at Harvard in 1875 (Harper 1950), he resisted the slippage into objectification committed by the experimentalist, whose

attitude toward cognition . . . is a thorough going dualism. It supposes two elements, mind knowing and thing known, and treats them as irreducible. Neither gets out of itself or into the other, neither in any way *is* the other, neither *makes* the other.

(James 1983, 214, emphasis in original)

For James, the duality imposes an irrevocable distortion:

The *great* snare of the psychologists is the *confusion of his own standpoint with that of the mental fact* about which he is making his report . . . . The psychologist . . . stands outside the mental state he speaks of. Both itself and its objects are objects for him. Now when it is a *cognitive* state (percept, thought, concept, etc.) he ordinarily has no other way of naming it than as the thought precept, etc., *of that object.* He himself, meanwhile, knowing the self-same object in *his* way, gets easily led to suppose that the thought, which is *of* it knows it in the same way in which he knows it, although this is often very far from being the case.

(James 1983, 195, emphasis in original)

Accordingly, the "psychologist's fallacy" confused what is experienced from within with the secondhand knowledge of an observer, whether external or the retro-introspective agent, herself. Both are guilty of "substituting what we know the consciousness *is*, for what it is a consciousness *of*" (James 1983, 196). The fallacy is more than a methodological error, for in the very act of parsing consciousness into segments, i.e., discrete parts,

the continuous flow of the mental stream is sacrificed, and in its place an atomism, a brickbat plan of construction is brought forward, and out of which no good introspective grounds can be brought forward, and out of which presently grow all sorts of paradoxes and contradictions, the heritage of woe of students of the mind.

(James 1983, 194–5)

Thus, the "objects" of self-consciousness are artifacts resulting when a given "bit" of experience is abstracted from the unified flow and retrospectively considered in the context of different relations. Characterizing consciousness as an indivisible unit, James reconceived the philosophy of mental experience by recognizing that a third-person perspective translates personal experience into a distorted objectification of parts. Such a representation is not the phenomenon itself, but only its *re*-presentation. So, James utterly rejected the schema upon which Freud based his psychology, and while Wundt and his German followers examined the mind by physiological parameters, James would characterize consciousness, that which is experienced, on its own terms.

Thus for James, the "objects" of self-consciousness are artifacts resulting when a given "bit" of experience is abstracted from the unified flow and retrospectively considered in the context of different relations. This is the basis of James's rejection of associationist approaches, which divided thought into discrete elements that would then be sorted and juxtaposed to picture mental function. Instead, he argued that *"however complex the object may be, the thought of it is one individual state of consciousness"* (James 1983, 266, emphasis in original) and to dissect such thought into components is to distort the experience of consciousness into a falsified series of segments: *"There is no manifold of coexisting ideas*; the notion of such a thing is a chimera. *Whatever things are thought in relation are thought from the outset in a unity, in a single pulse of subjectivity, a single psychosis, feeling, or state of mind"* (James 1983, 268, emphasis in original). James goes on to explain:

> The reason why this fact is so strangely garbled in the books seems to be what on an earlier page [James 1983, 195 ff.] I called the psychologist's fallacy. We have the inveterate habit, whenever we try introspectively to describe one of our thoughts, of dropping the thought as it is in itself and talking of something else. We describe the things that appear to the thought, and we describe other thoughts about those things—as if these and the original thought were the same . . . What a thought is, and what it may be developed into, or explained to stand for, and be equivalent to, are two things, not one.
>
> (James 1983, 268)

James made a serious indictment: consciousness as studied by the psychologist distorted the normal flow of the mind. He then recognized that the key issue was not methodological, but rather the very basis of the science employed. A different way of thinking about the mental was required.

James thus evolved from considering consciousness as a critical component of scientific psychology to a problem lying at the base of the metaphysics directing the objectification of the mind. From his early psychological
writings through the magisterial *Principles* (1890), he had misgivings
about psychology's conceptual foundations that grew from his resistance
to regarding the mind in physicalist terms. While material things or processes might be dissected into their various parts, he argued that subjective states cannot be broken into such elements. He vigorously rebutted
the so-called Mind-Stuff Theory, in which mind states are composed of
unconscious mental units, and instead insisted that conscious experience is
singular (*Principles of Psychology*, chapter 6). For example, green, composed of blue and yellow, cannot be divided into those primary colors but
are *experienced* solely as green; the separation of sweetness and sourness in
lemonade does not disentangle the unified experience of the drink, namely,
it is tasted as a singular experience (James 1992a, 1074). This position dates
to James's early psychology:

> When I think the seven colors of the rainbow, I do not have seven
> thoughts of a color, and then a thought of a bow; that would be eight
> thoughts. What I have is just one thought of the whole object. And the
> first reasonable word has yet to be said to prove that such a "thought"
> as this is not, when considered in its subjective constitution, and apart
> from its cognitive function, also a "feeling," as specific and unique as the
> simplest affection of consciousness.
>
> (James 1992b [1884], 996).

This "continuity thesis" underlies all later developments of James's psychology. More deeply, by emphasizing the continuity of experience, he
would not allow any inserted break introduced by reflexivity and concomi-
tant subject-object partition.

Introspection is by its very nature a secondhand report, where the initial feeling (the firsthand experience) is scrutinized and recounted as an
object of thought (Smithies and Stoljar 2012; Kriegel 2009). These are
the "bits," the extracted artifacts of self-consciousness James sought to
purge in his characterization of mental life. As he introduced the key
notion of "stream of consciousness," he emphasized the artifactual
nature of reviewing experience retrospectively that renders consciousness as appearing

> chopped up in bits. Such words as "chain" or "train" do not describe it
> fitly as it presents itself in the first instance. It is nothing jointed; it flows.
> A "river" or a "stream" are the metaphors by which it is most naturally

described. *In talking of it hereafter, let us call it the stream of thought, of consciousness, or of subjective life.*

But now there appears, even within the limits of the same self, and between thoughts all of which alike have this same sense of belonging together, a kind of jointing and separateness among the parts, of which this statement seems to take no account . . . Do not such interruptions smite us every hour of our lives, and have we the right, in their presence, still to call our consciousness a continuous stream?

This objection is based partly on a confusion and partly on a superficial introspective view.

The confusion is between the thoughts themselves, taken as subjective facts, and the things of which they are aware. It is natural to make this confusion, but easy to avoid it when once put on one's guard. The things are discrete and discontinuous; they do pass before us in a train or chain, making often explosive appearances and rending each other in twain. But their comings and goings and contrasts no more break the flow of the thought that thinks them than they break the time and the space in which they lie.

(James 1983, 233, emphasis in original)

That insight originated in James's earliest thoughts on the matter and guided his later philosophical development.

Ralph Barton Perry, James's student, colleague, and key biographer, quotes from an early notebook (1870) in which James devotes thirty pages to the status of what was called "natural realism" as expounded by Samuel Bailey in *Letters on the Philosophy of the Human Mind* (1855): physical reality is immediately presented in perception and thus prior to the reflexive act in which the mind becomes aware of its own states. James, in his consideration of Bailey's realist argument, focused on the status of representation:

The act of knowledge never knows itself, though it may be known by a later act of the same subject:—Be your reflection as agile as it may, you can never make it seize upon its very self, never make the instant act of thinking become the thing thought of, any more than the man in Chamisso's could overtake his pigtail by rotating. In other words, we never overtake the immediate in thought, the essence of whose form, consequently, is to posit an object distinct from itself. Thus the very form of thought implies a duality. While you think, you think of an object, be it a thing or idea, and not your instant thinking. *This* the idealist must admit . . . Logically analyzed . . . the *act* of knowledge always skips one step forwards and outside of the object of knowledge, which therefore remains an object ever.

(Perry 1935, 576, emphasis in original)

Thus, very early in his career, James recognized the irreducible subject-object structure of self-reflection, a second-order (retrospective) process; first-order (un-reflected) consciousness has no such division. He carried this observation into his maturity, where it served to undercut the claims of scientific introspection, and, more broadly, it set the groundwork for deconstructing the presumptions of selfhood as a definable entity, as to *what* is *me* as a product of self-consciousness:

> If they really were the innermost sanctuary, the *ultimate* one of all the selves whose being we can never directly experience, it would follow that *all* that is experienced is strictly considered *objective*; that this Objective falls asunder into two contrasted parts, one realized as "Self," the other as "not S;" and that over and above these parts there *is* nothing save the fact that they are known, the fact of the stream being there as the indispensable subjective condition of their being experienced at all. But this *condition* of the experience is not one of the *things experienced* at the moment; this knowing is not immediately *known*. It is only known in subsequent reflection. Instead, then, of the stream of thought being one of *con*-sciousness, thinking its own existence along with whatever else it thinks . . . it might be better called a stream of *Sciousness* pure and simple, thinking objects of some of which it makes what it calls a "Me," and only aware of its "pure" Self in an abstract hypothetic or conceptual way. Each "section" of the stream would then be a bit of sciousness or knowledge of this sort, including and contemplating its "me" and it's "not me" as objects . . . but not yet including or contemplating its own subjective being. The sciousness in question would be the *Thinker*, and the existence of this thinker would be given to us rather as a logical postulate than as that direct inner perception of spiritual activity which we naturally believe ourselves to have.
>
> (James 1983, 290–1, emphasis in original)

Accordingly, the Thinker, the self-aware putative *self*, becomes "a phase of the stream of consciousness, a phenomenon among the stream's phenomena, capable of being treated as a datum within experience and having the same basic nature as other data accessible to psychological inquiry"—an *object* of thought, not of thought itself (Myers 1986, 263). Such an agent is inextricably entwined within a stream of thought jumping between first- and secondhand accounts of consciousness. In other words, "the self" is *of* consciousness, and *sciousness*, immediate experience, *exists* unmediated. In short, "a subject-spectator watching the 'real world' must be given up if we are to understand that what goes on not *in* but *as* consciousness" (Barzun 1992, 905, emphasis in original).

Although James characterized the self in its various modalities (empirical, social relational, indexical, etc.; see Chapter 5), the core matter would reside as a deep mystery and thus undefined:

This attention to thought as such, and the identification of ourselves with it rather than with any of the objects which it reveals, is a momentous and in some respects a rather mysterious operation, of which we need here only say that as a matter of fact it exists; and that in everyone, at an early age, the distinction between thought as such, and what it is "of" or "about," has become familiar to the mind. The deeper grounds for this discrimination may possibly be hard to find; but superficial grounds are plenty and near at hand. Almost anyone will tell us that thought is a different sort of existence from things, because many sorts of thought are of no things—e.g., pleasures, pains, and emotions; others are of non-existent things—errors and fictions; others again of existent things, but in a form that is symbolic and does not resemble them—abstract ideas and concepts; whilst in the thoughts that do resemble the things they are "of" (percepts, sensations), we can feel, alongside of the thing known, the thought of it going on as an altogether separate act and operation in the mind . . .

If the stream as a whole is identified with the Self far more than any outward thing, a *certain portion of the stream abstracted from the rest* is so identified in an altogether peculiar degree, and is felt by all men as a sort of innermost centre within the circle, of sanctuary within the citadel, constituted by the subjective life as a whole. Compared with this element of the stream, the other parts, even of the subjective life, seem transient external possessions, of which each in turn can be disowned, whilst that which disowns them remains. Now, *what is this self of all the other selves?*

(James 1983, 284–5, emphasis in original)

With this question, the intractable character of consciousness, its resistance to scientific scrutiny (at least from the first-hand perspective), and the enigma of its evasive character that comprises our very sense of selfhood converge in James's reconceptualization of the mind. Accordingly, our sense of personal identity is a product of a second-order contemplation and as such, a construction or, at best, a presumed way of organizing consciousness in the familiar Cartesian subject/object structure of perception. As discussed in Chapter 5, Freud proceeded with unexamined assumptions about the knowing ego, while James followed the philosophical consequences of a flawed dualism to a radically different conclusion.

I postpone further discussion of this matter and suffice it to note here that James abdicated finding correlations or speculative mechanisms that would account for consciousness, much less unconscious mentation.[4] He repeatedly admitted that "the relations of a mind to its own brain are a unique and utterly mysterious sort" (James 1983, 212). And while he continued to study those relationships, for him, the two domains remained distinct and indeterminate in their interaction. And no wonder, for James recognized that consciousness is not an entity or something introspectable (Taylor and Wozniak 1996a, xiv). Although understood as analogous to sense perception, there is no *object* as such to be scrutinized. "No subjective state, whilst present, is its own subject; its object is always something else" (James 1983, 189), for "introspection is really immediate retrospection" (Myers 1986, 66). He was acutely aware of the confusion between the thoughts themselves comprising the stream of consciousness as subjective experience and the things of which the subject is aware that, unlike the stream, are discrete and discontinuous (James 1983, 233). With that recognition, James understood that the subject-object dualism that underlay the science of psychology could not account for the primary *experience* of the conscious subject.

The metaphysical turn

The Principles of Psychology, beneath its review of the discipline's advances and unresolved issues, obliquely referred to the philosophical problems lying at the base of the science of the mind. In the Preface, James clearly (perhaps defiantly) declared,

> Men must keep thinking; and the data assumed by psychology, just like those assumed by physics and the other natural sciences, must sometimes be overhauled. The effort to overhaul them clearly and thoroughly is metaphysics; but metaphysics can only perform her task well when distinctly conscious of its great extent.
>
> (James 1983, 6)

Such a revised metaphysics arose from his earlier declaration that the doing of the science could not solve the basic philosophical impasse imposed by an inadequate metaphysical foundation. So, by 1895 he concluded that the

> whole business of ascertaining how we come to know things together or to know them at all [fell well beyond psychology] considered as a natural science. Such considerations, I said, should fall to metaphysics. That we do know things, sometimes singly and sometimes together, is a

fact. That states of consciousness are the vehicle of the knowledge, and depend on brain states, are two other facts. And I thought that a natural science of psychology might legitimately confine itself to tracing the functional variations of these three sorts of fact, and to ascertaining what determinate bodily states are the condition when the states of mind know determinate things and groups of things. Most states of mind can be designated only by naming what objects they are "thoughts-of," i.e., what things they know.

(James 1992a, 1074)

Moreover, gathering such "facts" proved not only futile but misdirected. Alas, he was

giving it up. I have become convinced since publishing that book [*Principles of Psychology*, 1890] that no conventional restrictions can keep metaphysical and so-called epistemological inquiries out of the psychology-books. I see, moreover, better now than then, that my proposal to designate mental states merely by their cognitive function leads to a somewhat strained way of talking of dreams and reveries, and to quite an unnatural way of talking of some emotional states.

(James 1992a, 1075)

With that declaration, James, the psychologist, would develop a new philosophy of mind, and, in the process, save subjectivity.

As already explained, James argued that psychology misconceived its own agenda with a skewed portrait of mental life if it assumed that consciousness could be parsed into segments; or, put another way, that the reductionism applied to physiology would find comparable success in dissecting mental life into discrete components (Woodward 1983). Yes, science would advance, but not on the path leading to comprehending the *life* of the mind. Such subjective phenomena could not be captured from the psychologist third-person gaze. As discussed, for James, replacing the seeming disorder of mental sequences with a concocted template to order contrived "bits" (elements) distorted human experience. Accordingly, experience is unified, and by espousing the continuity of consciousness and recognizing the primacy of the unity of parts to form integral wholes, he rejected the "chopping up of 'the mind' into distinct units of composition or function, numbering these off, and labelling them by technical names" (James 1992c, 725).

As detailed in Chapter 5, James argued that the sense of continuity in which consciousness is viewed as a unified whole captures the sense of *me*. He derived this principle from Brentano's notion of inner perception, the reality of our sense of implicit coherence.[5] And that position in turn harkens back to Schopenhauer's view of the subject connecting the objects of his or her world through his or her own relation to them. The phenomenological challenge—that is, the issue of thought's intentionality—is developed by regarding the object, even when it is not directly linked to consciousness, as being an object of potential perception or action. Even outside the boundaries of immediate perception, the "hat in the cloakroom" (namely, what is not seen, but is known to exist) thus is allowed to exist.

With this orientation, James understood thought as "suffused with the consciousness of all that dim context" (James 1983, 227), namely, all that structures experience and that can only be analyzed reflexively. Selection (and ordering) of experience is present in every perception, and in fact we "actually *ignore* most of the things before us" (James 1983, 273, emphasis in original). Thinking thus involves choice, and interests are driven by those objects of practical or aesthetic importance, all integrated by a phenomenal totality (Seigfried 1990, 88). The need for selectivity of consciousness is an ever-changing flux of reality won by arbitrarily arresting experience. Conceptualization requires isolating and distinguishing some aspects, excluding others, and ordering reality not by hard and fast divisions, but by personal pursuit of meaning and goals. Experience, then, enters not as bare or raw data, but according to the needs of the one experiencing and thus organized to serve human needs, a thoroughly pragmatic conclusion.

A second aspect of James's advocacy for what he called the "stream of consciousness" drives another nail into the coffin of a Cartesian subject-object understanding of experience: if consciousness is a unity as presented, then no such "entity" as a synthesizing ego is required. Instead, phenomenological inquiries are focused on the interactive process of the subject with her environment.

On this view, the self—the abstracted agency of the mind—through active selection (guided by awareness and directed by intention) constructs its world from the bewildering complexity of the surrounding plenum. Accordingly, the acts of perception, recognition, and reaction portray the knowing agent in action, whose intention is key. As James wrote,

[Nature] is a vast plenum in which our attention draws capricious lines in innumerable directions. We count and name whatever lies upon the special lines we trace, whilst the other things and the untraced lines are neither named nor counted. There are in reality infinitely more things "unadapted" to each other in this world than there are things "adapted"; infinitely more things with irregular relations than with regular relations between them. But we look for the regular kind of thing exclusively, and ingeniously discover and preserve it in our memory. It accumulates with other regular kinds, until the collection of them fills our encyclopedias. Yet all the while between and around them lies an infinite anonymous chaos of objects that no one ever thought of together, of relations that never yet attracted our attention.

(James 1987f, 394)

This discussion originates from a long line of argument about "natural kinds." Are "things" we dissect from the panoply of experience individual elements that may be counted, or are they differentiated and acknowledged as items by consensus? Much of contemporary post-positivist comment builds on the understanding that "natural" categories are imposed, and while used because of their functional utility, their authenticity is always in question.[6] James argued that the furniture of the world is delineated by human interest and need—i.e., "things" do not arise naturally, but are accounted by making and categorizing choices:

We carve out groups of stars in the heavens, and call them constellations and the stars patiently suffer us to do so,—though if they knew what we were doing, some of them might feel much surprised at the partners we had given them . . . What shall we call a thing anyhow? It seems quite arbitrary, for we carve out everything, just as we carve out constellations, to suit our human purposes . . . The permanently real things for you are your individual persons. To an anatomist, again, those persons are but organisms, and the real things are the organs. Not the organs, so much as their constituent cells, say the histologists; not the cells, but their molecules, say in turn the chemists. We break the flux of sensible reality into things, then, at our will. We create the subjects of our true as well as of our false propositions. We create the predicates also. Many of the predicates of things express only the relations of the things to us and to our feelings. Such predicates of course are human additions.

(James 1987c [1907], 597–8)

And then James hammers against positivism's conceits:

there is no really inherent order, but it is we who project order into the world by selecting objects and tracing relations so as to gratify our intellectual interests. We carve out order by leaving the disorderly parts out; and the world is conceived thus.

(James 1987d, 634)

And to account for the direction of selection—its *telos*, so to speak—James invoked the exercise of choice determined by interest and utility.[7]

James wanted nothing less than to apply a "wrench to reality" (Bell 2014). He might well have referred to the innovation of Cubism, which has been called the greatest transformation in art since the Renaissance (Golding 1988, xiii). Coincident with James's own revisionary epistemology, Pablo Picasso and Georges Braque (in 1907–9) portrayed human figures merged into the background; their features, like the musical instruments or fruit of the still life pictures, lost their ordinary lines of demarcation. The portraits deconstruct individual attributes and place the subjects fully immersed in the world, albeit in idiosyncratic ways. As detailed in the next section, this is the world of James's radical empiricism presented in visual terms. Reality is assembled not by a prescribed form, but rather experienced and then sorted by human attention and ordered by individual interest. The Cubist thus declared (knowingly or not) James's vision: The world is in fact of one piece, and to whatever extent one sees discrete objects or persons, a particular schema imposes those characteristics. In addition, the products of those schema are not "true" in an ordinary, prescribed sense but, rather, possess relational characteristics derived from the viewer's culture and experience, for whatever ends and to whatever utility. Accordingly, the abstraction distills accidental details to reveal truths that lay beneath the surface (Poggi 1992, 129). In other words, the Cubists refracted reality based not on some universal "realist" (or mimetic) vision but, rather, on an individualistic construction of reality. Their pictorial manifesto asserts that (1) different perspectives yield different realities (already propounded by Nietzsche a generation earlier); (2) the world has no "natural kinds" (per James's own views [James 1987c, 597–8])—that is, humans see discrete objects and their relationships in different ways, and although there is a high degree of accordance, relativism has displaced the uniformity of some singular view of reality (Nisbett 2003); and (3) the subject is so integrated into her world that bordered definitions of identity are replaced with contextual schemes. Prioritizing his own inner experience, James fits snuggly in these redefined ways of seeing the world (James 1992a, 1075).

The trajectory of James's thinking may be fixed at one end by *Principles of Psychology*'s pragmatic view of consciousness, namely, that for which actions are "performed *for the sake* of their result" (James 1983, 21]), which, by 1904 (as discussed in the next section), had been radically dismissed to become "the name of a nonentity and has no right to a place among first principles" (James 1987a, 1141). So, having moved from orthodox psychology to what he himself called metaphysical considerations, James promoted "a kind of pluralism according to which there is no one phenomenal property and no definable list of such properties, shared by all conscious states" (Klein 2020, 296). Moreover, consciousness *as experienced*, falls into a domain beyond scientific study, resolutely resistant to analysis by imposing a system of representation or measurement. Indeed, how would psychologists characterize inner thought when what James called a constitutive "vagueness" resisted the concretization required for objectification? Simply, laboratory investigations were confined to a narrow spectrum of phenomena that could be studied, but which James regarded as tangential to the true characterization of psychic life.

This basic tenet is perhaps best illustrated by James's refusal to segregate any form of personal experience from study, even if clearly inaccessible to scientific methods. For example, we glimpse how he threw off the yokes of conventional science in his later "psychic research" (paranormal activity, telepathy, hypnotism), in which he sought in the world of the séance and the mystic to break the natural versus supernatural opposition for a *tertium quid*, a third way (Knapp 2017; James 1986b). Philosophy could not carry him forward in that domain, at least not the philosophy that sought analytical "solutions." At the risk of being scorned by more conservative colleagues, James actively pursued the investigation of that which eluded positivist assessment in his attempt to legitimate such experience that found no language (certainly no philosophical analytical basis) for its expression. His fascination with experience beyond the confines of scientific examination exemplifies how James refused to draw boundaries of validity around experience, for all was fair game for his inquiries. And beneath his intellectual curiosity, James sought to answer the call of the existential, a primary experience that he would legitimate as best he could. If we would assign a first principle to his thought, it must be the primacy of all-inclusive experience, which in turn required a radical empiricism, one un-mediated by an injected logical or ideological partitioning.

After completing *The Principles of Psychology*, James further developed a pluralistic view of the mind around the centrality of the subjective. Although he does not carefully distinguish them,

he made four different claims about the feeling intellect that he discerned: (1) the *phenomenological* claim that thoughts are inseparable from feelings, (2) the *causal* claim that feelings produce or determine our thoughts and beliefs, (3) the *epistemological* claim (so common in Romanticism) that we know the world as much through feeling as through thought or sensation, and (4) the *metaphysical* or *existential* claim that in certain circumstances our feelings produce not thoughts but the objects that our thoughts or feelings posit, anticipate, or acknowledge.

(Goodman 1990, 70, emphasis in original)

By presenting a thoroughly pluralistic conception of mental life, James sought to understand subjectivity on its own terms, a project he developed in critical opposition to the new scientific discipline he helped found (Perry 1935; Myers 1986; Richardson 2006). With that agenda clearly in sight, he required an epistemology appropriate to the task. To that venture we now turn.

Consciousness eclipsed: radical empiricism

Like his Romantic forebears, James sought ways of "seeing" the world unmediated by a distorting Cartesian bifurcation of *me* and the *world*, in which objectification becomes the inevitable product of knowing. With "radical empiricism," the primacy of experience—personal experience—James sought to displace the dualism underpinning the objectivity of science for the primacy of one's own vision. The pluralism he advocated was neither a rejection of objectivity nor the scientific worldview (later bemoaned by Heidegger [1977a, 1977b]), but rather a celebration of multiple ways of articulating meaning and the legitimacy of subjective experience. His philosophy was not *either/or* but rather governed by *and*, a conjunction of diverse experience and kinds of knowledge.

The antecedents of what became radical empiricism appeared a decade before James's change of course. Already in *The Principles of Psychology*, he noted the artificiality of characterizing the stream of consciousness in terms of what he called "the resting places," or substantive parts, to the exclusion of "the places of flight," or the transitive parts (James 1983, 236).

The resting-places are usually occupied by sensorial imaginations of some sort, whose peculiarity is that they can be held before the mind for an indefinite time, and contemplated without changing; the places of flight are filled with thoughts of relations, static or dynamic, that for the most part obtain between the matters contemplated in the periods of comparative rest . . . It then appears that the main end of our thinking is at all times the attainment of some other substantive part than the one from which we have just been dislodged. And we may say that the main use of the transitive parts is to lead us from one substantive conclusion to another.

(James 1983, 236)

James had identified a critical component of thought by emphasizing that *relations* are as integral to experience as are the objects of cognition. By 1884, he wrote, "we ought to say a feeling of *and*, a feeling of *if*, a feeling of *but*, have a feeling of *by*, quite as rapidly as we say a feeling of blue or a feeling of cold" (James 1992b, 990, emphasis in original; repeated in "The Stream of Thought" chapter in *Principles of Psychology* [1983, 238], and again in the *Briefer Course* published two years later [1992d, 162]). Accordingly, the stream of consciousness is not solely composed of punctuated substantives but constitutively includes the transitional elements as well. Indeed, the mind itself is "the equivalent of a transitive state" held by conjunctives of "ands," "ifs," "buts," and a host of prepositions that motor the movement of unarticulated thought (Davis 2022, 40).

> Now it is very difficult, introspectively, to see the transitive parts for what they really are. If they are but flights to a conclusion, stopping them to look at them before the conclusion is reached is really annihilating them. Whilst if we wait till the conclusion be reached, it so exceeds them in vigor and stability that it quite eclipses and swallows them up in its glare . . . As a snow-flake crystal caught in the warm hand is no longer a crystal but a drop, so, instead of catching the feeling of relation moving to its term, we find we have caught some substantive thing, usually the last word we were pronouncing, statically taken, and with its function, tendency, and particular meaning in the sentence quite evaporated. The attempt at introspective analysis in these cases is in fact like seizing a spinning top to catch its motion, or trying to turn up the gas quickly enough to see how the darkness looks.
>
> (James 1983, 236–7)

And with this emphasis on *relation*, James set the groundwork of radical empiricism, whose succinct description first appeared in the Preface to *Will to Believe* (1896), a collection of essays that

> taken together express a tolerably definite philosophic attitude in a very untechnical way. Were I obliged to give a short name to the attitude in question, I should call it that of *radical empiricism*, in spite of the fact that such brief nicknames are nowhere more misleading than in philosophy. I say "empiricism," because it is contented to regard its most assured conclusions concerning matters of fact as hypotheses liable to modification in the course of future experience; and I say "radical," because it treats the doctrine of monism itself as an hypothesis, and, unlike so much

of the halfway empiricism that is current under the name of positivism or agnosticism or scientific naturalism, it does not dogmatically affirm monism as something with which all experience has got to square.

(James 1992h, 447, emphasis in original)[8]

Thus for James, the stream of consciousness included the prepositions that linked objects of thought, but this proved only an intermediate step to discarding the segmentation of experience. As already discussed, consciousness described in terms of any objectification—even including the connections of "bits"—distorted personal experience. Accordingly, he attempted to redirect psychology from an exclusive study of sensory inputs and responses to an altogether different concern, namely, characterizing pure experience of the immediate moment (Taylor and Wozniak 1996a, xv).

The "solution" to the failure of capturing experience in a first-order fashion by introspection was to collapse the distinction between consciousness and content into *experience*. James was led to this revision by his underlying opposition to a duality in which consciousness arises from a second-order description in which primary experience becomes the object of some knowing agent. "It is an experience, after all, that we introspect to see whether it includes consciousness, discovering that it does not. This fact alone proves that an experience is logically a more basic concept than consciousness" (Myers 1986, 79). In its place, James substituted *pure experience* as the most basic unit of the psyche, which he hoped would become the basis of analyzing what happens both within the mental realm (its qualities, including continuity) and outside in configuring its relations.

"Thoughts" and "things" are names for two sorts of object, which common sense will always find contrasted and will always practically oppose to each other . . . [but] if we start with the supposition that there is only one primal stuff or material in the world, a stuff of which everything is composed, and if we call that stuff "pure experience," then knowing can easily be explained as a particular sort of relation towards one another into which portions of pure experience may enter. The relation itself is a part of pure experience; one of its "terms" becomes the subject or bearer of the knowledge, the knower, the other becomes the object known.

(James 1987a, 1141–2)

By depicting *experience* as undivided, *mind* and *body* are but different aspects of what is basically unitary. Accordingly, mind and body were only different "arrangements" of "stuff," which are myriad.[9] There are as many stuffs as there are "natures" in the things experienced. If one asks what any one bit of pure "experience is made of, the answer is always the same: 'It is made of that, of just what appears, of space, of intensity, of flatness, brownness, heaviness, or what not'" (James 1987a, 1153). Seemingly resistant to clear definition, "pure experience" has been described as "a very odd metaphysical concept," one hotly debated between those who see James embracing panpsychism (e.g., Gale 1999) and those who interpret him as a metaphysical realist and phenomenologist (Ford 1982, 75–80; Putnam and Putnam 1996). I regard radical empiricism in the latter modality, in which pre-reflective experience (or what James called "unverbalized sensation" or subconscious mentation) is "pure" in the sense it resides in a non-analyzed domain free of "culturally specific ways of understanding" (Ford 1982, 81).

Despite the restrictions imposed by the ordinary logic in which pure experience is reported, James held to this account and suffered scathing criticism (Taylor and Wozniak 1996b). Most generously, we might admit that he was fighting the entrenched dualism of our predicate language and the metaphysics in which we have grown accustomed. He was grasping to articulate contentless thought. In that effort we perceive an epistemology in which Cartesian dualism has been abandoned. Before the subject-object divide, he attempted to point to *experience*, which lies under language, beyond articulation, in an ineffability resisting concretization. In Chapter 4 we will consider how James found some approximation in what he called "the vague," but this too has resisted firm definition.

James is unrepentant in his own conceptual imprecision. He reminds that the authority for his notion of pure experience resides within our own "mentalese," and he simply alerts his reader to the obvious:

As "subjective" we say that the experience represents; as "objective" it is represented. What represents and what is represented is here numerically the same; but we must remember that no dualism of being represented and representing resides in the experience per se. In its pure state, or when isolated, there is no self-splitting of it into consciousness and what the consciousness is "of." Its subjectivity and objectivity are functional attributes solely, realized only when the experience is "taken," i.e., talked-of, twice, considered along with its two differing contexts respectively, by a new retrospective experience, of which that whole past complication now forms the fresh content. The instant field of the present is at all times what I call the "pure" experience. It is only virtually or potentially either object or subject as yet.

(James 1987a, 1151)[10]

James clearly understands that the logic of accustomed thinking opposes the heart of his proposal. Shedding dualism once and for all, he must also deflect the Reason that supports the discarded metaphysics:

> Rationalistic thought, with its exclusive interest in the unchanging and the general, has always de-realized the passing pulses of our life. It is no small service on empiricism's part to have exorcised rationalism's veto, and reflectively justified our instinctive feeling about immediate experience.
>
> (James 1987e, 1038; 1979, 59)

And, of course, if the logic of consciousness is abandoned, so must consciousness be discharged as well:

> For twenty years past I have mistrusted "consciousness" as an entity; for seven or eight years past I have suggested its non-existence to my students, and tried to give them its pragmatic equivalent in realities of experience. It seems to me that the hour is ripe for it to be openly and universally discarded. . . . Let me then immediately explain that I mean only to deny that the word stands for an entity, but to insist most emphatically that it does stand for a function.
>
> (1987a, 1141–2)

Note, James did not deny that conscious thought exists, but he would "discard all curious inquiries about certainty [of consciousness] as too metaphysical" (James 1983, 185) and concluded that "the attributes 'subject' and 'object,' 'represented' and 'representative,' 'thing' and 'thought' means, then, a practical distinction which is of a FUNCTIONAL *order only*, and not at all ontological as understood by classical dualism" (James 1977, 194, emphasis in original).

> Consciousness, James now contended, is not an entity, but a function within experience, the function of knowing, which is added to it rather than a precondition of it. The "double-barreled" meaning of experience, at once subjective and objective, is an expression of its originally holistic and relational character. Conceptual knowing or "knowledge about" is one step removed from the more basic perceptual knowing or "knowledge by acquaintance," in which there is no reflective separation of subjective knower and object of knowledge.
>
> (Jay 2005, 280)[11]

Much of later twentieth-century philosophy of mind then argued this functional thesis.

The development of radical empiricism roughly coincides with a shift in James's appreciation of contentless thought and the arena of subconscious (if not unconscious) mentation. His thinking about unconsciousness falls into two phases, roughly marked by his "turn" to metaphysics after publishing *Principles of Psychology* in 1890. The first position is marked by his insistence on an *esse est sentiri* epistemology ("to be is to be sensed"), in which only conscious awareness qualifies as mental. Accordingly, James dispenses with unconsciousness as a category of the mind. From this position, he promoted the concept of a continuous "stream of consciousness" to characterize the mind as freely flowing from one intention to another, but always maintaining an indivisible unity of its own making (James 1983, 233).

The "The Mind Stuff Theory" chapter of *Principles* lists ten arguments against the unconscious. Some have argued that James held this position throughout his writings (e.g., Cooper 2002; Klein 2020), while others interpret discussions in *Principles* as supporting unconscious processes, and later writings more explicitly acknowledge "a secondary consciousness" and "subconsciousness," as well as "subliminal," "split," and "dissociation" states, all of which have been included in what later were modeled as unconscious mental phenomena (e.g., Taylor and Wozniak 1996a; Reed 1997; Weinberger 2000). The latter group of critics justifiably claim that James was well aware of "subconscious" thinking, which he regarded as both readily accessible to recall or utilization as required.

That interpretation is then strengthened when examining James's views during his later metaphysical phase, when he declared a new enthusiasm for unconscious aspects of mental processes. In the *Varieties of Religious Experience* (1902), he explicitly described how the subliminal serves as a reservoir of different states of experience (e.g., religious or mystical).

If the word "subliminal" is offensive to any of you, as smelling too much of psychical research or other aberrations, call it by any other name you please, to distinguish it from the level of full sunlit consciousness. Call this latter the A-region of personality, if you care to, and call the other the B-region. The B-region, then, is obviously the larger part of each of us for it is the abode of everything that is latent and the reservoir of everything that passes recorded or unobserved. It contains, for example, such things as all our momentary inactive memories, and it harbors the springs of all our obscurely motivated passions, impulses, likes, dislikes, and prejudices. Our intuitions, hypotheses, fancies, superstitions, persuasions, convictions, and in general all our non-rational operations come from it. It is the source of our dreams, and apparently they may return to it. In it arise whatever mystical experiences we may have, and our automatisms, sensory or motor; our life in hypnotic and "hypnoid" conditions; our delusions, fixed ideas, and hysterical accidents, if we are hysteric subjects; our supranormal cognitions, if such there be, and if we are telepathic subjects. It is also the fountainhead of much that feeds our religion. In persons deep in the religious life, as we have now abundantly seen,—and this is my conclusion—the door to this region seems unusually wide open; at any rate, experiences making their entrance through that door have had emphatic influence in shaping religious history.

(James 1987f, 433–4)

Indeed, having identified the "subliminal" as the locus of the mystical, the sense of the divine and the origins of a spiritual identity, he enthuses about its discovery:

> I cannot but think that the most important step forward that has occurred in psychology since I have been a student of that science is the discovery, first made in 1886, that, in certain subjects at least, there is not only the consciousness of the ordinary field, with its usual centre and margin, but an addition thereto in the shape of a set of memories, thoughts, and feelings which are extra-marginal and outside of the primary consciousness altogether, but yet must be classed as conscious facts of some sort, able to reveal their presence by unmistakable signs. I call this the most important step forward because, unlike the other advances which psychology has made, this discovery has revealed to us an entirely unsuspected peculiarity in the constitution of human nature. No other step forward which psychology has made can proffer any such claim as this.

(James 1987f, 215)

What a reversal, one that fits snugly into his promotion of a new portrayal of mental life based on the rejection of Cartesian metaphysics.

Varieties was written as James was developing his ideas about radical empiricism, and one may fairly conclude that these writings about the source of mystical and religious ideation served as a key example of pure experience. With James's philosophical transition of interests from *consciousness* to *experience*, and then to *pure experience*, he *had* to admit the unconscious domain into his schema. James's version of *experience* is prior to consciousness and therefore cannot be articulated. Precisely because it has no content, pure experience remains unknown except for its manifestations in feelings. James, like Freud, can only point to this nebulous source of subjectivity and thought as the reservoir of consciousness that must arise from somewhere, but that somewhere remains beyond formulation. Only when thought is concretized does this unconscious substratum become conscious. In short, James could eschew *the* unconscious as subject to investigation, but he could not deny its presence in the mental apparatus. Thus, ironically for James, pure consciousness presupposes the "something" Freud had described as "the Unconscious;" their difference was that the psychoanalyst proposed a model as to *what* it was and *how* it operated, while James basically forecast Wittgenstein's sage advice, "What we cannot speak about we must pass over in silence" (Wittgenstein 1974, 74).

Comment

James sought nothing less than to dislodge Cartesian metaphysics, and by following the logic of his revision, retrospective or second-order consciousness was displaced as the primary mental phenomenon for undifferentiated *pure experience*. And when experience is considered retrospectively, a contortion appears that arises from two differing perspectives: a new, second-order experience (voiced as self-consciousness) is one step removed from the original experience itself that exists undisturbed in a "pure," unarticulated state.[12] On this view, if experience is allowed to rest within its own domain, undisturbed by reflexive reconsideration, the problem of dualism fails to appear, because in the immediacy of pure experience,

> there is no *inner* dualism of knower and known. Separation of knower and known only occurs when a given "bit" is abstracted from the flow of experience and considered in the context of different relations, relations that are external to that experience taken singly but internal to the general flow of experience taken as a whole. For James, the dualism of knower and known is an *external* dualism of experienced relations not an *inner* dualism of substance. This is the fundamental metaphysical postulate of James's radical empiricism.
>
> (Taylor and Wozniak 1996a, xvi, emphasis in original)

The unity of experience (despite its characteristic punctual character that jumps to and fro) must reside in acknowledging the pluralistic character of consciousness and its nature of shifting relationships. Absent a dualism of substance, the subjective, then, cannot be captured by objective analysis.[13] As Wundt and his followers would have to readily admit, all the particulars may be studied, but none individually, nor their sum, depicts the *experience* of subjectivity. With this description, James easily claims standing as an early phenomenologist.

To summarize, the Cartesian "dualism of body and soul had been transformed into one of knower and known or consciousness and content," whose essence "lay in a reification of consciousness and a separation of consciousness from its content" (Taylor and Wozniak 1996a, xiv). In its place James proposed radical empiricism built from six key tenets (Crosby and Viney 1992, 102–4): (1) *experience* is James's metaphysical ultimate, i.e., everything real is an aspect of experience; (2) the distinction between subject and object, knower and known, is made within the field of experience; (3) instead of a correspondence theory of truth, pragmatic criteria hold—adequacy of experience or workability in practice;[14] (4) *relations* are as real in experience as the *things* that are related (anti-nominalist); (5) experience is a "concatenated" unity that requires pluralistic methods of inquiry; and (6) experience is the sole warrant of any claims and intellectual constructions (e.g., monism, pluralism, materialism, idealism, theism, and naturalism) must be tested against experience (James 1977). With that formulation, he would address the subjective on its own terms.

Notes

1 "The Metaphysical Club" was comprised of a group of thinkers at Harvard in the 1870s, who assembled to informally discuss philosophy under the leadership of Chauncey Wright. They included the luminaries who would eventually be regarded as the early authors of pragmatism—besides Peirce and James, most notably Wright and Oliver Wendell Holmes Jr. (Weiner 1949; Madden 1963; Menand 2001; Ryan, Butler, and Good 2019).

2 Referring to Theodor Adorno's *negative dialectics*, *excess* addresses the limits of a representational conception of mind and the consequences of subject-object predicate thinking. For him, in any experience, the mind selects, sorts, and orders objects from an undifferentiated state of being. Objects thus become *objects* only as differentiation occurs, a reduction that occurs by a "selective negation." Accordingly, a process of "subtraction" occurs to transform a state of undifferentiated being to fashion a human-perceived object through the imposition of order, identity, difference, relation, etc. Such a concept with distinguishing characteristics is generated through "negation," which precipitates the object from the plenum of being. As the "thing-to-become-objectified" emerges, an undifferentiated space is left behind. This inevitable remainder is the *excessive* portion of the set, which thus consists of the conceptualized object and the excessive residua, or what Rothenberg calls the "empty set" (2010, 36). The empty set has no positive properties and, by adding its own emptiness, unglues and separates objects from the undifferentiated plenum (Tauber 2013a, 67–8).

3   James's contemporary, J. T. Merz, summarized the problematic status of such a depiction:

> The analytic process is irreversible. The point at which we start to synthesise or put together is purely arbitrary, fixed by our knowledge or rather our ignorance, and the product of such synthesis is accordingly artificial, not natural: the world of things, images of thought or practical constructions, is accordingly artificial.
>
> (Merz 1965, vol. 4, 776)

4   James was unsympathetic to *the* unconscious as conceived by Freud (James 1983 207ff., 221–4; 362ff.). James allowed that we may be inattentive to certain experiences and allow them to reside unattended, and in pathological cases of hysteria (following Pierre Janet), a split in personality divides conscious experience between two different conscious beings. Freud, of course, rejected "unconscious consciousness." For him the unconscious was an impersonal realm, and to the extent it might be experienced, such manifestation occurred irrespective of conscious awareness (Freud 1925a, 59).

5   By joining the early phenomenologists Brentano (1973) and Mach (1914), James shed the scientific approach of his earlier work (James 1992f [1879], 970–1). The key characteristic of these phenomenological accounts is a demurral on investigating *how* mind functions.

> Consciousness is to be understood as an activity that arises in natural circumstances in the natural interaction of sentient being with its environment. The interaction and distinction between subject and object occurs, then, within the whole field of experience, not, as traditionalists had it, with the object within and the subject without . . . James insisted that to ask what the nature of experience itself is, is a misleading question. For it assumes already that some pure general, single nature of experience exists. For James, experience had no specific general nature . . . It is rather a word, a metaphor, a figure of speech like "self" and "world" used heuristically to name the field or context of activity of the functionally (not ontologically) distinguished elements of subject and object etc. These categories of subject object thought/thing and so on are relational to each other.
>
> (Wheeler 1993, 93–4)

6   Originally posited by Plato in *Phaedrus* 265d–266a; for modern accounts, see Campbell, O'Rourke, and Slater 2011.

7   This position built from James's resistance to the lingering Aristotelian notion of natural kinds, where the "thing-hood" of nature's objects that science examines seem self-evident. These entities are assumed to exist as contained within a simple location of placement that in turn depends on a certain understanding of the space-time continuum (Whitehead 1925, 69–70, 1929). However, just as James promoted his radical empiricism, twentieth-century physics up-turned a universe of discrete objects existing in fixed coordinates of space and time. With a simpler mechanical philosophy of physics, the real is effectively localized and captured as objective *entities*. Such "things," waiting in nature for human discovery, rested upon what Whitehead called the "Fallacy of Misplaced Concreteness" (Whitehead 1925, 72, 82). In other words, the abstract

descriptions of nature arising from modern science have paradoxically been conceived as concrete realities, when in fact they are "constructions" of human invention. They are "real," but their reality depends on how they have been partitioned from the array in which they exist. Simply put, humans apply the partitioning borders of "things" through measurement or definition, which in turn is constructed with human tools (machines) (Whitehead 1925, 72). Although the newly discovered physics described by Einstein and Planck did not figure in James's thought, he argued precisely this point in his criticism of a science of the mind based on mental "bits" that were artificially partitioned from an integrated whole and were, he maintained, only artifacts of a second-order evaluation.

8 In a second Presidential address to the American Psychological Association in 1904 (published as "The Experience of Activity" 1987h [1905]), James continued the theme introduced a decade earlier and then published a series of essays that were posthumously anthologized in 1912 in *Essays in Radical Empiricism* (1976 [1912]) (Perry 1935; Myers 1986; Richardson 2006). For the contemporary reception of James's philosophy, see Taylor and Wozniak (1996b).

9 "Pure experience" is fraught by James's own descriptive inconsistencies, and the confusion hinges on how he meant the so-called "stuff" of which pure experience is composed. Richard Gale offers a trenchant clarification by noting the differences between "metaphysical stuff" (fully indeterminant and thus "potential") as opposed to "general stuff" having empirical characteristics; nevertheless, other fundamental problems emerged, and James abandoned the formulation after writing the essays of 1904–1905, although he never abandoned radical empiricism (Gale 1999, 199–215). Gale's description is based on what he regards as James's irreconcilable portraits of a self depicted either in terms of an "ontological relativism" in which "all reality claims must be relativized to a person," and a mystical self in which non-relativized claims are based on mystical experience (Gale 1999, 19). While Gale attempts to find a synthesis, he basically sees James as beleaguered by this "aporia," one that James Pawelski attempts to integrate (Pawelski 2007, 104–30).

10 As Dianda observed:

> James proposal is not, as has sometimes been thought, to eliminate the distinction between thought and thing by returning to an undifferentiated experience or feeling, but to reinterpret the traditional subject/object distinction in terms of contexts and functions" [J. E. Smith 1970, 31]. Terms such as "subject" and "object," "thought" and "thing," or "perception" and "conception" don't stand for various aspects of reality. They are additions that we build into experiences as a means of explaining them. Context determines what we call subject or object . . . [and] the division between thought and thing is not found in experience, as such, but emerges retrospectively.
>
> (Dianda 2023, 197)

11 Jay highlights the indebtedness to Shadworth Hollway Hodgson (1832–1912), whom James first met in 1880 (Jay 2005, 278–83). Hodgson forecast key ideas that James also developed, most importantly discarding the atomized view of consciousness into discrete sensations for the fluid stream metaphor. Hodgson

also questioned the independent existence of substances and subjects in favor of the relations that subtended them. By 1885, Hodgson wrote James that he had abandoned the idea of Mind as agent, or rather,

> it was got rid of before I came into the field at all; I found it *gone*, broken up by its inherent contradictions; and generating nothing but skepticism by its putrefaction. This being so, I resolved to base philosophy (no longer on an assumption but) on *experience*. *That* is the history and reason of my method. My aim is not to get rid of mind as agent, but to replace it; to have a philosophy based, not on it, but on experience.
>
> (letter from Hodgson to James, Feb. 14, 1884; quoted by Jay 2005, 278–9, emphasis in original)

By 1895, James began moving beyond Hodgson in developing his own non-dualist understanding of experience, and subsequently, their comradeship waned. (See Perry 1935, I:611–53 for correspondence that reveals James's early affinity and later dissatisfaction with Hodgson.)

12 Alexis Dianda (2023) has provided an extensive review of James's notion of "experience," a construction that evoked criticism from its earliest presentation (Taylor and Wozniak 1996b) and extended into our own era (e.g., Bernstein 2010, 128). The most prominent rejection of *experience* as James used it occurred with the rise of the "linguistic turn" by which neo-pragmatists (principally Sellars and Rorty) rejected James's notion of experience, which, they maintain, "is always already mediated by language, [and] if experience cannot play the role of 'furnishing' the mind with ideas or data, securing objectivity, then it has no valid *philosophical* status . . . There is little room for doubt that experience cannot play the role cast for it at the dawn of epistemology, nor can it live up to the hopes empiricists once invested in it"

> (Dianda 2023, 21–2, emphasis in original; see Rorty 1980, 1999; Sellars 1997; Misak 2013)

Rather than dismiss James's understanding and use of *experience*, Dianda argues that neo-pragmatic inquiry became preoccupied with traditional epistemological inquiry and thus subverted the fecundity of James's psychology and its larger philosophical significance (Dianda 2023, 10).

In a broader review of *experience* in twentieth-century philosophy, Marianne Janack concurs, as she sets the context in which she would reintroduce experience as philosophically useful in the humanist tradition James himself invoked:

> By the late twentieth century . . . "experience" had been demoted, if not completely displaced from the realm of philosophical concern. In Quine's story about science and epistemology, "experience" is just shorthand for the stimulus input to our sensory faculties . . . The situation was little different among those who rejected epistemology entirely: "experience," Rorty argued, was a term better left behind, abandoned for the term "discourse" . . . or left on the side of the nondiscursive, where it could only refer to meaningless causal prompts . . . The idea that there is need of an interface between self and world called "experience" is a relic of the Descartes-Locke-Kant

tradition and the idea of the mind as mirror that animates that tradition. The faith in the therapeutic role that experience could play in bringing philosophy back from the brink of arid scholasticism, a faith that was alive and well in the early twentieth century, was apparently lost by the end of that century, replaced by a new vision of the human mind and the self that had no place for the concept of experience . . . A similar romance and breakup with "experience" was playing out . . . in feminist theory and in other disciplines in which the question of racial, sexual, or gendered identity was a central concern in discussions of politics and knowledge. Discussions of women's experience and the experiences of marginalized others populated the discourses of identity politics in the 1960s and 1970s, but by the 1990s, Joan Scott was putting "experience" in scare quotes to signal that the term was intellectually and politically suspect. (Janack 2012, 17)

13 See especially James's analogy to the separation of pigment from the menstruum of paint (James 1987a, 1144–5).

14 The standing of various pragmatic notions of truth underlies post-Kuhnian critiques of science, which generally reflects the Jamesian viewpoint of an evidentiary notion of truth (Tauber 2022, 199–205; Zammito 2004). The realist, in stating the truth conditions of a theory, cannot affirm whether those conditions are satisfied because even the best confirmed theories may still be false. Truth then becomes "some sort of (idealized) rational acceptability," or essentially an epistemic notion based on our state of knowledge and thus not achievable in any finalized sense (Putnam 1981, 49; see also Putnam 1997, 2005). That is not to discard truth (Putnam 1990a, 222–3), for

> James's pragmatism has the merit of having safeguarded the concept of truth by assuming it, like Peirce, in terms of a regulative ideal essential to every kind of cognitive activity, whether scientific or any other field—even though he believed absolute truth to be "humanly" unattainable. (Calcaterra 2022, 67)

This deflationary position holds that truth has no essential feature, and indeed, there is no single robust property or underlying nature to characterize it. So, instead of searching for such an attribute called "truth," the deflationist would argue that truth should be regarded as fulfilling an epistemological function as a guide for seeking correct or reliable statements in the effort to optimize certainty (Horwich 2005; Armour-Garb and Beall 2005). That is enough, for in terms of success, while aspiring to an idealized finality of Truth, scientific practice, pragmatic and dynamic, has proven itself capable of establishing standards adequate for its own pursuits, for self-appraisals and constant scrutiny are constitutive to scientific methodology (Fisch and Bebaji 2011).

> To say that we should drop the idea of truth as out there waiting to be discovered is not to say that we have discovered that, out there, there is no truth. It is to say that our purposes would be served best by ceasing to see truth as a deep matter . . . as a term which repays "analysis." "The nature of truth" is an unprofitable topic, resembling in this respect the nature of man and "the nature of God," and differing from "the nature of the positron."
>
> (Rorty 1989, 8)

Truth then becomes a pragmatic standard, a guiding or regulative principle of the scientific enterprise without metaphysical standing. Rorty further developed this position (e.g., 1998, chapters 1–4), which generated heated debate (e.g., Brandom 2000; Auxier and Hahn 2010; Putnam 1990c, 2017) about a slippery slope that could eventuate with "truth" dispensed altogether while holding onto an instrumental understanding that prefers explanations to the best approximation and thus foregoes some idealized standard of true. On this view, while science still claims its exultant epistemological status, its product, true knowledge, is an approach to the asymptotic, or idealized limit. Instead of some finality, the pragmatist is satisfied with practical results and the successes based upon them. Accordingly, beliefs have as firm a basis as can be established with pragmatic assessments. Of course, a "true" result may occur for the "wrong" reasons, but to say (as does Rorty) that truth only serves to order the scientific enterprise does not make true arbitrary. The attempt to reduce all knowledge acquisition to "just" interpretation and thus subject to relativism is simply wrong, a position with which Rorty agreed (Putnam, 2017; Rorty 2002).

> I think it's important for pragmatists to say that the fact there aren't any absolutes of the kind Plato and Kant and orthodox theism have dreamt doesn't mean that every view is as good as every other. It doesn't mean that everything is now arbitrary, or a manner of the will to power, or something like that. That, I think has to be said over and over again.
>
> (Rorty 2002, 375)

Chapter 3

Concerning subjectivity

The deep divide separating Freud and James resides in their disparate *philosophical* positions concerning *agency*: Freud's entire scientific edifice rested on the Cartesian-Lockean concept of an autonomous (metaphysically separated) subject who could observe nature objectively. Freud, a loyal enthusiast for objectivity, consistently presented psychoanalysis as a science of the mind accompanied by deterministic psychic forces. James, while an early devotee, eventually demurred and developed a philosophy of mind eschewing the methods of the laboratory, the efforts to concretize experience in objective terms, and the determinism inherent in that program. Although they both thought (at least initially) that they were forging a new science, a novel way of understanding human being, even Freud eventually understood that the science was inadequate to his original purpose (Tauber 2010, 17, 66–7, 81–4). Today, the particulars of Freud's mechanistic descriptions and meta-psychological constructions have been largely dismissed, even by the psychoanalytic community (see Introduction, note #17). After all, even Freud himself regarded his theory as only a preamble to future models of the mind (Freud 1926, 266),[1] and by 1932 his excuses appeared lame. In a famous exchange, Freud reminded Einstein that in the end all science rested on some untestable metaphysical foundations and noted that "does not every science come in the end to a kind of mythology like this? Cannot the same be said to-day of your Physics?" (Freud 1932, 211), by which he referred not only to the provisional character of scientific theory but also to a metaphysical boundary, a domain beyond human understanding that Freud believed underlies all human knowledge. In this sense, Freud thought he had plumbed the depths of the psyche and seen – perhaps, intuited – the dynamics governing behavior, but only to a level that human reason permitted. The unique grammar and semantics he had devised were only "logical" inventions to describe that-which-had-no-logic. At this deepest level, Freud reached into the mythic to express the inexplicable, one that was in kind

DOI: 10.4324/9781003565413-3

no different from the limits of the metaphysics supporting contemporary physics. However, Freud's circumspection hardly validates the philosophical assumptions of psychoanalytic theory nor its clinical claims!

Freud never abandoned his commitment to scientific knowledge and, perhaps more importantly, scientific reason and the applicability of scientific models more generally. His analytic extensions, in which assessing subjective states and memories might be processed with the same effective rationality assigned to other kinds of cognition, proved to be a far-reaching supposition with little basis in scientific fact. After all, as Freud himself acknowledged, selective and fallible memory and self-appraisal are weak tools for objective accounts, not to speak of deeper philosophical obstacles (Freud 2003). Nevertheless, he expected that future developments in neuroscience would advance knowledge about psychic dynamics according to the positivist principles to which he was committed. And more generally, Freud affirmed that "our best hope for the future is that intellect—the scientific spirit, reason—may in the process of time establish a *dictatorship* in the mental life of man" (Freud 1933, 171, emphasis added). He thus confirmed his most basic premise: the inner life of subjectivity could be examined objectively through representative modalities (language, symbols, secondary manifestations), which he identified (defined) as epiphenomena of unconscious processes (Tauber 2013a).

Freud went to great lengths to show how *different* the unconscious is from the dynamics governing the conscious ego (i.e., the lack of intelligible notions of time and space; the seeming a-rationality and a-morality of dreams; the inscrutable disjunctions of sequences that pass for loss of causality). Nevertheless, he declared in the key meta-psychological paper "The Unconscious" that despite all distortions of reasoned thought, unconscious "mentation" could be treated in the same terms conscious thought is characterized, namely, by interpreting the assigned representations of the psychoanalytic drama (Freud 1915b, 168). In other words, he made the unconscious discernable in the same terms used to describe consciousness. And then *interpretation* is required to unlock the meaning of those symbols inasmuch as such representations have only inferred objective status. Is that *science*?

Despite the hermeneutical connotations of "interpretation," Freud relentlessly presented his project as a science governed by positivist principles, namely, an analysis that objectified unconscious motivations and uncovered hidden meanings. That he sided with the scientist persona as opposed to the clinician is supported by many references, but perhaps is most clearly stated in a late overview of psychoanalysis, where he wrote, "The future will probably attribute far greater importance to psychoanalysis as the *science* of the unconscious than as a therapeutic procedure" (Freud 1926, 265, emphasis added). So, for Freud, the therapeutic result was construed as a fortunate product of a successful analysis, but the scientific status of the analysis remained his primary concern.

> It must not be supposed that these very general ideas [referencing depth psychology] are presuppositions upon which the work of psychoanalysis depends. On the contrary, they are its latest conclusions and are in every respect open to revision. Psycho-analysis is founded securely upon the observation of the *facts* of mental life; and for that very reason its theoretical superstructure is still incomplete and subject to constant alteration.
>
> (Freud 1926, 266, emphasis added)

Freud, thus ever conscious of disparaging criticisms (Gay 1988), admitted the shaking grounds upon which he stood in regard to the scientific pose:

> Our justification for making such inferences and interpolations and the degree of certainty attaching to them of course remain open to criticism in each individual instance; and it cannot be denied that it is often extremely difficult to arrive at a decision—a fact which finds expression in the lack of agreement among analysts. The novelty of the problem is to blame for this—that is to say, a lack of training. But there is besides this a special factor inherent in the subject itself; for in psychology, unlike physics, we are not always concerned with things which can only arouse a cool scientific interest.
>
> (Freud 1940, 197)

Here, in his last testimony, Freud acknowledges the irresolvable tension, arising between a scientific explanation and a hermeneutical interpretation. Stan Draenos succinctly states the conflict, one deeply embedded in psychoanalysis:

> A contradiction runs through Freud's writings like a fault line. It arises from the fact that psychoanalysis presents itself as knowledge of two different kinds. On the one hand, psychoanalysis takes the form of an understanding of mind obtained through the disclosure of hidden meanings in dreams and neurotic symptoms. On the other, psychoanalysis takes the form of an explanation of mind secured in the elucidation of the mechanisms and systematic relation of a "mental apparatus."

To bring these two forms of knowledge together within one science is like trying to square a circle. For they carry with them visions of mind that are fundamentally at odds. In seeking to understand mind through interpretation of meaning, Freud takes the mental as a property of a subject and his inner life. In seeking to explain mind as a mechanism, he places mental phenomena among the natural objects of the external world. Mind as meaning and mind as mechanism, however, lie on opposite sides of a great divide first enunciated by Descartes's famous dualism, in the distinction between *res cogitans* and *res extensa*, consciousness and matter, subject and object.

(Draenos 1982, 7)

Freud, of course, straddled the line, and when dealing with the emotions, the fault line starkly appears. James understood the misstep of such scientific accounts and deliberately outlined the philosophical requirements to deal with examining the psyche. He did so by drawing on a philosophical tradition at odds with the positivism that had so readily applied its precepts to characterizing the physical and mental universes.

How consciousness is debated in current discourse reiterates the James-Freud argument (Dennett 1991; Chalmers 1995; Flanagan 1997) and, more particularly, are representational models of the mind employed by computers relevant to the complexity of human cognition and the *experience* of subjectivity (Fodor 1980, 1981; Putnam 1988; Dreyfus 1992)? As the power of artificial intelligence looms before us, we ask, ever more urgently, does the cognitivist model reveal natural brain functions or do computers only mimic certain mental operations that follow different principles of organization and regulation? And lodged deeply within these debates the question that has accompanied the rise of positivism since the early nineteenth century persists: can subjectivity be saved within the growing hegemony of the psyche's objectification?

James, a Romantic

At the core of the James-Freud confrontation is the reification of subjectivity and then the legitimization of an analytic kind of understanding. Where order by objectivity and reason had prevailed in the Enlightenment, a different epistemology would emerge in reaction. The Romantic Revolt (1780–1830) that launched resistance against positivist aspirations (if not imperialistic dominance) of what constituted true knowledge comprised a challenge with repercussions throughout Western culture. Nothing less than *reality* was at stake—ways of knowing, ways of being. And in that opposition, we find the dramatic meeting of our protagonists.

The roots of Comtean positivism originate in the Age of Reason, whose basic Enlightenment precepts maintained that certain knowledge is a virtue, which meant that all genuine questions can be answered through correct reason, as opposed to revelation or authority. "Correct" reason, of course, conformed to the mathematization of nature and the logic of objective analysis, which, by its very stricture, bracketed subjectivity as a source of bonafide knowledge. Romanticism arose in opposition: the forms of validated Reason were too confining and denied the legitimacy of emotion, aesthetic sensibility, and, in the final throes of God's funeral, religion. So construed, Reason was a kind of confinement to be supplemented by creativity and imagination and personal authenticity. Emotionalism celebrated the subjective at the expense of the analytic; the sanctity of the inexpressible and its transmission through art captured the deepest human realities; the protest against universality elevated individualism and self-assertion; and, perhaps most central, the primacy of one's own subjectivity that displaced objectivity as the final arbiter of reality. Here, the conflict of the sciences contra subjective interpretation commenced, because according to the Romantics, physics cut "reality into some kind of mathematically symmetrical pieces, whereas reality is a living whole" (Berlin 1999, 58). *Ergo*, science could not deal with a huge swath of human interest and, furthermore, distorted (even nullified) the authenticity of personal experience.

The objection originates with the Cartesian *res cogito/res extensa* formulation that sundered the metaphysical unity between knower and known. The Romantics remonstrated that when one is in dialogue, the experiencing self is absorbing and responding. So, in the process of *experience*, which became the watchword of Romanticism, the very idea of a set identity, one fixed and unchanging (and thus unable to develop), becomes anathema (C. Taylor 1989; Jay 2005). Growth and creative expansion were idealized, whether in personal terms or in one's relation to the world at large. Accordingly, *relation*, more specifically, dialectical exchange, redefines the subject-object relationship as ever-changing—dependent on context, history, psychological state, etc. The dynamics of such intercourse replace a static worldview and, for that matter, the status of the autonomous self that would know the world and itself also assumed a dynamic character. Romantic philosophers—and by extension, or perhaps in concert, the poets—were attempting to break the confining impasse in which the self had been placed by Locke's construction of a detached, observing "eye" that would perceive the world, know it directly, and retain its objective autonomy (C. Taylor 1989). His philosophy argued for the ability of the individual to detach from the world, and from himself, and observe each objectively (Tauber 2001, 199). The Romantics rebelled against this formulation of identity.

Yes, they prized individuality, but they rejected the metaphysical rift that set them apart from nature and the ideal of the Whole.[2] Always aware of separation, and appropriately so, since science would purge itself of subjective contamination, this "subject-less subject" faces the metaphysical challenge of finding herself in the world described without her (Fox Keller 1994). The question then loomed: how to overcome the Cartesian/Lockean subject/object divide? What are the philosophical possibilities and consequences of shifting the human "stare" *at* the world to human placement *within* it? Once the very foundation of agency began to shift, *everything* was at risk, and much was overturned.

The "great break in European consciousness" inaugurated in the Romantic era moved "away from the notion that there are universal truths, universal canons of art, that all human activities were meant to terminate in getting things right, and the criteria of getting things right were public, were demonstrable" (Berlin 1999, 14). The massive cultural shifts associated with modernism (and then postmodernism) had their roots in these Romantic ideas: (1) per Nietzsche's proclamation that humans define themselves through self-chosen values and goals; (2) because there is no preexisting structure to which adaptation is required, perpetual self-creation expresses the dynamism of nature and the unpredictability of human activities; (3) knowledge and its telos, certainty, is sacrificed and replaced with the human reality depicted by art and myth; and (4) instead of the unification of knowledge, disunity characterizes the world and our understanding of it (Tauber 2022, 39). James in many respects was a Romantic, and his vision of the plurality of knowledge and the *sui generis* of subjective experience serves as a contra-position to Freud's approach to the psyche, one based on positivist principles and the hegemony of a particular kind of reason that imposed, what Heidegger called, the scientific "world picture" (Heidegger 1977a, 1977b).

James built upon Kierkegaard's observation of how the objective and subjective aspects of experience can easily be conflated. In "The Task of Becoming Subjective" of the *Postscript*, Kierkegaard wrote,

[T]he subjective problem is not something about an objective issue, but is the subjectivity itself. For since the problem in question poses a decision, and since all decisiveness . . . inheres in subjectivity, it is essential that every trace of an objective issue should be eliminated. If any such trace remains, it is at once a sign that the subject seeks to shirk something of the pain and crisis of the decision; that is, he seeks to make the problem to some degree objective.

(Kierkegaard 1941, 115)

In other words, subjectivity does not adhere to the demands of objectivity. And more to Kierkegaard's point, assuming an objective view of one's own life and determining its "intent" based on such criteria both distorts and misdirects the subjectivity that constitutes one's core being. James was intent to rectify this conflation and set subjectivity on its own grounds. Indeed, the consequences of displacing the Cartesian metaphysics underwriting psychoanalysis with a radical alternative and rescuing subjectivity in the process are immense.

The Romantics valorized the individual perspective and thereby rejected the universal "world picture" science presented. This general orientation frames our reading of James's philosophy and the derivative depiction of the mind that contrasts so starkly with Freud's own positivist conceits. Simply, Freud drew from a scientific philosophy that required that subject-object separation, while James sought to replace it.

These contrasting portraits of the mind draw from the unsettled status of self-consciousness. Freud assaulted complacent notions of self-knowledge. *Who am I?* assumed new dimensions within the psychoanalytic dominion. And James, by recasting the very metaphysical foundations upon which self-consciousness rests, attempted to rescue subjectivity from the distortions imposed by the assumptions of "objective" scrutiny. The key innovation, in each case, concerned the self's relation to its addressed object. For Freud, the innermost *me* is objectified, while in James's program, subjectivity resides in primordial experience awaiting expression. James thus fell into a long Romantic line of thought that legitimated the subjective on its own terms, while Freud followed the underlying positivism that guided the scientific psychologists of his era. Hatched from the laboratories of physiology and newly created specialties of neuroanatomy and psychology, science would be applied to the *psyche*, not the *soul*, thereby configuring the *mind* according to the methods available (Reed 1997).

With the attempt to "save" subjectivity, James's metaphysics of pure experience attacked modernity's dualisms: of mind and body, of subject and object, of representation and represented, of thought and content. For him, "there is no separation of knower and known. Indeed, in a real sense, there is no knower and known, there is only experience" (Taylor and Wozniak 1996a, xvii).

The phenomena of consciousness were viewed as *entering* consciousness as content and consciousness itself was construed simply as that *within which* the phenomena of consciousness occur, *within which*, as James puts it, "awareness of content" takes place. . . . It is this reified consciousness, separated from its content, whose existence James denies; and it was to transcend this dualism of consciousness and content that James articulated his doctrine of "pure experience."

(Taylor and Wozniak 1996a, xiv, emphasis in original)

To countermand the second-order *re*-presentation of experience, James sought to capture the world of the personal that is *present* in its full immediacy:

"Other world?" says Emerson, "there is no other world,"—than this one, namely, in which our several biographies are founded . . . The belief in the genuineness of each particular moment in which we feel the squeeze of this world's life, as we actually do work here, or work is done upon us, is an Eden from which rationalists seek in vain to expel us, now that we have criticized their state of mind.

(James 1987e, 1038–9; 1979, 60)

Emerson's godson had pushed the Transcendentalist aspiration, what Emerson called in *Nature*, "the transparent eyeball," to its inevitable conclusion—overcoming the dualist Cartesian construct of consciousness and content (Emerson 1971; Van Leer 1986; Jay 2005).[3]

This key Romantic ethos serves as the scaffolding of James's thought (Gale 1999, 220–34; Rorty 2007; Schulenberg 2015, 2022). As we unpack his principles of psychology and the philosophical structure of his ideas about selfhood, consciousness, freedom of the will, and truth, we will find his Romantic temperament manifest, which both directed his interests and oriented his conclusions (Madelrieux 2022; Gunnarsson 2022).

James's Romantic forebearers, facing the objectification of world and *self*, asked (as he would) how to legitimate the subjective—feelings, intuitions, and memories—in a milieu in which the human being was increasingly defined in terms of scientific objectification. The answers, of course, were varied, but all fixed on the centrality (and authority) of the knowing subject, and then the problem became how to express and thus in some sense *know* the unformulated of personal experience. Thus was introduced the problem of consciousness—more specifically, self-consciousness. As Coleridge asserted, "self-consciousness is the fixt point . . . . [It] is not a kind of being, but a kind of knowing, [and while the] objective is assumed as the first, we yet can never pass beyond the principle of self-consciousness" (Coleridge 1983, 285).[4]

As already discussed, although consciousness would serve as James's starting point for his own considerations of subjectivity, he would eventually dismiss the entire matter. The reality of subjective experience was never in question, but for James, its objectification in some scientific pose could only appear distorted and thus misrepresented. Upon abandoning scientific psychology, he sought a deeper conduit into the mind than offered in consciousness or the workings of Reason. In this regard, he snugly fits into the Romantic Quest.

Subjectivity, *sui generis*

James reconfigured subjectivity by prioritizing *experience*—primary, immediate, and unreflected; consciousness (and most profoundly, *self*-consciousness) then becomes derivative of a deeper mental stratum. With that distinction, he highlighted the struggle of finding the explicit in which the formulation of an idea, the concretization of an intuition, the expression of feelings reflects a *poesis* at work. Rather than draw upon Reason, he placed an emphasis on the imaginative, flexible, and ambiguous process of creating meaning. For that endeavor, he presented an epistemology based on a roughly etched notion of a "potentiality"—the unformed and ambiguous—that then becomes articulated in the emergence of creative consciousness. He thereby expounded a philosophical formulation of what Coleridge (1983 [1817], chapter 13) had called *imagination* and Novalis, *romantic*.[5] For them and a host of fellow travelers, the creative poet confers special qualities upon the world and in that process *manufactures* meaning.

The "world picture" depicted by science provides just one of several ways to describe reality, both psychic and physical. That mode of knowing was too narrow for James. He shared the Romantic notion "of the priority of imagination over reason—the claim that reason can only follow paths that the imaginations has broken" (Rorty 2007, 105).

Insisting upon the making of reality, James, like Emerson, Nietzsche, and Schiller, holds that the world is unfinished, incomplete, malleable, and thus waiting for humans to add something to it. James is a poet-philosopher who maintains that the subject's creativity is capable of shaping and enriching the world that it finds. Furthermore, his thought is directed against apriorism, dogmas, fixed principles, and timeless absolutes. This implies that he critiques the gesture of a convergence to the antecedently real or good, as well as the correspondence theory of truth.[6] The subject must not seek to faithfully and objectively imitate what it finds, but it should try to enrich and elevate reality. James's humanism is moreover directed against systematic thought, the idea of *prima philosophia*, and theoretical abstractions. His brand of pragmatism illuminates the significance of creativity, praxis, plurality, and perspective; that is, it demonstrates that in a world without foundations, essences, substances, and immutable principles, only the finite world of change, contingency, and creative praxis is real.

(Schulenberg 2022, 367)

This generative capacity of the knowing agent to establish meaning is the crucial Romantic step, for "untreated" nature, nature without human complementarity, has no value. So, where science seeks to eliminate subjective judgment, Romantic resistance allows for exercising free will, and in that metaphysical facet alone, James radically diverges from the determinism lying in the very foundations of Freud's putative natural science.

In highlighting the subjective, James is, in fact, offsetting the encroachment of "intellectualisms," but not at the expense of the inescapable processing that accompanies introspection or self-awareness more generally. In essence, he is arguing for a spectrum of "thought" stretching between the inarticulate feeling to the concept.

> From the cognitive point of view, all mental facts are intellections. From the subjective point of view all are feelings . . . And then we see that the current opposition of Feeling to Knowledge is quite a false issue. If every feeling is at the same time a bit of knowledge, we ought no longer to talk of mental states differing by having more or less of the cognitive quality; they only differ in knowing more or less, in having much fact or little fact for their object. The feeling of a broad scheme of relations is a feeling that knows much; the feeling of a simple quality is a feeling that knows little. But the knowing itself, whether of much or of little, has the same essence, and is as good knowing in the one case as in the other.
>
> (James 1983, 452)

By emphasizing that thoughts and feelings are two *aspects* of experience, neither to be taken in isolation from the other, James described the mind in terms that preserved its irretrievable unity and the inviolate standing of unmediated subjectivity (Dianda 2023, 102).

James not only denied the concretization that would displace subjectivity with an objectivizing Cartesianism, but he also asserted the active role of the individual in creating the world in which the subject lives. Thus, James depicted experience as an *active* and *lived* process, by organizing "our environment, arrange phenomena, and focus on some aspects of our reality, while ignoring others, for reasons more than mere physical need" (Dianda 2023, 108). And because we manipulate experience to serve interests, ends, needs, wants, desires, and wishes, our choices are not simply spontaneous reaction to stimuli. On this reading, James regarded the mind as a creative faculty, one that exercises choice in service to pragmatic well-being. Or as Dewey, following James, stated later,

> Mind is no longer a spectator beholding the world from without and find-ing its highest satisfaction in the joy of self-sufficing contemplation. The mind is within the world as a part of the latter's own ongoing process. It is marked off as mind by the fact that wherever it is found, changes take place in a directed way, so that a movement in a definite one-way sense . . . takes place.
>
> (Dewey 1984, 232)

The Romantic ethos of individuality and valorization of imagination inspired this view of the dynamic mind.

James engaged two ventures, coupled but distinct in the pursuit of devel-oping this romantic view of the mind in the face of the positivist challenges of his own era. The first was as a psychologist, which, in several respects, he completed with *The Principles of Psychology* in 1890. That work assessed the basic findings of the science of the mind while recognizing the limits of that approach. In the second phase, pursued as a metaphysician, James attempted to reconcile the problems raised by the mind-body dualism of his earlier portrayal. Indeed, psychology as a newborn science could not escape that duality in the effort to characterize perceptions, feelings, cognitions, and reasonings coupled to their physiological conditions. Then, by explic-itly rejecting the mind-body duality for the primacy of *consciousness*, and then placing *experience* as the organizing principle of his "radical empiri-cism," James combined the metaphysical claim that reality is not monistic but composed of pluralistic experience(s) with such concepts as *knowledge, meaning*, and *truth* that must be understood as essentially concerned with the *relations* between experiences (Myers 1986, 14).

And a second converse issue is how James strained against this same dualism in legitimating the melding of self and Other in mystic revelry. He endorsed those psychic realms well beyond rational discourse, and the panpsychism of his thought certainly drew from those sentiments (Ford 1982; Gale 1999). In many different contexts, James argued that concretized consciousness is but a distillation of a greater reality (one in which the subjective is subordinated to objective accounts), and religious experience (more particularly, the mystical) held special importance in his thought. Although James (falsely) claimed no firsthand knowledge, the mystic served him especially well as a model of radical empiricism in action, namely, by exemplifying experience outside the structure of self-consciousness.

James found the opportunity to expound on the matter during the Gifford Lectures (1901–2) (later published as *Varieties of Religious Experience*). He included two chapters on mysticism and concluding remarks emphasizing the authenticity and noetic quality of such experience.[7]

> The further limits of our being plunge, it seems to me, into an altogether other dimension of existence from the sensible and merely "understandable" world. Name it the mystical region, or the supernatural region, whichever you choose. So far as our ideal impulses originate in this region (and most of them do originate in it, for we find them possessing us in a way for which we cannot articulately account), we belong to it in a more intimate sense than that in which we belong to the visible world, for we belong in the most intimate sense wherever our ideals belong. Yet the unseen region in question is not merely ideal, for it produces effects in this world. When we commune with it, work is actually done upon our finite personality, for we are turned into new men, and consequences in the way of conduct follow in the natural world upon our regenerative change. But that which produces effects within another reality must be termed a reality itself, so I feel as if we had no philosophic excuse for calling the unseen or mystical world unreal.
>
> (James 1987f, 460–1)

And, he might well have added, valuable.

As James reminds his audience, he had initiated "all this empirical inquiry not merely to open a curious chapter in human consciousness, but rather to attain a spiritual judgment as to the total value and positive meaning" of the religious (James 1987f, 239). And as he himself understood, that meaning extended well beyond the confines of the spiritual and undergirded epistemology, Romantic and otherwise (Tauber 2001, 2012a). As James himself noted, "The human mind always has and always will be able to interpret facts in accordance with its moral interests."[8]

> The whole drift of my education goes to persuade me that the world of our present consciousness is only one out of many worlds of consciousness that exist, and that those other worlds must contain experiences which have a meaning for our life also; and that although in the main their experiences and those of this world keep discrete, yet the two become continuous at certain points, and higher energies filter in. By being faithful in my poor measure to this over-belief, I seem to myself to keep more sane and

true. I can, of course, put myself into the sectarian scientist's attitude, and imagine vividly that the world of sensations and of scientific laws and objects may be all. But whenever I do this, I hear that inward monitor . . . whispering the word "bosh!" Humbug is humbug, even though it bear the scientific name, and the total expression of human experience, as I view it objectively, invincibly urges me beyond the narrow "scientific" bounds. Assuredly, the real world is of a different temperament,—more intricately built than physical science allows. So my objective and my subjective conscience both hold me to the over-belief which I express.

(James 1987f, 463)

This passage highlights cardinal features of James's thought: the underlying psychology that directed his thinking (Leary 2022; Madelrieux 2022); the legitimization—indeed, valorization—of the subjective; and the subordination of consciousness (per self-consciousness) that interferes with the primacy of personal feeling (viz. religious, non-objectified). He placed the religious realm within the "subconscious" that mediates between the ineffable "more" and conscious awareness or articulation and argued for its reality on the pragmatic basis of effects and the epistemological pluralism that undergirded his philosophy.[9]

Indeed,

how can one provide a description of *more* than reality? One can describe more than reality if reality isn't all there is. There is also unreality. And part of the extreme pluralist view that lies behind James's metaphysics is just that: reality isn't all there is, that there is also unreality, or rather that there are "intentionally, at any rate," unreal entities.

(Putnam 1990b, 237, emphasis in original)

As already discussed, *experience* is articulated only as a second-order conscious phenomenon, and that expression may take a form other than the mediation of relationships in the natural or social worlds. However, religious experience is categorically different as James defined that "*experiences of individual men in their solitude, so far as they apprehend themselves to stand in relation to whatever they may consider the divine*" (James 1987f, 36, emphasis in original), which he further delineated as a consciousness of union with the "More" (James 1987f, 435ff.). By moving from the public to the private experience of religious experience in *The Varieties*, James no longer dealt with the subject/object dualism of ordinary processing, but rather focused solely on the privileged personal. As discussed in the previous chapter, to reach that source, he repeatedly alludes to the "subliminal" as the reservoir of the sense of the divine (James 1987f, 215, 384, 433, 457). Indeed, the mystical experience is a phenomenon that resists normal language as repeatedly attested in James's citations and thus represents another kind of experience that expands his epistemological agenda to a consideration of the beguiling Sisyphean search for the center of human subjectivity, the source of one's sense of personal being (Jay 2005, 275–6). Accordingly, *Varieties* holds a special place in James's opera, for there he allows himself to freely explore this unstructured territory of experience. Simply, the mystical abandons secondary predicate processing of perceptions to the inner cosmos of unmediated feelings.[10]

Allowing the subjective its full due, James would not allow a stultified philosophy to deny the validity of feelings irrespective of their epistemological status. Accordingly, James's philosophical explorations reached well beyond intellectual analytics to deal with various emotional and existential crises, and those analytics were followed with radical consequences. In following his spiritual intuitions, James expressly forfeited logic and perhaps philosophy as generally conceived. In his last work, published posthumously, *Some Problems of Philosophy*, James shifted (as did Heidegger a generation later) from "philosopher" to "thinker":

> The question of being is the darkest in all philosophy. All of us are beggars here, and no school can speak disdainfully of another or give itself superior airs. For all of us alike, Fact forms a datum, gift, or *Vorgefundenes* [existing], which we cannot burrow under, explain or get behind. It makes itself somehow, and our business is far more with its What than with its Whence or Why.
>
> (James 1987e, 1006; 1979, 30).

Couched in terms of metaphysics, James's temperament and emotional wonder found logic's limits, and again like Heidegger and Wittgenstein,[11] he sought its expression in philosophy's negation:

> There is a *plus ultra* beyond all we know . . . The ontologic emotion of wonder, of mystery, has in some minds such a tinge of the rapture of sublimity, that for its aesthetic reason alone, it will be difficult for any philosophic system completely to exorcise it.
>
> (James 1992f [1879], 979–80)

Note, in that pursuit, the ego would be eclipsed. That collapse clearly (and dramatically) illustrates how the self-conscious subject is deeply beholden to Cartesian metaphysics (Tauber 2013a).

In conclusion, *Varieties of Religious Experience* holds a special place in James's oeuvre. By avoiding the philosophical technicalities of radical empiricism, it became his most accessible treatise on the lessons derived from his revamping the metaphysics of experience: the subjective cannot be captured by objective analysis; all the particulars may be studied, but none individually, nor their sum, depicts subjective *experience*. By explicitly rejecting the mind-body duality of *consciousness* for the primacy of *pure experience* as the organizing principle of his late philosophy, James made the fundamental metaphysical claim that reality is not monistic but is composed through pluralistic experience(s), and such concepts as knowledge, meaning, and truth must be understood as essentially concerned with the relations between experiences of diverse kinds (Myers 1986, 14).[12]

Capturing the emotion, or not

Despite reservations about the Freudian model, certain key insights remain intact, namely, mental functioning occurs on parallel tracts:

1. A continuous unconscious stream of uninterrupted mental events follows its own "logic," which may be discerned by episodic manifestations in conscious thought, emotion, and behavior;
2. interspersed in this unbroken flow, punctuated consciousness skips from one intentional object to another as determined by external stimuli and unconscious motivations; and
3. whether assessed through cognitive science studying perception or contemporary cognitive psychology examining human motivation, rationality, memory, attention, creativity, unconscious reasoned choices require delegation to unconscious sorting, relational, and rational deliberation (e.g., T. D. Wilson 2002; Dijksterhuis and Nordgren 2006; Sio and Ormerod 2009; Hayles 2017; Reber and Allen 2022; reviewed in Tauber 2014).

Accordingly, the mind is fundamentally a continuous unconscious mental stream that erupts in discontinuous foci of consciousness, and thus the conscious mind is intrinsically incomplete. On this view, consciousness is a fragment of the mind. Absent the highlighted conscious/unconscious configuration, the mind continuously functions as any physiological system, albeit in different modalities of perception and response.

However, deeper issues about the very character of human being that emanate from this description remain decidedly unresolved, specifically the place of the affections in Freud's theory. We lack convincing evidence of what James thought about psychoanalysis. We know of his interest in Freud's early studies of hysteria, and he smiled benignly upon Jung and Ernst Jones in Worcester. However, considering James's larger agenda, it seems reasonable to surmise that psychoanalysis as a scientific venture would have evinced James's scornful dismissal. That judgment is based not only on the various reasons James rejected the positivist descriptions of experience, generally, but on a deeper antithesis about metaphysical claims draped in the guise of the factual in which the subjective found no ready home. So how, in fact, did Freud deal with emotions in his conception of psychoanalysis?

As detailed in Chapter 1, the psychoanalytic unconscious is a product of the representational mind, one with a particular philosophical orientation: As "the other" of the conscious mind, and most evidently as deciphered by psychoanalytic interpretation, the unconscious mirrors the semantic structure of consciousness, which, according to a Jamesian perspective, follows from the disjunction (and distortion) imposed by the Cartesian metaphysics of the ego scrutinizing itself. (Indeed, that objection becomes the key tenet of James's later philosophy.) To achieve this formulation, Freud adapted the Kantian epistemological scheme by postulating that

1. the unconscious is noumenal, composed of drives seeking their release;
2. the drives have ideas attached to them, and psychoanalysts discern these ideas through interpretations of various manifestations, e.g., dreams or parapraxis;
3. such phenomena are then considered as derived from the unconscious, but in such representation, the direct expression of the unconscious drive is not represented, only the associated *idea*;
4. thus, psychoanalysis is based on discerning the *idea*, calibrating its associated drive, and explaining the repression that has led to psychic disequilibrium (neurosis).

With such insight, the tyranny of the despotic unconscious would be broken by *analysis* mediated by reason's autonomy, that is, by the ego's ability to free itself from disguised or hidden psychic forces. Reason would discern deterministic causes of overt behaviors and thoughts that hitherto were inaccessible or disguised. Most importantly, the discernment offered by analysis would hopefully result in some form of emotional release and resolution of neurosis.

This scheme is perhaps Freud's deepest commitment to a Cartesian understanding of the subject—namely, to the mind-body divide, which included (at least implicitly) a correspondence theory of truth that accurately relates the mind's representations with the phenomena under scrutiny. Given that "phenomena" are not the thing-in-itself, he then makes the intimacy of psychic experience a special case; i.e., the immediacy of personal feeling provides more direct epistemological knowledge and thus a lesser "problem" than faced with the cognitive mediation of exterior nature (see Chapter 1, note #17). This is where, at the base of modern Western metaphysics, his theory was most vulnerable. That affections are immediately experienced does not mean that they then can be related to oneself (much less to others) as *representations*.

The tension between the dominance of the unconscious and the autonomy of the ego remains unresolved in Freud's theory and leads to a bi-partite strategy to resolve psychic conflict: First, the emotional disturbance is deciphered to translate the affects into terms susceptible to analysis; and then in a second step, such knowledge brings the analysand to recognize the emotional trauma directly, i.e., without intellectual mediation. And once repression loses its hegemony, the affections may be confronted directly. Upon the ego's analysis, a recalibrated *emotional* response constitutes the psychoanalytic therapy. The underlying premise holds that emotional recognition and rational insight leads to personal freedom. Accordingly, insight becomes the therapeutic means towards psychological and existential health. The interpretive process serves as a ladder to the emotional platform, where the curative psychodynamic work occurs. Schematically, a fivefold progression is at work: Repression → Recognition → Release → Reflection → Resolution. *Understanding* the affective is crucial, but in service to the essential emotional engagement that results from the analytic strategy of identifying the repression, the conflict, and finally the "cause" of anxiety. Thus, the traditional analytic fulfills one function; the cathartic insight fulfills another. Given the centrality of emotions in this psychoanalytic process, how were they placed in the psychoanalytic schema?

Freud dealt with emotions most directly in terms of the psychodynamics of repression, in which the *idea* associated with the drive is repressed; if the emotion remains inaccessible to conscious processes, its motivational effects remain mysterious (see Chapter 1). Note that repression, working to control emotion, works on the *idea* associated with that affect. In other words, uncovering the repressed idea assigns meaning to the emotion, and such interpretation of those representations (posing as "ideas") provides "the royal road to the unconscious" (Freud 1900, 608).[13] Accordingly, the representations of unconscious drives are used to configure affections into a translation composed of concepts, symbols, and complex interpretations of instinct-linked "ideas" contextualized within an intellectualized story. "The work of psychoanalysis is to restore the original meaning of the representation, i.e., more closely link the idea to the affect and correct the mis-construal and thereby relieve repression and ultimately anxiety" (Freud 1916, 403–4, 409; Tauber 2015).

Emotion thus finds an interpretation through an analytic procedure of rendering multiple faculties, e.g., memory, associations, dreams, and parapraxis into psychoanalytic ideation. Strikingly, instead of "emotion" accounted on its own terms, they become transported as "ideas" and, as Freud acknowledged, treated as conscious thought. After all, if emotions remain inaccessible to conscious processes, then their motivational effects remain mysterious. Intervention then depends on "articulating" emotions and thus making them conscious. Upon this theoretical platform, Freud built psychoanalysis.

Note that Freud does not maintain that unconscious emotions do not exist, but rather that we cannot gain direct access to them for analysis (Tauber 2013a, 36–8). Once identified, the affect must remain conscious for the repression to be broken:

It is surely of the essence of an emotion that we should be aware of it, i.e., that it should become known to consciousness . . . If we restore the true connection, we call the original affective impulse an "unconscious" one. Yet its affect was never unconscious; all that had happened was that its *idea* had undergone repression.

(Freud 1915b, 177–8, emphasis in original).

Without such exposure, "the possibility of the attribute of unconsciousness would be completely excluded [if not attached to an idea] as far as emotions, feelings, and affects are concerned" (Freud 1915b, 177). So, the challenge becomes how to bring emotional trauma to consciousness through an analysis of the available "idea" (representations of emotional desiderata) derived from analysis of the symbols embedded in dreams, jokes, slips of the tongue, various neurotic behaviors, and so on. In short, the interpretative process putatively reveals unconscious conflict by studying the hidden links of the newly revealed *ideas*.

Basically, Freud intellectualized emotions by linking them to ideas and thus made them subject to other *conscious* mental processes, most prominently a "science" that would decipher the unconscious into the linguistics of consciousness whereby the emotion is translated through the ideas and thus *known* as a derivative of the primary affect. So, whereas James gave primacy to the immediacy of primary experience (the emotions), for Freud, emotions become *derivatives* of rational thought. Accordingly, for Freud, emotional life is understood only in conscious terms, and analysis effectively "rescues the rationality of an emotion" (Lear 1990, 90). That move highlights the basic premise of Freudian psychoanalysis that endeavors to translate the unconscious into conscious "ideas" and thereby converts that which has no language into terms the ego may manipulate. The skeptic notes that even though "the unconscious is not susceptible to colonization by Knowledge," the introspective psychological eye

> has complied with the demands of the ego (and its will to power) seeming without reflection. . . . But it cannot be a given that psychological categories should offer the best means for locating and conceptualizing the unconscious. In fact, this very inclination constitutes a danger in that it threatens psychoanalysis with a dead-lock. For ultimately, when one has preordained the unconscious to be a representative of the categories familiar to consciousness, it will be very difficult to discover and investigate anything other than the already well-known and reasonable world of the ego.
>
> (Reeder 2002, 18–20)

In other words, Freud's science of the mind portrays the psyche in its own rational terms, and the argument from the earliest days of his presentation revolves around the justification of that rendering.

We must not construe Freud's idea of the affects as the same "bodily feelings" James ascribed to emotions. On James's account (presented in "The Emotions" chapter of *Principles of Psychology*, 1890), emotions are "nothing but the feeling of a bodily state, and [have] a purely bodily cause" (James 1983, 1074). In other words, emotions are reduced to physiology, whose manifestations are interpreted at higher cognitive levels as feelings—fear, love, anger, etc. He reversed the commonsensical notion that the emotion causes a bodily change that expresses it. Instead, James insisted that a person who sees a charging lion, runs, and the running, with its associated bodily changes, is experienced as fear: "*bodily changes follow directly the perception of the exciting fact*," and the resulting feeling of those changes is the emotion (James 1983, 1065, emphasis in original). Accordingly, emotions as *feelings* are derivative of physiological responses and thus have no motivational force. Accordingly, James accepted emotions as such, and therein lies the upshot of their conflicting philosophies of mind and the psychologies derived from those constructs.

Freud offered a radically different account: the lynchpin of psychoanalytic theory is that conscious or not, emotions have intentions (given their association with the drives), whose elucidation provides the meaning to the feelings and behaviors of the ego. After all, psychoanalysis is devoted to uncovering those intentions and explaining the motivational drive of unconscious drives. Although the affects are taken as expressions of some primitive psychic apparatus, Freud regarded emotions as part of the *conscious* cognitive mind, whereby an emotional response is either a discharge of energy caused by an idea or the awareness of the discharge (Freud 1915b, 178; Lear 1990, 87). Simply put, whereas James assumed a physiological orientation where cognitive states generate emotion, Freud made emotions subject to other conscious mental processes. If this distinction is maintained, then Freud's notions of hate, love, anger, and so on must be understood as *ideational* states, and when associated with trauma, repression is the requirement for maintaining emotional homeostasis.

Freud provided sparse theoretical consideration concerning the character of emotional intentionality, i.e., what establishes a vector of expression, or what constitutes an emotion's distinctive relation to its object (Deigh 2010, 24). A tale of obstructed energies and rising tensions hardly fulfills the requirements of a metapsychology that might account for the so-called primitive affective life (Freud 1895). He thus left undeveloped a theoretical conception of emotions *qua emotions*, and the various formulations of the pleasure principle seeking its fulfillment were, in parallel, left ambiguous.

This lacuna is an ironic aspect of Freud's thinking. After all, psychoanalysis originated in the diagnosis of psychosomatic illness—the spasm, cough, paralysis, pain afflicting his patients. These symptoms, according to his interpretations, pointed to a psychic origin that were in some profound sense contained within the mind, when in fact they were bodily expressions of emotional trauma. But because he worked as a dualist and consequently restricted his vision to the unconscious psychic reality, he demarcated these "mental expressions" from brain states and certainly the soma itself. Instead of anchoring the ego in some melding of mind and body, "an ego that would be body, of a body that would be ego—he dissociates it. He makes it into a 'mental projection' of the corporeal surface, its transposition on the psychic plane" (Rogozinski 2010, 73). He thereby forsook any attempt to develop a unified theory that would integrate the emotions (the body) with the mental.

This construction was derived from Freud's dualist metaphysics that placed mind and body (emotions) in separate domains, and their linkage was then achieved by the representations of the affects to consciousness. Note that Freud created a model of the mind to *re-present* that which is experienced *without* mediation. To represent affections served his science, but such a stratagem intellectualized and thus veiled the emotion itself.[14] In effect, the psychoanalytic library is limited to the representations of various phenomena characteristic of the psychopathology of everyday life (signi-fied by symbols, uttered as word distortions or misapplications, displaced objects, forgotten commitments, etc. [Freud 1901]) that are then subject to interpretation. The entire enterprise is thus an elaborate translation system. On this view, we arrive at an ironic result: While representations and their repressed ideas point to an intra-psychic "Other," the *affective* unconscious appears only as the artifact of its representational status (Henry 1993, 287–8, 298–300, 315).[15]

On empathy

Affects present themselves directly as experience without representa-tion. And this too is a way of *knowing*, albeit not readily conceptual but rather manifest as a direct visceral experience of feelings that range from non-descript moods to complex emotions. In this arena, psychoanalysis attempts to provide an account of the origin and cause of what is *felt* but not formulated. The process by which the affect is presented occurs through the transference between analysand and analyst, a pivotal mode of communica-tion in the therapeutic process. Simply put, the analyst's insight is based on empathy (albeit informed by Freudian precepts).

As already detailed, in the psychoanalytic scenario, the same subject-object divide that appears so clearly in the Kantian schema of cap-turing external reality also applies to representing psychic life. But inner states are different in character from discerned (potentially public) knowl-edge of external reality. One difference pertains to the "product" of the cognitive process: Physical objects may be objectified; namely, different observers might agree on what the object is. Of course, that agreement may or may not correspond to the same assessment, and in the end, measure-ment may be the only criterion for some "final" objective account. Yet, whatever the basis of agreement, verified knowledge rests on *shared* expe-rience. With subjective states, one's representation to oneself is private, and when articulated, it becomes a second-order report and *never* complete. So, while subjective experience might be expressed in the same represen-tational language used to discuss the external world, the feeling or emotion exists as such, constrained (if not trapped) within the private experience of the individual. And if that experience remains unarticulated, in what sense is it "mental"?

When one becomes cognizant of an emotional state—namely, when the affect has moved into self-consciousness—mental characteristics may be attributed. When someone says, "I am happy," an ego, "me," is identified, and a conscious evaluation is made about his or her state of being—both the subject assessing herself and the other person being addressed. That self-awareness becomes a perception of sorts. Freud struggled with ways of accounting for that movement and the basis of sharing the emotion with the analyst. The issue constitutes a central theoretical concern, for the entire endeavor of making the unconscious, conscious, depends on a reliable means of capturing the emotion in terms that allow for deliberation and yet leave the affect "true" to itself. That Freud claimed affections are immediately known does not mean that they then can be depicted and then related to oneself (much less to others) as *representations*.[16] Only upon reflection does the emotion require (and acquire) ideas (and their corresponding representations). At this point, the problem of the representation itself is at issue, and the way Freud dealt with this matter illuminates the representational character of his theory and its failings.

Freud, while steadfastly holding onto an epistemology that would serve his science, understood the limitations of his theory. Given that the unconscious is not governed by logic, time, causality, or *teloi* characterized by rational thought, how would this domain register in the realm of reason? The challenge is analogous to how one would describe the taste of an apple, or a Mozart sonata, or a feeling of disgust. In each case, a subjective report has a word representation to convey the experience. As Wittgenstein pointed out at the beginning of *Philosophical Investigations*, the simplistic model of associating an object (e.g., apple) with a word is inadequate to capture the complexities of experience and its expression. For example, the *experience* of eating remains one's own. The taste of the apple is mine and may not correspond to yours. Diverse emotional experience fails precise articulation; describing the experience of hearing a work of Mozart defies language. Musicologists may discuss the structure of the music and critics may opine about a performance, but who can describe the *feelings* of hearing Cossi fan Tutte? My appreciation of the opera is mine alone; yours is yours.

The key challenge rests on the quandary of how an analysand might adequately convey her own state of feelings. One might describe pain and find language incapable of capturing the experience, as the phobia of Little Hans has no conceptual intermediaries for the child (Freud 1909). To be reassured by the analyst, "I know what you mean," is based on the intricacies of transference and trust, but does the analyst really *know* what her client is feeling? The analyst has her own perspective and narrative, a frame of reference that may differ widely from the analysand's. All rest on complex levels of "cognitive empathy," and while a powerful means of communication, the trauma or dream in its full array remains largely sealed within the analysand's memory and unspoken experience. The ineffable character of inner mental states requires another mode of transmission, whereby the analyst may join the analysand in some shared experience. Analysis alone is insufficient; indeed, an altogether different kind of "knowing" is required, one in which the subjective plays its irrepressible evaluative role as a cognitive faculty. Indeed, empathy may be regarded as a form of "emotional reasoning," not in the same way as logical precision commands but as a lens by which perceptions are refracted by mood, personal experience, and temperament (Nussbaum 2001; Tauber 2013a, 224).

Freud recognized that the medium of affective transmission is unconscious in the sense of not being represented by any conceptual structure. Rather, affectivity is expressed directly through the "passions," all of which fall well beyond rational discourse. Freud, stepping outside his scientific comfort zone and accepting the pragmatic therapeutic requirements of his method, understood this cardinal fact and taught the analyst to be sensitive to her own unconscious feelings as a receptacle of affective transmissions of the analysand. Accordingly, the analyst "must turn his own unconscious like a receptive organ towards the transmitting unconscious of the patient . . . so the doctor's own unconscious is able, from the derivatives of the unconscious which are communicated to him, to reconstruct that unconscious" (Freud 1912, 115–16). The translation of those feelings into language was to heighten awareness of emotional content, but in the end, this translation only served a deeper affective recognition process. Because "representability as such allows only one of all available psychical contents to be known to consciousness" (Henry 1993, 288), Freud widened his approach. Indeed, the commitment to the affective domain shifted his therapeutic strategy from a primary focus on the rational reconstruction of psychic trauma to the instrumental use of reason as a step towards establishing direct emotional contact with the affect that has been repressed through its association with a psychic "idea." Put another way, only through the affect might engagement with the unconscious occur.

As already discussed, to discern the economy of the psychic drives that escape the laws of consciousness, Freud employed what he thought were reliable representatives of the obscure drives, namely, the ideas to which the drives associated. So, through drive-idea association, he might "know" the unconscious. By making the mental state an object of scrutiny—and thus *objectified*—he donned the role of the scientist, because for him, knowledge existed only as positivist knowledge. Accordingly, he would press the unconscious into an objective mold. That required *re*-presenting what was

presented directly, the emotions. By assigning ideas to the affects, a manipulation is at work: *ideas* are not the affections with which they associate but
remain only their *re*-presentation. Then, one may reasonably ask, how is the
emotion experienced without mediation?

For Freud, the ends of interpretation are emotional recognition and
rational insight directed towards change. Beyond the analysis *qua* analysis, a revised interpretation of one's personal history, behaviors, choices,
maladjustments, conflicts, and neuroses allows some reconstructed understanding of one's personal identity, goals, and placement in the world.
A normative ideal organizes the therapeutic goals, as Freud quite explicitly
observed: "Analysis replaces repression by condemnation" (Freud 1909,
145), by which he meant that the ego asserts control on acting out desires
or breaking constraints. That goal defines the trajectory of analysis and the
possibility for a therapeutic outcome (Tauber 2010, 12).

By focusing on the pursuit of better-balanced emotional dynamics
through reasoned self-knowledge, insight putatively modulates (even
resolves) guilt and ultimately relieves the analysand from dysfunctional
behaviors. In other words, reason serves to awaken an emotional awareness, and that recognition serves to release the subject from the tyranny
of the traumatic past. The work of psychoanalysis occurs in transference
and countertransference, where the emotional ties established between analyst and analysand allow for reenactment, identification, reconfiguration,
or redistribution of emotional trauma, with the eventual release of repression and anxiety (Rubovits-Seitz 2001). Reason thus recedes, for in the
transference, psychoanalysis enacts a transformation of psychic reality,
not its domination—at least in theory. Because conscious recognition and
recollection are insufficient for psychic cure, effective therapy ultimately
requires a corresponding affective response linked to the analytical recall
and insight. Simply, intellectual analysis alone fails to curatively modify
the analysand's *emotional* life. With this emotionally based strategy, unconscious drives putatively are met on their own grounds in the transference,
whose effective enactment becomes the ultimate goal of psychoanalysis.
Here, human subjectivity—redacted, redirected, and reformed—might find
its fuller expression. In the end, Freud's "science" devolves to an interpersonal interpretation about feelings. How does that occur?

Accessing the unformulated

Much of post-Freudian theorizing has delved into the cognitive processes in
which the clinical encounter emerges. In the context of our discussion, the

most pertinent are the array of conjectures that would characterize states of mind that escape the symbolic representative model undergirding Freud's original thesis (Levine, Reed, and Scarfone 2013; D. B. Stern 2019). Arising from many theoretical sources and diverse psychoanalytic schools, they hold in common a reconfiguration of Freud's original goal of revealing hidden or distorted, preexisting mental contents to the revised task of finding a conduit to the unconscious through shared analysand-analyst experience. Such states are understood as unformulated and thus unrepresented. Lacking "shape" or articulation, they must be "created" or given meaning in the analytic exchange. All agree that this reservoir of feelings and memories has a formative influence on human understanding, behavior, and adjustment, but their discernment is approached differently from the elucidation of their putative symbolic content.

The task is for the analyst to share the unformulated experience dwelling in the primordial emotional stratum of the analysand's unconscious and to assist in making it meaningful. In other words, analysis becomes possible only with the articulation of the unsayable. The unformulated *as such* thereby assumes crucial theoretical interest.[17] On this view, the ego and self psychologies that have dominated North American theories—"diluted forms of psychoanalysis" (D. B. Stern 2019, 29)—must be aligned with what Lacan called "back to Freud," which, while recalling the original intent of revealing the unconscious, remains an ironic motto given Lacan's utter rejection of Freud's original design.

The "movement" from inchoate unconscious feelings to their articulation was schematized by Harry Stack Sullivan, who divided cognitive states into three developmental phases (D. B. Stern 2019, 3–4): (1) *prototaxis*, the most primitive mode of the infant, in which the world is disorganized as the "blooming, buzzing confusion" described by James (1983, 462); (2) *parataxic* experience, which has some temporal order but meanings cannot be specified and remain unformulated (the domain of the unconscious and the hidden meanings of the interrelational); and (3) *syntaxic*, the modality in which experience is validated consensually and thus articulated, which may occur in the public domain or privately. Based on this partition, Donnel Stern has elaborated a theory of unformulated experience to take account of the role of nonverbal experience in the psychoanalytic encounter (D. B. Stern 1983, 1997, 2010, 2015). In brief, he views the unconscious as a reservoir of inarticulate experience, and as it is converted from a parataxic to a syntaxic expression, meaning is generated. Language, then, is not only a medium for representing meaning that already exists; the articulation *creates* meaning. This so-called "constitutive theory of language" (C. Taylor 2016) strikingly contrasts with Freud's point of view.

> For Freud (1915b), language is inadequate to unconscious meaning ("thing-presentations"), which are only one step removed from things-in-themselves. Unconscious meanings, that is, cannot be accommodated by words. There is a loss of meaning when "thing-presentations" are linked to language, thereby becoming "word-presentations." Word-presentations, the only form in which meaning can enter consciousness, are a paler version than the form they represent.
>
> Language, that is, inevitably presents an impoverished rendition of the nonverbal meanings that it labels.
>
> (D. B. Stern 2019, 6)[18]

In contrast, not only do the constitutive theories deny that language sacrifices meaning, but articulation actually contributes to the construction of meaning by giving form to the unformulated. On this view, instead of consciousness as "the paler form, a dilution of the meaning that exists in the unconscious," meaning emerges as it moves from unconsciousness to consciousness (D. B. Stern 2019, 7). Thus, for Stern, psychoanalysis is designed to provide the setting by which the (parataxic) unformulated may find its syntaxic organization and thereby coalesce and become articulated into fully appreciated meanings. In short, "clinical psychoanalysis is devoted to the recognition and encouragement of such opportunities" (D. B. Stern 2019, 7).

Although unacknowledged, Stern has followed James's footsteps. Whereas Freud would transcribe symbols with entailed meanings, James left meanings "open," ready to assume form and significance within the context of experience. The correspondence shared by James and Stern concerning the inner creative potential of the unexpressed is striking. Indeed, James could not have more clearly described their shared insights and conclusions than his ingenious protégé, and, because of his cogency, I quote the psychoanalyst in full:

> One of the most compelling and mysterious aspects of our experience is its emergent, unbidden quality (D. B. Stern 1990, 2015). We have no idea what we are going to think or feel next. We are observers of our own continuous acts of psychic creation, and these acts of our minds have an undeniable spontaneity. We do not know, and cannot know, that our sense of spontaneity is "true" (that is, we cannot know for sure that we are right to accept the impression that experience really is emergent)—because

we are locked out of the nonconscious parts of the operations of our own minds. It is at least hypothetically possible that our sense of spontaneity—that emergent, antic, unbidden quality that our experience has—is illusory, and that if we knew the invisible workings of our minds we would see that every thought and feeling is predetermined.

But that seems highly unlikely. Such a characterization contradicts not only our sense of ourselves, but also denies the significance of context. Can it be that, without being affected by context, our experience just unfolds from within, like widgets being stamped out on an assembly line? I think that no one would make such a claim, despite claims in the Freudian literature of the past that all experience is predetermined. Nor does such a view allow for novelty. Yes it is true that psychoanalysis teaches us that we re-create the same meanings over and over again; but of course we also create new meanings. Our psychoanalytic observation of the most conservative parts of our functioning is important, because these observations allow us to see the ways we trap ourselves in old, self-destructive ways; but our observations of the temptations of our own conservative casts of mind are also significant because it is only against their background that we see that we can sometimes transcend them . . . .

[W]hen I refer to unformulated experience as potential experience, what I mean is that *the final form of the articulated experience always remains to be determined*. There is always "wiggle room." This perspective has often been called "constructivism" in psychoanalysis, especially by analysts generally identified as relational (D. B. Stern 1983, 1992, 1997; Mitchell 1993; Hoffman 1998). The core of this idea is that experience always begins with ambiguity that is resolved into a particular meaning via an interpretive, hermeneutic process.

(D. B. Stern 2019, 7–8, emphasis in original)

Stern goes on to deny relativism and then emphasizes that the unformulated is defined by "inherent constraints on what it can become . . . Reality is not directly received, that is, but interpreted" (D. B. Stern 2019, 9).[19]

And then Stern makes the relational move with a twist:

The factor that determines which potential experience comes to be articulated in consciousness is the interpersonal field, especially its unconscious aspects. That is, it is the immediate human context between patient and analyst that determines what they can experience in one another's presence.

(D. B. Stern 2019, 10)

Upon that interpersonal platform, classic Freudianism shifts to "object relations," in which the dynamics of transference and countertransference assume the contours of various forms of intersubjectivity theory. Accordingly, sub- or unconscious exchange that eventually generates meanings occurs through the interaction of analysand and analyst typically opaque to both and thus unspoken until some unexpected insight or emotional event triggers *meaning*. The entire success of the psychotherapy is based on the expression—mental or emotional—of some *potential* experience that has taken form. In short, the "vaguely organized, primitive, global, non-ideational, affective states" finally emerge in a formulated, meaningful state (D. B. Stern 2019, 12).[20]

The transition from the inarticulate to the expressed remains an enigma, but two elements seem crucial: First, the analyst's sensitivity to the analysand, the empathy required for the receptive experience of the other, is crucial and rests firmly and irrevocably in the subjective. And second, effective psychoanalysis must "destabilize the status quo and thereby open the mind to novel possibilities. The new meanings . . . are the patient's to create—although inevitably in partnership with the analyst" (D. B. Stern 2019, 16–17).

Without further delving into Stern's description and the particulars of how he is placed within the context of contemporary psychoanalysis, suffice it to note that the horizons of this approach to unlocking the secrets of our inner emotional lives already appears in vivid relief, an expansive view that resonates with James's overall attitude to human potential and flourishing:

> In psychoanalysis, I believe that the most important question we can ask about psychic phenomena is not whether they are symbolized in verbal or nonverbal terms, or even whether they are conscious or unconscious, but instead whether they are *meaningful*. The question in psychoanalytic treatment is whether psychic phenomena are transformed from their initial, nonmeaningful state into *either* a verbal or a nonverbal meaning. For me, that initial state is unformulated experience;. . . [and] meaningfulness . . . would be defined by our capacity to employ psychic material in the composition of waking dream thoughts. For me, the critical thing is whether the material can be used in the construction of spontaneous, creative living.
>
> (D. B. Stern 2019, 21, emphasis in original)

To close, let's shift from Stern's psychoanalytic context to a wider philosophical framework in which his ideas easily fit.

Dewey, inspired by James, stated Stern's ode to *meaning* almost a century earlier when he asserted that "meaning is wider in scope as well as more precious in value than is truth" (Dewey 1931). Dewey was making both an epistemological observation and a moral claim based on his exuberance about the possible. The primacy of meaning might be easily misunderstood, and rightly rejected, if truth is not included as occupying a central place in the constellation of what constitutes meaning. But for Dewey, *meaning* must be the end point of knowledge, as the individual interprets the world as a product of the present moment within the context of prior experience. In this fashion, meaning becomes the cognitive glue in which experience coheres. This attitude, developed by pragmatists (and contemporary cognitive scientists), serves to capture human intention, because without the search for meaning, the motivation for integration and coherence would have no basis and experience would have no structure (Flanagan 2007).

On this view, a "foundational" epistemology has been replaced with a Jamesian-inspired pluralistic, functional philosophy, a pragmaticism of situating meaning-seeking ventures in ordinary experience (Tauber 2005, 235–7). At that juncture James and Stern's kindred neo-post-Freudians meet in common purpose. They share the promise of an open universe of potentialities concretized by human creativity that is opened by acknowledging, nay embracing, what James called the vagueness that infuses the turmoil of all experience (discussed in the next chapter). Reaching from our inner individual consciousness to the external world where chance and indeterminate causality are constitutive of natural phenomena, he would marshal the heretofore unformulated. And in such a cosmos, human freedom may fulfill its pursuits.

James's idea of freedom grew from "the fundamental idea of an open universe in which uncertainty, choice, hypotheses, novelties and possibilities" framed his vision of human creativity in a world devoid of enchantment (Dewey 1984, 440; quoted by McDermott 1967, 8). He demonstrated the Herculean effort required to penetrate the philosophical obstacles thwarting such fulfillment. His testimony still brightly illuminates our own path. I am alluding to how modern psychology, the current fragmented science of the mind, is

deeply divided against itself, split into myriad subdisciplines. Some of these subdisciplines focus on aspects of the mind, such as cognition or emotion; others focus on aspects of the body, such as neurotransmitters or reflexes; still others, such as psychoanalysis, focus on the unconscious. From James's point of view these foci are all, equally, abstractions drawing us away from the reality of living, breathing, acting, and experiencing.

A science such as James advocated, one based on concrete, lived experience, remains conspicuous by its absence . . . I believe that the Romantics were right to call for a science of the soul, and that James was right to seek to implement this idea through his science of experience. Once the science of psychology arrogates the right to reject out of hand the content of a person's experience—because it is too inchoate, mystical, or whatever—it can no longer pronounce on the meaning of that experience. Psychology in its present divided state applies at best intermittently and incompletely to the lives most of us lead.

(Reed 1997, 220–1)

James and Freud escape this indictment. They shared a common humanist commitment in their respective pursuits, albeit with very different modes of study. James turned to "metaphysics" in dissatisfaction with "the crumbs that fall from the feast" of experimental psychology (James 1983, 266), while Freud endeavored to discover new insights about human motivations and complex emotional behavior. In each case, the search for *meaning* directed their efforts. Despite the philosophical pitfalls that eventually doomed psychoanalysis as a science, we must acknowledge the humane ethos of Freud's endeavor (Tauber 2010). After all, he sought to find meaning within the turbulence of psychic forces by making sense of nonsense. His influence can hardly be exaggerated as psychoanalysis became a crucial component of modernism's various ways of "liberating the individual from the tyranny of his culture" and asserting individual "autonomy of perception and judgment" (Posnock 1991, 70, citing Trilling 1965, xiii). So, in the "maelstrom of modernism" (Richardson 2006), James and Freud joined in the struggle with the "duality of *rationalization* and *subjectivation*" that was being played out in the "increasing divorce between the *objective* world created by reason in accordance with the laws of nature, and the world of *subjectivity*, which is primarily the world of individualism" (Touraine 1995, 4, emphasis in original). The very divergence of their respective approaches and conflicting philosophies reflects the obstinacy of the challenges they faced and the spectrum of responses offered. Re-examining their divergent philosophies illuminates their trials that remain ours as well.

Notes

1 For instance, when Freud posited a metaphorical censor, "the watchman," to preside over a gateway that determined which psychic contents pass from the large unconscious "entrance hall" to the smaller "drawing-room" in which consciousness resides, he observed, "I know you will say that these ideas are both crude and fantastic and quite impermissible in a scientific account. I know that

they are crude: and, more than that, I know that they are incorrect. . . . They are preliminary working hypotheses" (1916, 296). Admitting that his science was still inadequate to explore the unconscious directly (and presuming that new scientific methods would alter his theory), he nevertheless proceeded as if his method and theory had scientific credibility (Tauber 2010, 57–8) on the basis that his constructions were required to help establish psychic laws (Freud 1940, 158). Moreover, he maintained that such theorizing followed the same basic procedures employed by natural scientists, who used similar approximations to link their findings into some coherent model useful to order phenomena otherwise uncoordinated (Freud 1940, 159; Tauber 2013a, 213–14).

2 Romantic holism grew out of the seventeenth-century debate over the metaphysical structure of nature, where Spinozean pantheism became the direct antecedent of the romantic notion of nature's unity and, by extension, human integration into that larger whole (McFarland 1969; Israel 2001). Positivists were also guided by that ethos, but without including the cognizant agent.

3 James's relationship to Emerson has been extensively discussed. See Goodman (1990); Jay (2005, 273–4).

4 Thus, the self-consciousness *of* self-consciousness, what Søren Kierkegaard later described as the endless regress of a self reflecting upon itself, articulates the Romantic conception of subjectivity (Tauber 2006). The self for Kierkegaard shifts from an analytical focus to a subjective one, and, more fundamentally, it rests on a metaphysics of irreconcilable difference between subject and object (in contradistinction to Hegel's pursuit of dialectical synthesis). Accordingly, the authentic self is a logical product of the absolute separation of the subject from others (M. C. Taylor 1980, 162ff.). For Kierkegaard, the self becomes a recursive reflection upon itself that has no end (as culmination). Self-consciousness is "decisive . . . . The more consciousness, the more self; the more consciousness, the more will; the more will, the more self" (Kierkegaard 1980 [1849], 29). Indeed, reflexivity, the process of relating, *is* the self. In other words, reflexivity has displaced circumscribed entity with infinite process. This much seems clear. But Kierkegaard goes further: he has turned reflexivity upon itself in an endless regress only to turn it outward: "The self is a relation that relates itself to itself or is the relation's relating itself to itself in the relation; the self is not the relation but is the relation relating itself to itself." From the twentieth-century vantage of a phenomenologist, this process-oriented construction is reaffirmed in another philosophical genre: "The self is literally no-thing . . . self is precisely the peculiarly complex reflexivity itself . . . In that sense, self turns out to be the *eidos* of human life" (Zaner 1975, 168).

5 "The world must be romanticized . . . When I confer a higher meaning upon the commonplace, a mysterious aspect upon the ordinary, the dignity of the unknown upon what is known, or an appearance of infinity upon what is finite, I romanticize it" (Novalis, quoted by Cardinal 1997, 150).

6 As explained by Putnam, the crucial element in the correspondence theory of truth is "the assumption that there is a way the world is independent of how we think (or say) it is; true beliefs then are said to correspond to that way" (Putnam 2017, 90). The alternate position holds that

> there are mountains in Jordan' is true "in virtue of the way things are," provided that "in virtue of the way things are" is understood as "in virtue of the way our current descriptions of things are used and the causal interaction we

have with these things;" [Rorty] disagrees if it means "*simply* in virtue of the way things are, quite apart from how we describe them." He rejects the latter because there is no way of describing the way things are independently of describing them, no way to distinguish the role played by our language and the role played by the rest of the universe "in accounting for the truth of our true beliefs."

> (Putnam 2017, 91; see Rorty 1998, chapters 1–4; also see my discussion of Rorty's view of science's truth claims, Tauber 2022, 198–205)

As Putnam himself put it, humans organize and know the world by conceptual functional frameworks (akin to Kant's) inasmuch as "the mind and the world jointly make up the mind and the world" (Putnam 1981, xi). He would significantly revise that position as he moved closer to a realist view (Putnam 1994, 2015, 94–7; reviewed by Rochefort 2021). He critiqued my own interpretation (Tauber 2009a, 201–5) in the ongoing effort to clarify his position (Putnam 2012, 103–8).

7 The contiguity of the essays comprising *Radical Empiricism* (largely composed 1904–5) and *Varieties* (1902) suggests that the latter work informed the former, although incipient ideas of what became James's late epistemology can be traced back to the earlier *Principles of Psychology* (1890) (McDermott 1976; Crosby and Viney 1992).

8 From an 1877 lecture delivered by James ("Recent investigations on the brain") at the Harvard Natural Historical Society (quoted by Perry 1935, II. 27, cited by McDermott 1967, 27).

9 In marked contrast, Freud utterly rejected any legitimacy to what he called the "oceanic feeling" of religious experience and tracked it to the "primitive ego feeling" of infancy and thus to the deep fantasies and desires of the unconscious (Freud 1930, 11–13, 68).

10 Martin Jay tracks the lineage of this primordial source to James's godfather, Emerson, who in the celebrated essay "Experience" describes that undefinable center of human experience, the intuited ineffable source of selfhood that lay just beyond consciousness (Emerson 1983). The essay famously describes how experience, all experience including the terrible loss of Emerson's first-born, is ultimately disconnected from the core of his being (Tauber 2006). Depicting a bifurcation, Emerson identifies a core "self" residing isolated and inured from a world that it calmly and imperturbably surveys, and a second, more superficial self-conscious ego that experiences the everyday events of life including the anguish of loss. The first sense of identity is impersonal and exists in communion with the rest of nature, unawares of its unique individuality ("Nature" [Emerson 1971]). This metaphysical assertion is disjointed from the human existential stance of personal experience ("Experience"). Strikingly, the core is "unknown" in its splendid isolation and remains unknowable—ever-present, but possessing a function and organization alien to human understanding or finite consciousness. Thus, the Emersonian self is layered: an "outer" stratum experiences and self-reflects—aware of itself, the world—and a second perplexing, isolated, deeper source, the primordial self. This core is disturbingly aloof and leaves its bearer with precious little connection to his own inner workings. It remains as a distinctive expression of certain existential truths concerning the essential isolation of man's being and the jealous guarding of his vitality. This view of the self is recurrent in Emerson's writings and not

just the product of a tormented man attempting to deal with a personal tragedy (Tauber 2006).

When Emerson writes, "souls never touch their objects" (Emerson 1983, 29), he is making more than an epistemological claim: not only is human consciousness separated from nature and thus impelled to read her as one would read a text, but one lives at a remove from the heart of one's own most intimate sense of being. The core self lies just beyond the limit of self-consciousness, the place where reflection ends and our mysterious *isness* resides. Jay infers that James internalized Emerson's construction to the extent that his philosophy of "pure experience" represents not only a philosophical exit from Cartesian dualism, but also an existential quest in answer to his own depressions and flirtations with nihilism.

> Without claiming that James in any way derived his own animadversions on this theme from reading this essay, it is striking that in his usage, the term "experience" often betrays a yearning for something lost or suppressed in the modern world, something occluded by conventional ways of grasping and ordering reality . . . Experience was the paradoxically foundationless foundation that provided an answer, or at least sparked the persistent questioning that drove his work for much of his career.
>
> (Jay 2005, 276)

11 Heidegger and Wittgenstein converge in recognizing the legitimate call of the existential, which they each claimed philosophy had failed to adequately face (Braver 2012; see Friedl 2018, 212–14).

12 Note that, for James, consciousness, and its directive potential framed by values ("moral epistemology" [Tauber 2022, 249ff.]), remained derivative to primary (pure or unmediated) *experience* that resides in a domain devoid of values. Values find their expression in directing consciousness in what James called the "selective agency," in which

> meaning and truth appeared symbolically, and as practical matters could be dealt with pragmatically. But meaning and truth were not for James the bedrock of reality; they were not the core of his mind's felt experience . . . "things never have any point. The eye and mind slip over and over them and they only smile within the boundary of their form" [James, *Diary* 1868–1873]. Within the boundary of pure experience there was indeed no "point," simply the "form" of relationship . . . This valueless relational space might be imagined as the field out of which symbolic creation emerged.
>
> (Bjork 1988, 265–7)

Or, in the context of our theme, the site in which romantic imagination originates.

13 "Strictly speaking . . . there are no unconscious affects as there are unconscious ideas. But there may very well be in the system Ucs. affective structures which, like others, become conscious. The whole difference arises from the fact that ideas are cathexes—basically of memory-traces—whilst affects and emotions correspond to processes of discharge, the final manifestations of which are perceived as feelings. *In the present state of our knowledge of affects and emotions we cannot express this difference more clearly*" (Freud 1915b, 178, emphasis added).

14 At the risk of psychoanalyzing Freud, an interesting revelation about himself
    may shed light on the issue. Despite his own love of art and the aesthetic obses-
    sion of his social milieu, Freud makes a startling confession in "The Moses
    of Michelangelo": he enjoyed only those works of art that he could *explain*
    to himself *intellectually*, i.e., "to explain to myself what their effect is due to.
    Wherever I cannot do this, as for instance with music, I am almost incapa-
    ble of obtaining any pleasure" (Freud 1914, 253). Freud, who clearly enjoyed
    the arts and reveled in artistic achievements, admitted that he could enjoy art
    only through his intellect, and more specifically, through an *interpretation*. For
    Freud, it is only when art is turned into an articulation, an explicit, deliberate
    explanation, that he found pleasure: "Some rationalistic, or perhaps analytic,
    turn of mind in me rebels against being moved by a thing without knowing why
    I am thus affected and what it is that affects me" (Freud 1914). This intellec-
    tualization made literature most accessible to him, and music, the least (Freud
    1914). Perhaps the *rationalization* of Freud's experience might also explain his
    inability to have proposed a theory of the affects beyond translating that experi-
    ence into ideas and concepts (Tauber 2015).
15 Although Freud's representational philosophy of mind that directed his theory
    construction has been emphasized here, he also accounted for psychic drives as
    being experienced *directly* through the affects that express them qualitatively
    (Laplanche and Pontalis 1973, 13). But note that the analysis does not constitute
    knowledge in the usual sense, and Freud admits that the elaborate emotion-idea
    linkage is only one way of accessing the affective economy underlying psychic
    life: "If the instinct did not attach itself to an idea *or manifest itself as an affec-
    tive state*, we could *know* nothing about it" (Freud 1915a, 177, emphasis added).
16 This is the crux of Wittgenstein's critique of private language (Wittgenstein
    1968, 88e–104e), whereby inner states exist as such; their immediacy requires
    no mediation. He constructs this case as an attack on the Cartesian "object and
    designation" schema, where he shows that sensations are not objects, and thus
    he rejects "the grammar which tries to force itself on us" (Wittgenstein 1968,
    §304, 102e; see Tauber 2013a, 166 ff.).
17 This self-awareness draws together such diverse thinkers as Lacan, Wilfred
    Bion, Donald Winnicott, Peter Finagy, and Jean Laplanche, as well as some
    American theorists (e.g., Donnel N. Stern, Daniel B. Stern, and the Boston
    Change Process Group [D. B. Stern 2019, 20–31]). The focus of interest on the
    unformulated has percolated into contemporary relational-based psychoanaly-
    sis, not so much as a novel insight but as a heightened self-conscious element
    in the therapeutic encounter (e.g., Benjamin 2017; Kurchuck 2021).
18 In regarding language as limiting and thus restrictive to probing the unformu-
    lated, Stern cites Daniel Stern (D. N. Stern 1985; Stern et al. 1998), Wilma
    Bucci (1997), Philip Bromberg (2009), and Antonio Damasio (1999) (D. B.
    Stern 2019, 6, 23). For instance, Bucci argues that what is most significant in
    clinical work forms around phenomena that are generally affective in nature
    and present without symbolic representation in the "sub-symbolic" mode of
    information processing. And Bromberg describes the clinical process in which
    meaning grows from what is revealed to be transpiring between patient and
    analyst outside the reach of the symbolic, and not from the interpretation of
    unconscious symbolic content that is already present within the mind.

19 Stern goes on to explain:

> Our interpretive attitude is usually so deeply taken for granted that it is not itself taken, or even cannot be taken, as the object of our attention. That is what makes ideology so insidious and compelling: it is invisible (e.g., Foucault 1980) . . . We can say, then, that it is axiomatic in contemporary hermeneutic philosophy that the continuous interpretive attitude, ceaselessly exercised by all of us, almost always without awareness of what we are doing, is what makes experience possible at all. But it is just as important and characteristic of these hermeneutic views that, no matter how much we depend on our own interpretive powers in creating our experience, we cannot simply violate the constraints contributed by reality.
>
> (D. B. Stern 2019, 9).

20 The analytical philosophical literature addressing the unformulated, or what is called "contentless thought," was introduced by Gareth Evans in the context of biological perceptual processing (Evans 1982). In following informational links, he argued that initial nonconceptual information is initially unconscious but becomes conscious when it serves as input to a thinking, concept-applying, and reasoning system. That thesis has been widely extended to a theory that

> some mental states can represent the world even though the bearer of those mental states need not possess the concepts required to specify their content. This basic idea has been developed in different ways and applied to different categories of mental state. Not all of these applications are consistent with each other, but each offers a challenge to the widely held view that the way a creature can represent the world is determined by its conceptual capacities.
>
> (Bermúdez and Cahen 2020)

In other words, animals, including humans, can think without conceptual content and, correspondingly, without linguistic capacities, i.e., absent articulation/conceptual formulation (Bermúdez 2003; Fedorenko, Piantadosi, and Gibson 2024). How this set of ideas might be applied to psychoanalysis or to psychology more generally is well beyond the scope of this book, but it suggests a fecund avenue for further investigation.

Chapter 4

Attending to *thought*

The articulation of the unexpressed feelings and memories sequestered beneath consciousness is the goal of psychoanalysis. *Thought* as language has no form in the unconscious—pre-linguistic, a-rational, untrammeled by convention, grammar, logic, or time. Indeed, the process of bringing that which is unformulated into public discourse, framed by the demands of comprehension and truth, organized Freud's project. How does the analysand find her expression of the dream or the memory? This is hardly an exclusive psychoanalytic question. The poet struggles to find expression, as does the mystic, the lover, the angered, the bereaved, and the exultant. The bridge from feeling and memory to the *voice* spans a gap, and psychoanalysis offers a particularly rich approach to exploring that transition.

At the most basic level, psychoanalysis is about articulating the dynamics of unconsciousness for ego reflection. That moves pre-literate feeling to subconscious potential and to conceptualized language. Almost a century ago, with nary a nod to our protagonists, Lev Vygotsky, in *Thought and Language* (1986 [1934]), showed the development of this progression in the child. During early infancy, thought and language emerge separately, and only later in development do they merge. Their functional segregation suggests that word meanings and linguistic expansion follow a stepwise maturation: The model begins with evidence that thought and speech have different roots in ontogenetic and phylogenetic development, with distinctive pre-linguistic and pre-intellectual stages identified in the maturation of thought in the human child as well as in other species that do not develop language. Accordingly, the two functions develop along different lines and independently of each other until these lines meet, whereupon thought becomes verbal and speech rational. Although the two functions reciprocally influence one another, both lines of development proceed separately to a relatively high level before they can be joined at about the age of two. When the curves of development of thought and speech join, a new form of behavior emerges, and "the child

DOI: 10.4324/9781003565413-4

'makes the greatest discovery of his life' that 'each thing has its name' [W. Stern 1914, 108] . . . At this point, the knot is tied for the problem of thought and language" (Vygotsky 1986, 82–3).

The complex psychological unit of "word meaning" is the crucial product of this union of thought and speech, and it operates in both public discourse and what Vygotsky called "inner speech," which is an internalization of the communicative speech forms that are learned by the child. Inner speech differs from external speech forms in relying on predication alone rather than the subject-predicate structure required for communicative language. According to Vygotsky, such inner speech is the format of thought, the means through which the child represents all knowledge about the world and which she uses to control and direct herself. However, a huge lacuna remains unattended. As noted by Wilma Bucci (1997), Vygotsky's work was seminal in identifying the separate lines of development of thought and speech, but he omitted consideration of the continued separation of these functions throughout life and the wide range of information processing functions that have been identified as configuring the emotions. Vygotsky not only ignored emotional expression from the integrative union of vocalization and thought, but he also expressly excluded the subjective:

> The higher, specifically human forms of psychological communication are possible because man's reflection of reality is carried out in generalized concepts. In the sphere of emotions, where sensation and affect reign, neither understanding nor real communication as possible, but only affective contagion.
>
> (Vygotsky 1986, 8)

Thus, he relegates the expression of emotion to the pre-intellectual roots of speech differentiated from thought and restricts the powerful notion of developing word meetings to more neutral cognitive domains (Bucci 1997, 144). So much for poetry, art, music, and prayer! For Vygotsky, to think is equivalent to speak; without language, no thought. He obviously did not consider pre-linguistic forms of thought, including purposeful action, problem solving, and tool use, much less acknowledge emotion or intuition as forms of knowing. Nor did he explore the issue as did James and Freud, whose ways of dealing with the relationship of thought and language are important chapters in the history of this matter. Having discussed the psychodynamic theory and how James's notion of experience resonates with a broad construal of the unarticulated, this chapter reconsiders the deeper consideration of that domain as approached by our protagonists. We begin with Freud.

Das Ding

Freud's basic schema poses the mind's substratum as radically "other" to the conscious me. This domain, the *id* or "it," emerges as a stranger, whose various clues are subjected to psychoanalytic interpretation. For example, the latent dream, disjointed and chaotic, becomes the manifest dream in an account that draws lines of connection and associations. The ego apprehends such secondary manifestations as representations of this domain. Psychic experience, memory, and behavior are distilled, translated, and articulated (albeit filtered by various defense mechanisms) from the unconscious reservoir and placed within consciousness (and reason) for analysis.

In the psychoanalytic theater, three individuals lie on the couch: a "stranger"—personified as the id; the "voice"—the unmediated expression of experience; and finally, "me" (the "you" from the analyst's perspective)—the observing, interpreting, feeling, knowing person, often identified as the reflexive, self-conscious ego. Note that this contemplative subject scrutinizes both the "voice" and its preconscious states to apprehend the unconscious, albeit not in terms of the primordial states (as discussed in the preceding chapter), but in ways that conform to the normative standards of conscious reality. Psychoanalysis thus offers a fecund case study of the "dialogue" between these personas, which, according to Freudian dogma, eventuates in exposing (perhaps, releasing) the unconscious and the pre-conscious to full awareness and scrutiny.

The unself-conscious voice of experience knows no perspective and thus lacks the analytic standpoint. It experiences the manifestations of the unconscious in the same "lived" way I might walk in a room and seat myself: I do not reflect upon each element that constitutes my walking and sitting. I just perform the action through the tacit knowledge of experience. This "voice" partially fulfills the criteria of selfhood inasmuch as this is the presentation that articulates the person in social intercourse and the "object" of self-reflection. In terms of the unconscious exhibiting itself, for instance in a dream state, I similarly just dream. No "distance" exists between the subject and her voice: there is no Archimedean point by which a vantage might be gained to survey the "my-ness" of my dream, of my voice, or of my memory. In this posture, there is no capacity of representing that other (the id) to my self-conscious ego, simply because I am not self-conscious in this nonreflective state. In this modality, Freud deciphers the subject *qua* subject, not in some static subject-object relation, but rather as a subject in action, in emotion, in behavior. In this sense, the analysand exists first as the subject of experience, an articulation of the subjective private voice, a voice that makes no attempt to self-reflect. On the basis of free association, this voice becomes the conduit to the subconscious psyche and provides the material for the scrutinizing ego. Given this schema, how might one regard this natural "voice"? More specifically, what theory underlies the articulated movement of the unconscious to the ego's articulation?[1]

Of the extensive commentary about the core unconscious drive, we begin with a rather obscure passage in Freud's early work, *Aus den Anfängen der Psychoanalyse* (1895), that was published posthumously as *Project for a Scientific Psychology*. As mentioned in Chapter 1, the manuscript offers insight into Freud's early thinking about psychodynamics and has been acknowledged as an important key in deciphering his notion of the mechanical balance of forces that underlay later psychoanalytic models, in which he characterized the drive as having a source, an aim, and an object. We have also described Freud's schema by which the drives become "articulated," and here we ask, how did Freud conceive the sense of a drive's *initial* presence and demand before the *Trieb* is directed towards its object of fulfillment?

Jurgen Reeder explains that for Freud, the object is formed as an object from two components. The first is the original perception, and then a judgment of that object (e.g., good or hostile) follows.

> This activity of *erkennen* (of which judgment is one possibility) is described . . . as a "dissection" (*Zerlegung*—could also be translated as "splitting"). Through the act of *erkennen*, it seems that while on the one hand understanding and comprehension are attained, through the representational cognitive cluster something is at the same time split off and isolated. This latter is the incomprehensible aspect of the perceptual complex, a constant and unchangeable structure that evades or resists understanding, which Freud calls *das Ding*.
>
> (Reeder 2012, 37)

The word, *erkennen*, usually translated as "cognizing," for Reeder is better rendered as "becoming aware or attentive of something lying outside a limited subjective orbit" (Reeder 2012). *Das Ding*, "the thing," fits into the general Kantian formulation in which the *noumenon*, the thing-in-itself (*das Ding an sich*), is that aspect of the real world that knowledge cannot grasp and becomes the *phenomenon* only through its processing through the cognitive faculty

(Tauber 2010, 179ff.; Eriksson 2010). For Freud, *das Ding* is more hidden than lost and seems only to function as the beginning of the representation process in which the psychic drive is brought into psychodynamic play.

A more fecund account of *das Ding* was offered by Lacan as he refocused psychoanalytic theory from the ego to "back to Freud," prioritizing Freud's original attempt to characterize the unconscious (Boothby 2001; De Kesel 2009; Reeder 2012).[2] For Freud, *das Ding* simply disappears, but for Lacan, *Ding* constitutes a point of reference for a desire always aiming at something that is *not* there. Accordingly, the "lost object" is missing only retroactively as other representations are recognized. "*Das Ding* designates an incompassable aspect of every representation, a kind of ungraspable center of gravity that lends coherence to the various manifestations of an object while remaining itself ineluctably out of reach" (Boothby 2001, 204). Only through interpretations does *Ding* become recognized as represented through some selected object, which a psychoanalytic narrative organizes into its own context of understanding.

> *Das Ding* is a void that arises because a chain of representations *is representation* and not the represented. In this view, *das Ding* stands out as an effect of the subject's symbolic function and the retrograde projection of a *no-thing*, an empty core at the center of the object world that can be substituted only with the series of representations that have made it appear in the first place. In this capacity of a locus without proper content *das Ding* constitutes a point of reference for (the coordinates of) desire and the subject's realization of its existence.
>
> (Reeder 2012, 39, emphasis in the original)

Accordingly, *das Ding* initiates a dynamic that articulates a representation of some kind where an object is in a sense identified, and then the undifferentiated "the real" is fractured or cut. The result forms the represented object and a residue. This remainder is both outside (represented) and inside—a structure that holds the original place of the Other. Structurally, the Other orients the subject and the object, and dynamically, it serves as the nexus for the drives and thus the locus of desire. The psychodynamics of Lacanian theory follow (Tauber 2013a, 119ff.), but here we focus on the "residue," that which is left behind, and we do so beyond the psychoanalytic scenario to draw a more general epistemological principle, one far less speculative than a medley of psychic forces in play that are directed at some "object," which has no standing as an entity or any *thing* else (Tauber 2013a, 72–5).

The "excess"

As discussed, James's depicted the mind as an active selecting faculty attending to encounters with the environment that command attention for good or ill. For instance, as one looks at a painting, different perceptions are appreciated; as one watches an accident, different reports emerge; walking into a room, different observers will mark different elements of interest.[3] Reality thus becomes a synthesis between mind and nature, and mind, in the context of this discussion, draws upon its excessive capacity to make the imaginative refractions of the world from which new language, representations, and models are drawn (see Chapter 2, note #2). In short, no prescribed reality exists as such; rather, it is constructed by active human knowing, where the mind's "excess" becomes the creative resource for those constructions.

This constructivist understanding readily applies to psychoanalytic theory. What is captured in conscious thought and feeling comprises only a portion of untapped memory and emotion. The rest remains in an unaccounted reservoir. Freud himself recognized that *das Ding* could not be captured by representational language, or what Adorno called the concretization of identification (Adorno 1973). His philosophical analysis of conceptual thinking highlights the hurdles that obstructed Freud's attempts to probe the unconscious, a matter to which we again turn.

Adorno developed an alternative logic to the "identity thinking" that became nothing less than a full assault on representationalism. For Adorno, the *concept* fails to fit the object, which means that the object/concept cannot be fully captured by *any* re-presentation. Indeed, the represented composes only part of the original, and therefore leaves the original "object" fractured, and its representation distorted, or fantasized. The remaining unknown portion of the object, the missing aspects, then corresponds to that which is beyond the concept and thus unidentified (i.e., the non-identity). This hidden residue, the so-called "excessive space," is the site of the *not-yet-represented*, a residual inexpressible. Thus, the mental product that results from carving objects (or representations of those objects) out of some substrate implicitly and unavoidably includes an "excessive" component: "objects do not go into their concepts without leaving a remainder" (Adorno 1973, 5).[4]

Adorno called *negation* the process by which a concept is "precipitated" (the "thing-to-become-objectified" from the plenum of being), leaving a residual behind (see Chapter 2, note #2). This remaining additional capacity (or an undisclosed appendage) serves as a reservoir for further development of the concept. Asserting that representations can never be closed or complete allows for emendation, addition, and interpretation of concepts. Because such mental objects are only part of a larger set, the unused capacity (the so-called empty set or remainder) may then feed the development of the represented concept. As the process propagates, the identified object changes, for the excess from which such modification might occur serves as the ambiguous and imaginative component for the subject to frame and signify the world with a dynamic lacking in the simpler, and distorting, "mirror of nature" identity (correspondence) model (see Chapter 3, note #6).

Basically, *excess* addresses the limits of a representational conception of mind and the consequences of subject-object predicate thinking to offer a means for creativity and freedom of thought (Tauber 2013a, 67–82, 161–2, 203–4). Adorno formally referred to this process as a reduction, or what he called, a "selective negation," where negation refers to the process by which subtraction occurs to transform the mere state of being (through the imposition of order, identity, difference, relation, etc.) to fashion a human-perceived object (concept), i.e., something with distinguishing characteristics. James developed his own idea of "reduction": in any experience, the mind selects, sorts, and orders objects from an undifferentiated state of being. Accordingly, objects become objects only as differentiation occurs, for mere being must be transformed into objects, which (as discussed in the next section) leaves a reservoir, what James called "the vague." He would enlist this basic orientation to explain his own view of the mind as a generative cognitive faculty.

The emergent character of knowing the world required an expansive view in which the formulated, concretized concept allows for an untapped reservoir for further development. Because "the conditions of representation reside in the domain of knowledge rather than the world itself—it is possible for the subject to imagine what is not given" (Colebrook 2005, 16). The result of this separation opens subjectivity and its accompanying freedom to go beyond the given. In this latter formulation, the subject enjoys an "excess." This epistemological schema may be extended to configure the self into two components: (1) the known sense of *the I* or *me*, a conscious or possessive function; and (2) the excessive space or potential (function) (previously referred to as the unconscious), from which mental revisions are made. *Excess* in this context refers to how the representational structure of knowledge is expanded and leads to a self-determining subject, whose own boundaries are left open to possibilities—epistemological and moral. From this perspective, the hermeneutics of the interpersonal encounter and self-reflective inner dialogue allow for a nebulous cloud of meanings for both the subject and her other. "No object simply means what it is; every object becomes a site of excessive meaning" (Rothenberg 2010, 111), and correspondingly, one cannot control the meaning of oneself for another, and for that matter, one's own self-meaning—representation of *me* to "myself"—because in each orientation, irreducible excessivity precludes closure of signification.

Psychoanalysis implicitly employs such a formulation, for excessivity holds potential or undeclared meanings for interactions with others, as well as self-analysis of one's own actions and feelings. Freud did not fully develop his theory around such a potentiality, but James fully embraced it (D. B. Stern 2019, 8–10; Dianda 2023, 12–14, 27, 108, 113). The idea of "excess" was not foreign to Freud, but he was so fastened to the "end-product"—the word and its associations—that he did not fully draw from the conceptual "excess" well:

> The idea, or concept, of the object is itself another complex of associations composed of the most varied visual, auditory, tactile, kinaesthetic and other impressions. According to philosophical teaching, the idea of the object contains nothing else; the appearance of the "thing," the "properties" of which are conveyed to our senses, originates only from the fact that in enumerating the sensory impressions perceived from an object, we allow for the possibility of a large series of new impressions being added to the chain of associations (J. S. Mill). *This is why the idea of the object does not appear to us as closed, and indeed hardly as closable, while the word concept appears to us as something that is closed though capable of extension.*
> (Freud 1953 [1891], 77–8, emphasis added)

Freud has made a revealing comment. Because his philosophical commitments drove him to a conventional representational modality to tackle the dynamics of the unconscious/conscious interface, he elaborated a model of word associations (ideas fixed to drives) and the mechanisms of psychoanalytic interpretations in which those dynamics were described, all of which rested upon the "closed" character of *words*. In this regard, then, the articulation of the mind, and here I refer to the core psyche, *das Ding*, the unconscious (forgotten) source of drives and emotions becomes *language*. With articulation, we plainly see the instantiation of the concretization of feelings and their appearance in public exchange. How else would (could) Freud invent a science of the mind? James offers an alternative view of psychic life that followed a very different philosophy, one that anticipated Adorno's own version of non-identity thinking by half a century.

James and the emergence of thought

Humans navigate the world, not because they see the cosmos as it *is* in a first-order way, but because they construct the reality in which they *live* by employing their cognitive capacity to parse, relate, and discern the world's contents in reference to themselves. This orientation James called "human-ist." Today we refer to this cognitive process as a "constructivist" formu-lation of reality (see Introduction note #12; Tauber 2009a, 201–5). The information that lies in the world is latent and does not exist as such until the mind makes it coherent. In other words, the indeterminacy of how that world is understood depends on some process (e.g., conversion, distillation, representation) of perception (already a second-order presentation depend-ent on cognitive faculties that require integration of both analytic and emo-tional faculties [Ben-Ze'ev 2000]). Add to this process a tertiary functional capacity that arises from the excessivity of the cognitive process itself, from which further assessment leads to reactive or proactive behavior. The infor-mation, the world as it were, is present but in a latent form, waiting to be seen and organized by the mind according to its own dictates as determined by need (Tauber 2013a, 72–3). That reservoir James called *the vague*.[5]

One of the features that James emphasized in his circumspect view of an objectifying science of the mind revolved around the "vagueness" of sub-jective experience. The vague assumed two meanings for him: In the most obvious sense, consciousness has a center and a less focused periphery, a penumbra (Cooper 2002, 103). However, the second sense regards the vague as having an important constitutive functional role. Instead of the clear and distinct ideas required for a scientific psychology, he accepted that experiences "taken all together, [are] a quasi-chaos" that inevitably eludes segmentation in language (James 1987b, 886). The *quasi-chaos* refers to how the transitive and the substantive components play upon each other in a dynamic in which hierarchy and order assume the most fragmentary structure in time sequences (James 1987b, 885). As described in *Principles in Psychology: Briefer Course*, James would preserve that unformed domain of the mental—the pre-formulated, the pre-conceptual, the "vague and inarticulate" character of human *experience* as such (James 1992d, 164). For him, the vague was not the result of some incapacity or deferment, but rather an explicit acknowledge-ment of the inexplicit; the elusive connections of perceptions and impres-sions; the absent elements underlying a thought; the blurred outline of an idea which follows no prescribed order. Many critics have emphasized the role of the vague as underlying James's writings about religion, mysticism, and spirituality, where the "bottom of being is left logically opaque to us" and we are irretrievably stuck in an "ontological wonder-sickness" (James 1992e, 510–11; Gavin 1992, chapter 2). While the inexpressible and elusive easily resides in the spiritual and aesthetic realms, James thought such limits of articulation were matters of degree and regarded the nebulous, elusive com-ponents excluded from a thought (whether a full concept or articulation of an intuition or feeling) as constitutive to thought in general.

To concretize this maelstrom of experience is to inevitably corral it in a representation that by its very nature cannot be complete; and beyond its partiality, it is also susceptible to distortion or even falsification. Simply, the articulation translates the primary experience into something else, which (as discussed) Adorno called the "concept" and the residual "excess" (the unrepresented). The "limits" of such processing (Adorno's "reduction") is not an incapacity that might be overcome, but rather the unavoidable "remainder" resulting from creation of the representation; the irreducible inexplicit; the elusive connections of perceptions and impressions; the absent consciousness underlying a thought; the blurred outline of an idea that follows no prescribed order.

In discussing vagueness, James highlighted how consciousness itself is characteristically elusive to *ourselves* and, moreover, how one's own attempt to articulate feelings and ill-formed ideas fails to both capture inner experience and, more broadly, express conceptual thought. For him, vagueness infuses the tumult of all experience, reaching from inner individual consciousness to the external world, where chance and indeterminate causality are constitutive of complex natural phenomena that eclipse the simple linear models of causation characteristic of Newtonian mechanics.[6] On this general view, the scientific study of consciousness is constrained by its objectification that, as James repeatedly observed, leaves the subjective irretrievably locked within its own domain: firsthand experience is always reported as a secondhand representation.

The vague follows the logic of James's initial insight about the "stream of consciousness," the ebb and flow of the mind, in two modalities, the *substantive* and the *transitive* (the "feelings of tendency"), which he claimed functioned together to produce the formulated.

> The traditional psychology talks like one who should say a river consists of nothing but pailsful, spoonsful, quartpotsful, barrelsful, and other moulded forms of water. Even were the pails and the pots all actually standing in the stream, still between them the free water would continue to flow. It is just this free water of consciousness that psychologists resolutely overlook. Every definite image in the mind is steeped and dyed in the free water that flows round it. With it goes the sense of its relations, near and remote, the dying echo of whence it came to us, the dawning sense of whither it is to lead. The significance, the value, of the image is all in this halo or penumbra that surrounds and escorts it,—or rather that is fused into one with it and has become bone of its bone and flesh of its flesh; leaving it, it is true, an image of the same thing it was before, but making it an image of that thing newly taken and freshly understood.
>
> (James 1983, 246)

The "fringes of consciousness" do not function as some kind of glue or linkage scheme, for each substantive is "steeped and dyed" in the free water that bathes it. As emphasized by Arthur Still (1991, 19), James corrects a critic by clarifying that the *transitive*

> is part of the *object cognized,*—substantive *qualities* and *things* appearing to the mind in a *fringe of relations*. Some parts—the transitive parts—of our stream of thought cognize the relations rather than the things; but both the transitive and the substantive parts form one continuous stream, with no discrete "sensations" in it. . . .
>
> (James 1983, 249, note #19, emphasis in original)

As James later wrote in "A World of Pure Experience" (1904), a seminal paper underscoring a more "radical empiricism," he claimed, "*the relations that connect experiences must themselves be experienced relations, and any kind of relation experienced must be accounted as 'real' as anything else in the system*" (James 1987i, 1160, emphasis in original).[7]

While a particular word, image, or sensation may dominate consciousness, other mental material surrounds or contextualizes the focused element. Although this "fringe" of relations surrounding each word or image of thought (what James also calls "suffusion" and "overtone") is, of course, difficult to conceptualize or capture by introspection (for then the focus shifts from the initial object of thought to its ending articulation), the central element never resides alone.

> It is just like the "overtones" in music. Different instruments give the "same note," but each in a different voice, because each gives more than that note, namely, various upper harmonics of it which differ from one instrument to another. They are not separately heard by the ear; they blend with the fundamental note, and suffuse it, and alter it; and even so do the waxing and waning brain-processes at every moment blend with and suffuse and alter the psychic effect of the processes which are at their culminating point.
>
> (James 1983, 249)

The "overtone" thus helps to drive thought to its next phrase or conclusion, whether articulated as a word or a more complex idea.

Moreover, the philosophical structure of thought and language places the fringe as critical to establishing meaning. In a key passage, James contrasts a geometer who has a figure before him and knows that it represents a universal relationship that may be applied without confusion, whereas when the word, *man*, is used, its meaning radically depends on the context in which it is deployed (James 1983, 446). That meaning is determined by "the fringe" that drives the dominant sense in one direction or another and supports the larger application.

With this focus on the transitive and the fringe, James criticized "orthodox" empiricism for reducing experience to a succession of stable, distinct, substantive elements—ideas, images, percepts, sensations-elements that can be held before the attention and introspectively examined. Such a punctate, discontinuous view of subjective experience overlooks and falsifies "immense tracts of our inner life," with the stream-like quality of consciousness (James 1992b, 987; Taylor and Wozniak 1996a). Thus, the "fluid" of consciousness in which the substantive presents itself cannot be accounted by the atomism of Cartesian-Lockean epistemology inasmuch as the transitive serves as the "vehicle" of meaning. In this construction, the explicit character of language is deconstructed. The substantive assumes a kind of transitive character as well, because the context and variability of representation bestows an irreducible contextualization, replete with flexibility, variation, and, not to overstate the point, an intrinsic "vagueness" (or "plasticity") to language (Still 1991, 19; Shanon 1993).

James thus highlighted the struggle of finding the explicit in which the formulation of an idea, the concretization of an intuition, the expression of feelings reflects a *poesis* at work, namely, the imaginative, flexible, and ambiguous process of creating meaning:

What is that shadowy scheme of the "form" of an opera, play, or book, which remains in our mind,

> and on which we pass judgment when the actual thing is done? . . . Great thinkers have vast premonitory glimpses of schemes of relation between terms, which hardly even as verbal images enter the mind, so rapid is the whole process.[8] We all of us have this permanent consciousness of whither our thought is going. It is a feeling like any other, a feeling of what thoughts are next to arise, before they have arisen. This field of view of consciousness varies very much in extent, depending largely on the degree of mental freshness or fatigue. When very fresh, our minds carry an immense horizon with them. The present image shoots its perspective far before it, irradiating in advance the regions in which lie the thoughts as yet unborn. Under ordinary conditions the halo of felt relations is much more circumscribed. And in states of extreme brain-fog the horizon is narrowed almost to the passing word . . . the slowness of his utterance shows how difficult, under such conditions, the labor of thinking must be.

(James 1983, 246–7)

With "the vague sense of a *plus ultra*"—a sense of forward movement of thought—James erected an epistemology based on a roughly etched notion of *potentiality*—the unformed and ambiguous—that then becomes articulated in the emergence of creative consciousness.

Let us recall the framework of scientific psychology in which James initiated his studies and then jettisoned during his philosophical dissection of consciousness. The critical finding of this period (from which German experimental psychology developed) was Helmholtz's 1851 discovery of the temporal gap between an electrical stimulus and the muscle contractile response (Schmidgen 2014). This finding revolutionized neurobiology, and it not only stimulated early academic psychology but prompted Bergson to highlight the philosophical significance of the brain exhibiting a physiological "gap, a hesitation and delay, 'an interval [écart], a void, nothing but a void between a stimulation and a response'" (Schmidgen 2014, 7). With only rudimentary knowledge of neurons and no inkling of synapses, the brain became a "black box," one James acknowledged and respected as he proceeded with his metaphysical descriptions. Nevertheless, despite the agnosticism demanded by the limited scientific understanding, James would employ the "reflex action" as a basic template of his model of the self (Pawelski 2007, 37–57, 108–13). In 1881, he described the reflex action as a triadic model of the self ("Reflex action and theism," later included in *The Will to Believe* [James 1992h, 54–65]), in which three "departments"—perception, conception, and volition—correlate to the basic neurological stimulus-response schema. "It is the means by which we transform our world in accordance with the desires of our volitional natures" and thus serves as the basis of James's commitment to the individuality of human will within a naturalistic construct (Pawelski 2007, 38). James imbues the "volitional" as the site of action and choice, the site in which free will is exercised:

> the immediate point of application of the volitional effort lies exclusively within the mental world. The whole drama is a mental drama. The whole difficulty is a mental difficulty, a difficulty with an ideal object of our thought. It is, in one word, an idea to which our will applies itself, an idea which if we let it go would slip away.
>
> (James 1992d, 419)

At the risk of oversimplification, *The Principles of Psychology* is organized around this central tenet (Pawelski 2007, 38).

Later, in developing radical empiricism and struggling with characterizing pure experience, the "temps perdue" of the stimulus-reflex arc would figure prominently. James was well aware of "the gap," and in his own accounting of the emergence of thought, he commented on the "space" between the unformulated and the articulated, whether concretized or left in the pre-verbal sense prior to explicit thinking. He uses the example of the "tip-of-the-tongue" phenomenon so common in everyday experience to show how the gap, in some sense silent, is a site of active retrieval as the mind seeks its avenue to further thought.

> Suppose we try to recall a forgotten name. The state of our consciousness is peculiar. There is a gap therein; but no mere gap. It is a gap that is intensely active. A sort of wraith of the name is in it, beckoning us in a given direction, making us at moments tingle with the sense of our closeness, and then letting us sink back without the longed-for term. If wrong names are proposed to us, this singularly definite gap acts immediately so as to negate them. They do not fit into its mould. And the gap of one word does not feel like the gap of another, all empty of content as both might seem necessarily to be when described as gaps.
>
> (James 1983, 243)

These gaps require reprieve, "striving to be filled out with words" (James 1983, 244), for

> a gap we cannot yet fill with a definite picture, word, or phrase, but which, in the manner described some time back, influences us in an intensely active and determinate psychic way. Whatever may be the images and phrases that pass before us, we feel their relation to this aching gap. To fill it up is our thought's destiny. Some bring us nearer to that consummation. Some the gap negates as quite irrelevant. Each swims in a felt fringe of relations of which the aforesaid gap is the term. Or instead of a definite gap we may merely carry a mood of interest about with us. Then, however vague the mood, it will still act in the same way, throwing a mantle of felt affinity over such representations, entering the mind, as suit it, and tingeing with the feeling of tediousness or discord all those with which it has no concern.
>
> (James 1983, 250)

James then expounds on the "fringe" he had described to show its *active* contribution in framing the expression of a subjective state, a feeling that, like a seed penetrating the soil in which it is covered, finds its larger world, a step in the endless sequence of the cascade into new (and renewed) thought.

> Relation, then, to our topic or interest is constantly felt in the fringe, and particularly the relation of harmony and discord, of furtherance or

hindrance of the topic. When the sense of furtherance is there, we are "all right;" with the sense of hindrance we are dissatisfied and perplexed, and cast about us for other thoughts. Now *any* thought the quality of whose fringe lets us feel ourselves "all right," is an acceptable member of our thinking, whatever kind of thought it may otherwise be. Provided we only feel it to have a place in the scheme of relations in which the interesting topic also lies, that is quite sufficient to make of it a relevant and appropriate portion of our train of ideas.

For the important thing about a train of thought is its conclusion. That is the *meaning*, or, as we say, the topic of the thought.

(James 1983, 250, emphasis in original)

Or, as he succinctly says, to fill the gap is "our thoughts' destiny" (James 1983, 250).

James draws an implicit parallel of this version of thinking with the striving of the organism and asks,

How does the pulling *pull*? How do I get my hold on words not yet existent, and when they come, by what means have I *made* them come? Really it is the problem of creation; for in the end the question is: How do I make them *be*?

(James 1987d, 808, emphasis in original)

James is attempting nothing less than to propose an outline of a life seeking its meaning and significance (a theme Dewey would later develop in similar terms; see the closing passage of the preceding chapter).

And what is the telos that orients the human query? James makes no pronouncement and, consistent with his pluralism, hastens to admit the individualism that alone dictates the course of the idealist optimism of choice James espoused (Pawelski 2007). No system, no prescription, no authority can trump the freedom of James's will to believe—and pursue. James likens human engagement with reality to some mysterious force analogous to iron bars oriented by a magnetic field of which we have no cognizance, "the agnostic sense of a reality that goes deeper than the ordinary sense" of human perceptive qualities (Davis 2022, 51).

It is as if a bar of iron, without touch or sight, with no representative faculty whatever, might nevertheless be strongly endowed with an inner capacity for magnetic feeling; and as if, through the various arousals of its magnetism by magnets coming and going in its neighborhood, it might be consciously determined to different attitudes and tendencies. Such a bar of iron could never give you an outward description of the agencies that had the power of stirring it so strongly; yet of their presence, and of their significance for its life, it would be intensely aware through every fibre of its being.

(James 1987f, 57)

Continuing his sensitive "literary reading," Philip Davis remarks that John Jay Chapman complained that James was not articulate, as might be expected of a philosopher, but rather exercised the gift of "suggestion" rather than well-defined expression, coming out of his "nature" rather than his "intellect," and was "never quite in sharp focus" (Davis 2022, 24). Davis not only endorses Chapman's appraisal but celebrates this quality, which James himself admitted as a virtue of a psychologist who seeks to gain access to

the *Binnenleben*, or buried life of human beings, [the] unuttered inner atmosphere in which his consciousness dwells alone with the secrets of its prison-house. This inner personal tone is what we can't communicate or describe articulately to others; but the wraith and ghost of it, so to speak, are often what our friends and intimates feel as our most characteristic quality.

(James 1992i, 827)

James is tapping into the emotional realm of understanding that holds a cognitive standing that must be accounted. He thus complains that

the merely descriptive literature of the emotions is one of the most tedious parts of psychology. And not only is it tedious, but you feel that its subdivisions are to a great extent either fictitious or unimportant, and that its pretences to accuracy are a sham. But unfortunately there is little psychological writing about the emotions which is not merely descriptive. As emotions are described in novels, they interest us, for we are made to share them. We have grown acquainted with the concrete objects and emergencies which call them forth, and any knowing touch of introspection which may grace the page meets with a quick and feeling response.

(James 1983, 1064)

James concludes that literary works are more effective in transmitting the character of emotions, for instead of parsing them into "individual things," feelings are treated by the poet or novelist in the vague sense in which they surround and mold experience. And from the point of view of cognitive processing, the emotional set-point orients experience as preliminary to its conceptualization.

Turning back to the transitive components of thought that James took such care in describing, we see how his insistence on the continuity of experience requires the transitive, and how difficult it is to capture the interstices of thought:

> Let anyone try to cut a thought across in the middle and get a look at its section, and he will see how difficult the introspective observation of the transitive tracts is. The rush of the thought is so headlong that it almost always brings us up at the conclusion before we can arrest it. Or if our purpose is nimble enough and we do arrest it, it ceases forthwith to be itself.
>
> (James 1983, 236–7)

Accordingly, "Life is in the transitions as much as in the terms connected" (James 1987i, 1181). Indeed, for James, "the connecting *is* the thinking" (James 1992i, 793), and by escaping the imperative of concreteness (contrary to Chapman's dismay), James sought to reinstate "the vague to its proper place in our mental life" (James 1983, 246; 1992d, 164).

Saving subjectivity

Un-reflected experience makes no distinction of mental content (perceived from the viewpoint of an observing subject) and the object of cognition. As already discussed, James chose experience as *experienced* and thus sacrificed the metaphysics inconsistent with that understanding and the science that would attempt to characterize the mind. Although interest in consciousness persisted throughout his career, he eschewed its definition and finally submitted to his own argument.

To be sure, James recognized the role of concepts in cognition: "*the only things which we commonly see are those which we preperceive,*" namely, things which "have been labelled for us, and the labels stamped into our mind. If we lost our stock of labels we should be intellectually lost in the midst of the world" (James 1983, 420, emphasis in original). However, he maintained that the application of such segmentation distorts primary experience. In the unfinished *Some Problems of Philosophy* (1910), he observed that not only do concepts incompletely capture the nature of reality, but they distort and even falsify the "perpetual flux" with the "static concept."

> Conceptual knowledge is forever inadequate to the fullness of the reality to be known . . . The flux can never be superseded, we must carry it with us to the bitter end of our cognitive business, keeping it in the midst

of the translation even when the latter proves illuminating, and falling back on it alone when the translation gives out. "The insuperability of sensation" would be a short expression of my thesis. To prove it, I must show: 1. That concepts are secondary formations, inadequate, and only ministerial; and 2. That they falsify as well as omit, and make the flux impossible to understand.

> (James 1979, 45; for the larger philosophical significance
> of this position, see Gale 1999, 293–302)

Already by 1907, James was fully committed to this "first-order" characterization of mental life:

> The essence of life is its continuously changing character; but our concepts are all discontinuous and fixed, and the only mode of making them coincide with life is by arbitrarily supposing positions of arrest therein. With such arrests our concepts may be made congruent. But these concepts are not *parts* of reality, not real positions taken by it, but *suppositions* rather, notes taken by ourselves, and you can no more dip up the substance of reality with them than you can dip up water with a net, however finely meshed.
>
> When we conceptualize, we cut out and fix, and exclude everything but what we have fixed. A concept means a *that and-no-other*. Conceptually, time excludes space; motion and rest exclude each other; approach excludes contact; presence excludes absence; unity excludes plurality; independence excludes relativity; "mine" excludes "yours"; this connexion excludes that connexion—and so on indefinitely; whereas in the real concrete sensible flux of life experiences compenetrate each other so that it is not easy to know just what is excluded and what not.
>
> (James 1987d, 746, emphasis in original)

With this redesign of conceptual thinking, James extended the earlier critique of breaking consciousness into "bits" that in turn derived from the objectification of predicate thinking. Indeed, if the subject and the object are made of the same ontological stuff, "pure experience," the unbridgeable ontological gap between them is mended (Gale 1999, 199).

> By transforming the problem of knower and known [through pure experience] James effectively pulled the ground out from under the distinction between consciousness (as the medium of introspection) and the

contents of consciousness (as scientific subject matter) on which the "new" psychology was based.

(Taylor and Wozniak 1996a, xviii)

In short, breaking conceptual thinking and the second-order basis of consciousness, results from the categorical denial of subject-object dualism.

Pluralism of method and orientation were key for James. For instance, in *Pragmatism* (1907), he wrote of how nature itself resists the explicit: "Profusion, not economy, may after all be reality's key note" (James 1987c, 570), and therefore, "may there not after all be a possible ambiguity in truth?" (James 1987c, 571). Note that James does not use "vague" in a pejorative sense as unclear, imprecise, or nebulous. The vague is directive; it points to the incomplete, the sense of something just beyond our consciousness or articulation, something yet to become detected, understood, or discovered (James 1983, 243; Seigfried 1990, 80).

> And has the reader never asked himself what kind of a mental fact is his *intention of saying a thing* before he has said it? It is an entirely definite intention, distinct from all other intentions, an absolutely distinct state of consciousness . . . How much of it consists of definite sensorial images, either of words or things? Hardly anything! It has therefore a nature of its own of the most positive sort, and yet what can we say about it without using words that belong to the later mental facts that replace it? The intention *to-say-so- and-so* is the only name it can receive. One may admit that a good third of our psychic life consists in these rapid premonitory perspective views of schemes of thought not yet articulate.
>
> (James 1983, 245, emphasis in original)

And then, in fully acknowledging the postscript nature of self-consciousness, James quotes Joubert's cogent observation: "We only know just what we meant to say, after we have said it" (James 1983, 270).[9] What could be a clearer statement about the second-order nature of reporting personal experience?

With this epistemology in place, James announced his final metaphysical position, an outlook that inflects philosophy as traditionally construed. He confessed in *The Pluralistic Universe* (1909), close to the time he met Freud in Worcester, "I have finally found myself compelled to give up the logic [of identity, of identification], fairly, squarely, and irrevocably. It has an imperishable use in human life, but that use is not to make us theoretically acquainted with the essential nature of reality" (James 1987d,

725–6; see also Chapter 2 of this book), and thus he followed Bergson in the attempt to recapture the "perpetual flux" of experience that conceptual thinking ("intellectualism") omits.[10] This renunciation of identity thinking captures the very heart of James's guiding philosophy:

> In principle, then, the real units of our immediately-felt life are unlike the units that intellectualist logic holds to and makes its calculations with . . . My present field of consciousness is a centre surrounded by a fringe that shades insensibly into a subconscious more. I use three separate terms here to describe this fact; but I might as well use three hundred, for the fact is all shades and no boundaries. Which part of it properly is in my consciousness, which out? If I name what is out, it already has come in. The centre works in one way while the margins work in another, and presently overpower the centre and are central themselves. What we conceptually identify ourselves with and say we are thinking of at any time is the centre; but our *full* self is the whole field, with all those indefinitely radiating subconscious possibilities of increase that we can only feel without conceiving, and can hardly begin to analyze. The collective and the distributive ways of being coexist here, for each part functions distinctly, makes connexion with its own peculiar region in the still wider rest of experience and tends to draw us into that line, and yet the whole is somehow felt as one pulse of our life,—not conceived so, but felt so.
>
> In principle, then, as I said, intellectualism's edge is broken; it can only approximate to reality, and its logic is inapplicable to our inner life, which spurns its vetoes and mocks at its impossibilities. Every bit of us at every moment is part and parcel of a wider self, it quivers along various radii like the wind-rose on a compass, and the actual in it is continuously one with possibles not yet in our present sight. And just as we are co-conscious with our own momentary margin, may not we ourselves form the margin of some more really central self in things which is co-conscious with the whole of us? May not you and I be confluent in a higher consciousness, and confluently active there, tho we now know it not?
>
> (James 1987d, 761–2, emphasis in original)

Then James hurls the challenge of a new consciousness, one that breaks the strictures of identification and concretization. Given the importance of this declaration, it is quoted in full:

> I am tiring myself and you, I know, by vainly seeking to describe by concepts and words what I say at the same time exceeds either conceptualization or verbalization. As long as one continues *talking*, intellectualism

remains in undisturbed possession of the field. The return to life can't come about by talking. It is an *act*; to make you return to life, I must set an example for your imitation, I must deafen you to talk, or to the importance of talk, by showing you, as Bergson does, that the concepts we talk with are made for purposes of *practice* and not for purposes of insight. Or I must *point*, point to the mere *that* of life, and you by inner sympathy must fill out the *what* for yourselves. The minds of some of you, I know, will absolutely refuse to do so, refuse to think in non-conceptualized terms. I myself absolutely refused to do so for years together, even after I knew that the denial of manyness-in-oneness by intellectualism must be false, for the same reality does perform the most various functions at once. But I hoped ever for a revised intellectualist way round the difficulty, and it was only after reading Bergson that I saw that to continue using the intellectualist method was itself the fault. I saw that philosophy had been on a false scent ever since the days of Socrates and Plato, that an *intellectual* answer to the intellectualist's difficulties will never come, and that the real way out of them, far from consisting in the discovery of such an answer, consists in simply closing one's ears to the question. When conceptualism summons life to justify itself in conceptual terms, it is like a challenge addressed in a foreign language to some one who is absorbed in his own business; it is irrelevant to him altogether—he may let it lie unnoticed. I went thus through the "inner catastrophe" of which I spoke in the last lecture; I had literally come to the end of my conceptual stock-in-trade, I was bankrupt intellectualistically, and had to change my base. No words of mine will probably convert you, for words can be the names only of concepts. But if any of you try sincerely and pertinaciously on your own separate accounts to intellectualize reality, you may be similarly driven to a change of front. I say no more: I must leave life to teach the lesson.

(James 1987d, 762–3, emphasis in original)[11]

And with that declaration, he, like Nietzsche, slammed the door on the house of scholars (Nietzsche 2006), more specifically those engaged in objectifying the mind and sacrificing the vibrancy of experience.

Comment

James's openness to experience, to that which rested beyond the articulate— the "excess"—closely resonates with Romantic sentiments. What was concretized in consciousness is only a distillation of a far greater resource that might be tapped. To misrepresent that flux by an imposed ordering template would, on James's view, distort the subjective into a mere shadow of primary experience.[12] He was reacting to a cultural current that was sweeping all before it. James, with his friend Henri Bergson, explicitly saw the demand for a renewed Romanticism in which

> only intuition, not abstract understanding, gives us access to the vital flux of raw reality . . . [As James wrote Bergson,] "You set things straight at a single stroke by your fundamental conception of the continuously creative nature of reality," . . . who returned the compliment: "You convey the idea, above all the feeling, of that supple and flexible philosophy which is destined to take the place of intellectualism. . . . When you say that "for rationalism reality is ready-made and complete from all eternity, while for pragmatism it is still in the making," you provide the very formula for the metaphysics to which I am convinced we shall come" (qtd. Perry 1935, 2:619, 621). The enemy for both Bergson and James was what the latter called "vicious intellectualism," which sacrificed the flux of experience to the stability of concepts.
>
> (Posnock 1991, 90)[13]

The positivism ascending in all disciplines prompted James to crusade for "the re-instatement of the vague" (James 1983, 246; 1992d, 164). Given that orientation, how would science characterize inner thought when the vague resisted the concretization required for objectification? Because James concluded that consciousness was irrevocably vague, the science was confined to a narrow spectrum of phenomena that he acknowledged the experimentalists could study, but their pursuits lay tangential to the fuller characterization of psychic life. When James writes of the need to preserve the vague, he is arguing against the concretization of experience, and the conceits of positivism with its the seductions of a "false clarity" and aspirations for "final certainty" (Gavin 1992, 2–3).

That conclusion was based on his understanding of consciousness as *experienced*, which neither Freud nor the German psychologists could capture by imposing a system of representation (Freud) or measurement (Wundt).

> James's desire to reinstate the "vague and inarticulate" is . . . not a defense of obfuscation or romantic cloudiness. Paradoxically, it is an effort to describe our experience as rigorously as possible and to avoid any procrustean cutting of experience so as to fit it neatly into what can be named and conceptualized . . . This in no way denies the legitimacy

and even necessity of extrapolating from or speculating upon our personal experiences. It does, however, caution against explaining away that which is present in our immediate experience.

(Gavin 1992, 3, quoting Fontinell 1986, 64).

In discussing vagueness, James highlighted how consciousness itself is characteristically elusive to *ourselves* and, moreover, how our own attempt to linguistically capture feelings and ill-formed ideas fails to both convey inner experience and, more broadly, express conceptual thought. As discussed in the preceding chapter, at this juncture of formulating the unformulated, he would find a growing cadre of twenty-first-century psychoanalysts making similar observations and closely aligning with his own intuitions as they struggle to find the expressive means of reaching into the deepest recesses of the subjective—their patients *and* their own (e.g., Levine, Reed, and Scarfone 2013; D. B. Stern 2019).

As discussed in several contexts, placing one's emotion in a representational mode makes the experience into something else. Not so much a distortion as simply another representation, an entity onto itself, within a frame of reference inevitably different from the original. After all, mental states are not objects, whose characteristics may be captured by objective means. The language of subjectivity is a *poesis*, approximations that rely on shared experience and extrapolations, because correspondence cannot be attained.

Subjectivity does not adhere to the demands of objectivity, and more to the romantic point of view, assuming an objective view of one's own life and determining its "intent" based on such criteria both distorts and misdirects the subjectivity that constitutes one's core being. Objectivity is an orientation towards reality based on abstracting away, in various degrees, from subjective experience, and from individual points of view. A subjective orientation, on the other hand, is based on an attunement to the inner experience of feeling, sensing, thinking and valuing that unfolds in our day-to-day living.

(Balog 2016)

But what does "attunement to the inner experience" mean? In philosophical terms, or analysis in general, subjectivity doesn't mean any *thing*, at least analytically. There is no referent other than *me*. The wording approximates an assertion that subjectivity has its own truth and standing. And more to the point, there is no basis for analysis, philosophic or otherwise. Attempting to capture subjectivity in objective terms, namely, in universal public talk, is a misplaced endeavor, radically misaligned with *who* one is. This is James's basic thesis, and he built it by erasing the subject-object duality altogether as a construct for human experience and thereby responded to Romanticism's pleas for a unifying philosophy.

If inner states cannot have the same object status as public phenomena, what is the standing of a language that endeavors to describe the experience beyond articulation—feelings of all sorts? Indeed, much of experience remains unsayable. The "gap" between thought and expression, between emotion and its verbal portrayal, is often stubbornly quiescent. The work of art, music, and poetry is the manifest attempt to recapture that experience resistant to enunciation. The Romantics were acutely aware that "a wordless or incommunicable vision" becomes distorted when transferred into a linguistic medium (Halliwell 1999, 21). Self-consciousness, and even the language in which such awareness might be expressed, is a bastardization of the primary experience or intuition. In other words, "a fundamental discrepancy always prevents the observer with coinciding fully with the consciousness he is observing" (de Man 1993, 12), even if the observer is oneself!

The same discrepancy exists in everyday language, in the intransigence of making the actual expression coincide with what has to be expressed, or making the actual sign coincide with what it signifies.[14] It is the distinctive privilege of language to be able to conceal meaning behind a misleading sign, as when we hide rage or hatred behind a smile (de Man 1993, 12). In short, no sign can represent anything ontologically prior to its use/appearance in experience, and there are no unmediated meanings outside the realm of signification, nor, for that matter, some transcendental consciousness of experience lodged in self-consciousness or any other faculty. As recounted here, James would endorse this understanding. He came to this set of issues through a meandering path, but once he cut through the obfuscations and made his own formulations, he reconceived these fundamental questions with ramifications stretching beyond psychology to philosophy and then into culture at large.

With this general outline of how James and Freud presented their respective theories of the inner sense of *me*, we turn to the "problem of the ego," its historical development, its problematic status, and, finally, its standing in its role of moral agency (Chapter 6). Again, although aligned in their promotion of liberalism (Diggins 1994; Tauber 2012b), Freud and James found themselves peering at each other across a wide divide to ask, doesn't the *mental* "belong" to a somebody? And what, then, does a "somebody" *mean*?

Notes

1 This discussion (adapted from Tauber 2013a, 15–16, 26–7) remains focused on this particular aspect of Freud's theory and makes no attempt to assess the place of representationalism in contemporary psychoanalysis, which is thoroughly reviewed by Perlow (1995, especially the discussion of Joseph Sandler's writings, 74ff., and subsequent theorizing, 121ff.; Sandler et al. 1997). The following discussion of *Vorstellungen* and *das Ding* is based on Tauber (2013a 32–3, 116–24).

2 In Lacan's formulation, the self-conscious, analytic ego has been subordinated to the unadorned voice of subjectivity, where the slogan "back to Freud" may be viewed as an explicit return to the "voice" of *das Ich* without the trappings of a controlling ego (Lacan 1991, 2006; Fink 1995; Chiesa 2007; Neill 2011). Ironically, by establishing the epistemological ambiguity of the ego, Freud perhaps inadvertently supported the "egocide" refutations and the revisionist programs that followed (Rogozinski 2010, 5). How and why Anglo-American psychoanalysis followed a different theoretical trajectory that defended, even valorized, the self-aware ego must delve back into English philosophy, where a strong empiricist tradition supported the focus on the knowing-agent (Reé 2019).

3 This basic constructivist phenomenological precept has been extended from the differing perceptions of individuals to contrasting cognitive strategies practiced by different cultural groups (Nisbett 2003).

4 Adorno's so-called "negative dialectic" described a process of dialectics without identity, an alternative non-identity thinking. The negative dialectic "confirmed neither concept nor reality in itself. Instead, he [Adorno] posited each in critical reference to the other. Put another way, each was affirmed only in its non-identity to the other" (Sherratt 2002, 63). Thus, Adorno sought to counter the "mathematization" of thought, which like a machine can only reproduce itself, and consequently, in its adjudication and dominance of thought, such identity thinking limits knowledge and ultimately stultifies experience.

5 The place of "vagueness" in philosophy has strong currents in American pragmatism, and given James's important role in the Metaphysical Club (see Chapter 2, note #1), we may fairly surmise that he would have found sympathetic reception to these ideas in Cambridge. Similar views are found in the writings of Charles Sanders Peirce (Gavin 1992, 4).

6 A well-known example of linear thinking was Freud's theory of psycho-mechanics, in which the push-pull play of unconscious forces purportedly explained the physiology of human neuroses (Kitcher 1992; Tauber 2010).

7 Beyond substantive ideas and images on which empiricist analysis traditionally focused, James insisted that experience includes the non-substantive transitions and relations:

> Every examiner of the sensible life in *concreto* must see that relations of every sort, of time, space, difference, likeness, change, rate, cause, or what not, are just as integral members of the sensational flux as terms are, and that conjunctive relations are just as true members of the flux as disjunctive relations are. This is what in some recent writings of mine I have called the

"radically empiricist" doctrine (in distinction from the doctrine of mental atoms which the name empiricism so often suggests).

(James 1987d, 757)

8 James illustrates with a footnote:

Mozart describes thus his manner of composing: First bits and crumbs of the piece come and gradually join together in his mind; then the soul getting warmed to the work, the thing grows more and more, and I spread it out broader and clearer, and at last it gets almost finished in my head, even when it is a long piece, so that I can see the whole of it at a single glance in my mind, as if it were a beautiful painting or a handsome human being; in which way I do not hear it in my imagination at all as a succession—the way it must come later—but all at once, as it were. It is a rare feast! All the inventing and making goes on in me as in a beautiful strong dream. But the best of all is *the hearing of it all at once.*

(James 1983, 247, emphasis in original)

9 James also cites M. V. Egger (*La Parole Intérieure* Paris 1881), "before speaking, one barely knows what one intends to say, but afterwards one is filled with admiration and surprise at having said and thought it so well" (James 1983, 270).

10 The issue of intellectualism leads from his

[anarchic] image of the world . . . characterized by flux and impermanence, a world that knows no fixed center or given telos . . . As much as James insists that we act in the world that we structure to suit our aims, it is also one that exceeds, overwhelms, resists, and frustrates our intentions. The error James signals with respect to what he calls "intellectualism" is that we tend to forget or overlook the human origin of this order, attributing it to some fact about the world itself, rendering the world too neat, too reasonable, too forgetful of its "game flavor."

(Dianda 2023, 173)

And, as discussed later, thus subject to human values, interests, and intentions.

11 For comment about the irony of James's submission to what some would call the irrational and his relation to Adorno's later elaboration of non-identity thinking, see Posnock (1991, 108ff.). For James's indebtedness to (and differences with) Bergson, see Friedl (2018, 307–20).

12 James wrote:

According to my view, experience as a whole is a process in time, whereby innumerable particular terms lapse and are superseded by others that follow upon them by transitions which, whether disjunctive or conjunctive in content, are themselves experiences, and must in general be accounted at least as real as the terms which they relate. What the nature of the event called "superseding" signifies, depends altogether on the kind of transition that obtains. Some experiences simply abolish their predecessors without continuing them in any way. Others are felt to increase or to enlarge their meaning, to carry out their purpose, or to bring us nearer to their goal. They "represent" them, and may fulfil their function better than they fulfilled it themselves. But to "fulfil a function" in a world of pure experience can be conceived and defined in only one possible way. In such a world transitions and arrivals (or terminations) are the only events that happen, tho they happen by so many sorts of path. The only function that one experience can perform is to lead into another experience; and the only fulfilment we can speak of is the reaching of a certain experienced end. When one experience leads to (or can lead to) the same end as another, they agree in function. But the whole system of experiences as they are immediately given presents itself as a quasi-chaos through which one can pass out of an initial term in many directions and yet end in the same terminus, moving from next to next by a great many possible paths.

(James 1987b, 885)

13 Bergson's concept of duration (*durée*) explicitly addressed the problem of representing a process that can be understood only in its entirety—for example, a melody—and centers on the inadequacy of a representational model to depict the ceaseless change of phenomena and experience in time. This attempt to describe what is essentially an *intuition* of duration shares the same general agenda with other philosophical attempts to capture consciousness framed by the same quandary of experience *in* time (e.g., Husserlian phenomenology) (Capek 1971, 83–186; Lacey 1989, 24–32, 88–98; Guerlac 2006; Allen 2023, 6–63). Accordingly, "there are no things, there are only actions" (Bergson 1911a, 248, quoted by Lacey 1989, 95). While Bergson opposed orthodox representative conceptuality, he was unable to free himself entirely of the representational modality. He saw metaphysics working best not so much when it dispenses with concepts as when it "frees itself of the inflexible and ready-made concepts and creates others very different from those we usually handle, I mean flexible, mobile, almost fluid representations" (Bergson 1946, 168, quoted by Mullarkey 2000, 152–3). These might be metaphors, similes, comparisons, or some intermediate Bergson labeled an *image* in the introduction to *Matter and Memory*: "[B]y *image* we mean a certain existence which is more than that which the idealist calls a *representation*, but less than that which the realist calls a *thing*—an existence placed halfway between the *thing* and the *representation*" (Bergson 2011b, xi–xii, quoted by Lacey 1989, 89). In seeking a compromise between realism and idealism, Bergson's influence had largely expired by World War II and had virtually no influence on psychoanalytic thinking (Herring 2024). While much has been written about the James-Bergson friendship and philosophical kinship, little scholarship has been directed at identifying resonances between Bergson and Freud (Guerlac 2006, 23, 110); and even Deleuze, when comparing Freud and Bergson, refers to how differently Bergson conceives the unconscious—to denote a non-psychological reality (Deleuze 1988, 56).

14 Of course, this extends even more to social communication:

In the everyday language of communication, there is no a priori privileged position of sign over meaning or meaning over sign; the act of interpretation will always again have to establish this relation for the case at hand. The interpretation of everyday language is a Sisyphean task, a task without end and without progress, for the other is always free to make what he wants differ from what he says he wants. [This state constitutes] a built-in discrepancy within the inter-subjective relationship.

(de Man 1993, 12)

Chapter 5

The enigmatic self

In a most commonsensical way, one generally thinks of the *ego* in terms of conscious awareness—feelings, thoughts, choices, actions, relations, emotions, which are then placed within three constructs of selfhood: (1) the indexical identity of a "me" or "I" that confers spatial, temporal, and relational structure to "my being in the world"; (2) a knowing subject who integrates experience and exercises memory; and (3) a moral agent who enacts identity and assumes personal responsibility. Whether assessed as conscious awareness of bodily actions or as an individual engaged in rational decision-making, the conscious self serves as a would-be judge of itself—both in terms of actions directed at the outer world and in regard to inner deliberative thought processes. In contrast, the Other comprises all those outside the personal domain, who confront, complement, dialogue, and exchange with the subject. This Cartesian schema presents the *I* as demarcated from the world and forming some integral wholeness unto *myself,* who resides in the world and negotiates its various activities as an individual.

The first-person viewpoint that demanded disengagement and ideally became a "view from nowhere"—neutral and universal, where no perspective was favored (Nagel 1986)—served as the fundamental agent of liberal democracy and scientific pursuit.[1] On this account, the observer would be so radically removed from the world that the ego would shrink to some "punctual point" and leave the scene of scrutiny undisturbed (C. Taylor 1989, 159ff.). This atomistic knower also achieved standing when extrapolated to the civil world as a political agent (the basis of citizen autonomy at the expense of monarchial authority) and soon became the ideal of individualized personhood in broader cultural and psychological respects. And when Descartes trained this view on himself, a gap appeared:

> "I" of the "I think" and the "I" of the "I am," which follows as a logical conclusion from the "I think." That is to say, either these two "I's" are

DOI: 10.4324/9781003565413-5

not the same thing or the second is already assumed in the positing of the first. "I think" already entails the subject "I" and, thus, the conclusion, "I am" is strictly superfluous. Descartes has not really proved or substantiated anything beyond what he had already presupposed.

(Chiesa 2007, 15)

So, the "I" which is said "to think" is already marked off from the "I" that affirms the thinking. And if the ego represents "himself" to "himself," or as he imagines himself, the "modernist fallacy" has been committed: such imagining must be based on *symbolizing* or representing himself to "himself" (Neill 2011, 17). Simply, the ego has been split, and subjectivity swings between the self-consciousness of *I think* and the being of *I am*. So, when I am not consciously thinking—i.e., when "I" is not (re-)presented in introspective thought, the subject extends *in* the world, unmediated by the self-consciousness of its own introverted thought.

In the barest sense, the self-recognition of a distinct, self-conscious *I* sunders the self's integration with both nature and, more intimately, one's own subjectivity. *I* is simply the voice of *me*. To communicate with "oneself" already entails a division. The very nature of such a monologue is, in fact, a dialogue, i.e., one who speaks to another or with "oneself" leaves the subject-object structure in place. And with that division, the *I* falls out of joint with the world because of the disjunction induced by radical individualization. Having been displaced from an integrated whole, the self-conscious knower then initiates efforts to repair that fragmentation. So, as a result of the *I* being atomized by self-conscious recognition, the ensuing rupture triggers the search for a "resting spot," where she no longer feels separated (even estranged) and thus alienated, disaffected, and disjointed. In that yearning, Romantic sensibility took form (Tauber 2022, 338–41).

The Romantics extended the analytical dualism problem into a subjectivist framework where self-consciousness becomes inextricable from personal alienation (Beiser 2002). Just as the world is objectified, so too am *I* as a subject made into an object by introspective reflection. Self-consciousness carries the same gaze that had been directed towards the external world inwards to look at oneself, as if *me* is something to be observed—seen or heard. Such objectification instantiates the self as another entity in the world; namely, one's intimate subjectivity becomes a "thing" of self-scrutiny (Tauber 2022, 288–9).[2] In this pose, the subject assumes objectification as reflected in a makeshift mirror that splits *me* into a subject observing another (*me*). From that externalized vantage point, self-consciousness may then "peer inside" to look for "me," or even style "me" as some-*thing*—an image or an ideal of some sort. In that exercise, "me-ness" then becomes a translation of a mirrored it. Simply put, subjectivity objectified presents the self as an object, where the *I* becomes an entity, a something that is separated from the world and navigates it as such.

James would eventually discard metaphysical dualism, and he did so to "save" subjectivity from the encroachments of misapplied objectification. In this chapter, we consider how his phenomenological revision required overthrowing a vast tradition of thought. Indeed, he was swimming against a powerful tide of philosophical and cultural commitments to the *individual* as presented in the Cartesian format.

James on the self

James's views on the self fell into two phases: the period in which he still regarded himself doing psychology (*The Principles* of 1890), albeit already disturbed by the limitations of positivist philosophy; and a second stage in which he shed the cloak of science for the robes of philosophy. While obvious correlations exist between mind and brain states, for James, mind-states do depend on brain states, but the nature of the mental is not *explained* by such a dependence (Myers 1986, 54ff.). That position never wavered. In the earlier stage, he accorded the self a *functional* status and thereby acknowledged the psychological necessity for unity and continuity afforded by consciousness (James 1992d, 197–8). *Psychology: The Briefer Course* (1892) offered a psychological description, not a philosophical explanation or analysis:

> But why should each successive mental state appropriate the same past Me? . . . My present Me is felt with warmth and intimacy. The heavy warm mass of my body is there, and the nucleus of the "spiritual me," the sense of intimate activity is there. We cannot realize our present self without simultaneously feeling one or other of these two things. Any other object of thought which brings these two things with it into consciousness will be thought with a warmth and an intimacy like those which cling to the present me.
>
> (James 1992d, 189–90)

However, by 1894, James recognized that putting one's faith in the coherence and the "warm intimacy" of self-consciousness as the substrate for identity was fraught with irresolvable difficulties.

James had considered several formulations of selfhood, and he did so without reconciling their philosophical differences. While acknowledging the constitutive social elements identifying the subject, his primary orientation during the period he was writing *The Principles of Psychology* wrestled with the problems arising from the underlying dualism embedded in the science of psychology and how to develop an epistemology extending Hume's depiction of self-consciousness arising from that introspective duality.

When Hume observed his own self-consciousness, he noted that what Locke had conceived as a stable continuity of experience and memory, the *self*, is but a "bundle . . . of different perceptions," and its handmaiden, consciousness, is only the piecemeal aggregate of those perceptions— fragmentary, often incoherent, frequently rationally disordered, and powerfully driven by the "passions" (Hume 1978, 252; C. Taylor 1989; Thiel 2011). Hume dismissed the notion of a self "insofar as it is accessible through inner experience" which consists only of perceptions. In other words, he sought an *epistemological* basis for identifying the self and noted that because his self-consciousness was comprised of fleeting perceptions or thoughts, he "never can catch" *himself* "at any time without a perception, and never can observe any thing but the perception" (Hume 1978, 252). This proved to be an insurmountable block to Hume's inquiry, for if the idea of the self is based on what introspection reveals, he could perceive only one thought or image jumping to another, seemingly without connection. Absent causal links, he could not establish the basis for integration of experience, and thus he dismissed *the* self as an entity, an imaginary construct, a fiction that permits the *sense* of an integrated identity that is conceived by the same criteria with which humans organize the world at large. He argued that the "me" of personal identity morphs from moment to moment, and thus the "I" is non-identical to itself. A bundle of perceptions has "no owner" as such—experiences and perceptions exist without a discernable subject. In short, the self, originally conceived as a postulated homunculus (what Descartes called the ego), lies beyond empirical characterization.[3] When Hume noted that the fleeting perceptions of his consciousness could not coalesce around a "self," he concluded that "all the nice and subtle questions concerning personal identity can never possibly be decided, and are to be regarded rather as grammatical than as philosophical difficulties" (Hume 1978, 262).

Hume's critique consists of two momentous moves. First, *the self* "has no clothes," i.e., no basis in fact. One only experiences fleeting thoughts and perceptions, and so was hatched the "hard problem" of consciousness (Chalmers 1995). Notwithstanding Descartes's certainty of an ego as some basic organizing principle for me-ness, he could not find *what* self-reflection *is*. And second, Hume maintained that notions of the self rest on a grammatical error (later developed by Wittgenstein; Tauber 2013a, 282–6; Wittgenstein 1960, 66). While experience must belong to someone, that someone has a grammatical pronominal position, whose predicates of consciousness remain constant whether reference is made to an I, he, she, or you. James's radical empiricism sought to address Hume's provocations.[4]

In *Principles of Psychology*, James described that knowing subject in two modalities, the *I* and the *me*: *I*, the knower, a unified subjective or personal center of thinking (i.e., the first-person subject), as opposed to *me* that stands for the self as known, the predicated object (James 1983, 279). The possessive sense of mind and character appropriately designates this "me-ness" as selfhood, the sense of myself as a person with an implicit sense of self-responsibility accompanying that appointment. If, after all, I am a "me"—and "me" connotes mine—then *I* assumes accountability that differentiates *me* as a being in the world. Simply, *me* refers not only to a different degree of intimacy with this identification, but also a sense of responsibility for this creature who walks among other similarly embodied minds. *I* then accounts for one's own identity through *me* broadly construed by identifying oneself with all that is hers or identifies of her nature—materially, spiritually, and socially. James cannot resolve these two senses of identity, and accepts the *I/me* distinction as given, derived from the common human experience of a predicated notion of selfhood derived from some notion of an inner dialogue between *I* and *me*. He concludes that personal identity resides as "an objective person, known by a passing subjective Thought and recognized as continuing in time. *Hereafter let us use the words ME and I for the empirical person and the judging Thought*," (James 1983, 350, emphasis in original). And then he admits,

> The identity which the *I* discovers . . . can only be a relative identity, that of a slow shifting in which there is always some common ingredient retained . . . Thus the identity found by the *I* in its *me* is only a loosely construed thing, an identity "on the whole," just like that which any outside observer might find in the same.
>
> (James 1983, 352)

Indeed, that "outside observer" is the *I* itself.

His waffling between first- and third-person constructions refers to the fundamental dilemma embedded in the Cartesian construction of splitting "I think" into subject and its own object (Chiesa 2007, 15–17). So, consistent with his psychologist role (at least as presented in *The Principles of Psychology*), he adheres to the traditional dualist schema despite deep misgivings.[5] James builds from his previous argument for the primacy of the stream of consciousness and builds his notions of selfhood within that construct. He returns to the primary sense of personal identity as deriving from the continuity of experience, while noting that such *"subjective synthesis* essential to all thought" is not the same as *"objective synthesis . . .* known among the things" (James 1983, 315, emphasis in original). Here the problematic predicated self-sensed subject/object divide appears, which he then explains follows from the same "synthetic form essential to all thought. It is the sense of a sameness perceived *by* thought and predicated of things *thought-about . . . .* The thought not only thinks them both, but thinks that they are identical" (James 1983, 315, emphasis in original). So, the primary principle of *identity*, inferred from experience, underwrites the sense of selfhood, for "continuity makes us unite what dissimilarity might otherwise separate; similarity makes us unite what discontinuity might hold apart" (James 1983, 317).

Note two key moves here. First, James uses this notion of identity to make the case that the self of yesterday is the same as today. However, the more profound claim concerns identity itself: the self does not exist as a *fact*, but rather as a *feeling* of continuity, sameness, personal identity (per the "warmth" cited earlier). James thus asserts that the sense of self is based on empirical and verifiable *experience*.

At this point he is left with the imbroglio of (1) a dualistic construction—the *I* thinking of *me*—which (2) leaves in abeyance the synthesis, i.e., the coherence of thought, the very basis of the continuity one senses and relies upon as the integration of personal identity. Consciousness does not provide an answer, for the subject-object dualism remains. *What*, in fact, is that object called *me*, or the *I* for that matter? In retrospect, we know that this impasse will eventuate in "radical empiricism" as the attempt to resolve the conundrum of identifying the "objects" of consciousness freed of the subject-object dualism embedded in the Cartesian ego. So, after considering and dispensing with theories of the soul, the associationist models, and the transcendental ego, James embarks on the course that will emerge as a new philosophy of mind.

In following the scientific program of *The Principles of Psychology*, James devised an illustration of four boxes that "contain the irreducible data of psychology": (1) the Psychologist; (2) the Thought Studied; (3) the Thought's Object; and (4) the Psychologist's Reality (the real world) (James 1983, 184). Having only introspection at his disposal, he briefly reviews its contested status (some like Brentano taking such as "true in themselves," while others like Comte who argue against introspective cognition altogether). James, as already discussed (Chapter 2), highlights the distortions resulting from the "psychologist's fallacy," namely, objectifying what is irreducibly locked in subjectivity of the first-person experience, but note, how he came to that conclusion. Bruce Wilshire cogently dissects the construction by noting that while James

> wants to study (2), the thought or mental state, so that he can correlate it causally to the brain state (4), he cannot specify the mental state until he specifies what it is of, that is, (3) The Thought's Object. And this "Object" cannot be a particular object, like a particular brain state—or a particular anything else. He means "all that thought thinks just as thought thinks it" [James 1983, 266]. An example he gives is hearing thunder. We do not perceive thunder pure and simple, but "thunder-breaking-in-on-silence-and-contrasting-to it. To specify the mental state, we must specify it in terms of this Object. The *particular* object it is of is only the "topic" of the total "Object" . . . The particular may just as well be a particular brain state or event as a particular clap of thunder.
>
> [Therefore] Thought's Object (3), described phenomenologically, engorges both (2) the mental state and (4) the brain state. It is the full sweep of the experienceable world.
>
> (Wilshire 1997, 107–8, emphasis in original)

This phenomenological orientation then extends to a characterization of the knowing agent and the basis of James's understanding of the self:

> But does the natural scientific investigator, (1) The Psychologist, not stand off from all this, a kind of self-constituting, self-reflecting, and inventorying consciousness somehow inside an organism? No. James launches an intriguing description of identity of self as "the passing thought." "The passing thought [then seems to be] the thinker" [James 1983, 324].
>
> (Wilshire 1997, 108)

After discarding the claims of the Soul, associative and transcendental theories, James argues that the "passing thought" (2) can be specified only in terms of (3), the total Object and, moreover, the Psychologist (1) is also absorbed into the Object and therefore cannot stand outside the phenomena to be described. And with that move, James endorses a phenomenological account of selfhood:

> The Object becomes all-engulfing: thinkers or experiencers absorbed in the experiencing-experienced-experienceable world. What started as

natural science becomes a world-view, with all the philosophical problems and opportunities attendant upon that. The way opens inexorably for James's later metaphysics, "A World of Pure Experience" [1987i], and for his phenomenology as the basis of this radically empiricist thought.

(Wilshire 1997, 109)

For example, as immediately experienced, the blue of the sky appears *as is*, neither confined to a subjective (mental) or an objective (physical) "compartment." "Only in retrospection, however rapid, is the pure or natural experience of blue sorted into the different contexts. In breathtaking immediacy and intimacy, experiencers belong in the experienced world, and that world belongs to them" (Wilshire 1997). In sum, James's failure, in *Principles*, to explain how mental states are about their object drove him to develop the doctrine of radical empiricism.

James forthrightly accepted that he could not account for how mental states are about their object and thus accepted a phenomenological account and the radical empiricism that supported it. The phenomenological description leaves the self as a functional organizing faculty (recognized retrospectively) in which ever-changing sense impressions cohere and take on meaning. That meaning, established in the very act of attention, is framed by the mind's *intention* and experienced in consciousness as the fleeting bundle of perceptions (whether interior or exterior) that Hume had described. James called consciousness in this phenomenological orientation as becoming a "selecting agency," "the very hull on which our mental ship is built," that forms the "nucleus of our inner self" (James 1983, 1421–3, 640; Linschoten 1968; Wilshire 1979, 1997; Edie 1987; Seigfried 1990; Taylor and Wozniak 1996a). Accordingly, selection and ordering of perceptions are prerequisites for experience. Most inputs are ignored, so thinking requires choice based on practical or aesthetic importance. Experience is thus arrested upon certain objects, whose conceptualization in turn demands isolating and distinguishing some perceptual aspects, excluding others, and ordering reality not by hard and fast divisions, but by active, selective processing. Experience, then, enters as bare or raw data, and then integrated and organized according to the intentions of the experiencing individual, who manipulates sensory data to serve personal needs.

The key element of this phenomenological account is the view of the mind in energetic engagement with the environment, where *I* selects and constructs *my* world from the bewildering complexity of the surrounding plenum and thereby differentiates *myself. I* do so only by active engagement. And by focusing on the act of perception, on the act of recognition, on the act of reaction, the subject is defined in action. In this sense, there is no *self* residing as some preexisting and specified ontological entity. In human terms, that cohesive "self" becomes an inviolate "I," a self-defining, unique individual. Note that consciousness ironically becomes another "object" of consciousness. This intentional "object," "self," is not consciousness itself. As an object, consciousness somehow resides separate, albeit close to one's true self, but always distinct. And underlying this conception of agency is an implicit sense of freedom of choice, an active aggrandizement that James would later ground his moral philosophy (see Chapter 6).[6]

In sum, consciousness is the stream of thoughts that, when contemplated as an object, must then be displaced by another core sense of selfness that unforgivingly retreats.[7] The self then cannot be purely experienced but is represented by the "sum total of all that he *can* call his" (James 1983, 279). These, of course, include emotional, spiritual, and material elements of identity beyond bodily sensations, but the embodiment reactions (according to James) serve as the foundation of consciousness and, *ipso facto*, selfhood. And note that consciousness is only known in retrospect: "[I]t is not one of the things experienced at the moment; this knowing is not immediately known. It is only known in subsequent reflection" (James 1983, 290). Consciousness, then, is the *process* of objectification, one irretrievably distinct from its ontological source, of which "selfness" emerges as a product of that functional exercise. In short, "the self" is, like other products of intentional mental activity, an *object* of thought that coheres in memory and linked behaviors and experience . . . but not objectified as an *entity*.

Comment

James held two key pragmatic observations about selfhood during his mature period: (1) the *I* cannot be characterized from an external or perceptual perspective (Shoemaker 1984, 105); and (2) the mind's fundamental function engages the world, not itself. People *live* unself-consciously. When healthy, their minds function within the world—coordinated seamlessly between themselves and their various modalities of otherness. When the moods, sentiments, emotions (the affects) demand attention, then consciousness performs its evolutionary function: facing a problem, it scrutinizes, analyzes, judges. Usually the target is the world, but in modern Western culture, it also includes the self-conscious mind itself.

The fundamental presupposition of "self-discovery" is that such a self exists as some entity. "Who am I?" may be answered by various social refractions, but that approach skirts the matter at hand, at least as posed by those who seek an introspective endpoint. As Kierkegaard had so well observed, the self is essentially that which reflects upon itself, what he called "a relation that relates itself to itself" (see Chapter 3, note #4). One's personhood then becomes an endless recursion; there is no entity; no core; no essence; no endpoint. Simply put, there is no objectification of personal identity, only self-reflection—a self-consciousness that splits "me" into a subject inquiring about itself, an introspective investigation adapted from a mode of acquiring knowledge designed for the external world. To apply the method of objective investigation to subjectivity ("modernity's mistake") is a profound category error. And that gaze, a Cartesian residue of a rebuked dualist metaphysics, focused James's critique. So, while neuroscientists investigated the mind as correlated brain states, psychologists examined the mind by deciphering cognitive mechanisms, and psychoanalysts interpreted the mind with a theory based on inferences, James would describe the mind phenomenologically.

As already discussed, James set his metaphysical sights on experience at the expense of consciousness, which he regarded as a secondary, derived phenomenon. And in characterizing consciousness, at least phenomenologically, he stressed its nature as "a teeming multiplicity of objects and relations, and what we call simple sensations are results of discriminative attention, pushed often to a very high degree" (James 1983, 219). And then he identified the principal features of conscious thinking: (1) a thought, to so qualify, is part of a *personal* consciousness that (2) is always in flux and (3) contiguous. Flirting with the dualism he was to later discard, (4) consciousness seems to deal with objects *independent* of itself, and therefore (5) a selective process, driven by interest, is always in operation (James 1983, 220). The knowing agent is thus portrayed as constantly attending to the perceptual world and actively re-constructing "reality."

To be fair, when he shed consciousness altogether, he did so not as a psychologist, but rather as a metaphysician. However, even in 1890, with an alternate tack, James would have arrived at the same port through a different course as did an array of twentieth-century philosophers who basically continued the philosophical trajectory set by that time. Certainly, by the end of the nineteenth century, the self conceived as an object or entity was no longer a viable formulation of personal identity. Hume had highlighted the missing object; Kant concurred and sought the necessary conditions for a cognizing agent, an organization with no empirical content other than his rich philosophical imagination; and Hegel turned the entire reflexive project from the inner sanctum of one's self-consciousness to the world at large.

In the famous Master/Slave allegory (*Phenomenology of Spirit*, 1807), Hegel mythologized a primordial scene in which two strangers meet. They recognize each other as the "other." In that recognition, they distinguish themselves as individuals. The confrontational scenario—one referred to as relational or dialogical—creates the self-consciousness of a distinct identity. In other words, one is not conscious of oneself until the Other appears. In that recognition, identity is formed through a novel self-awareness. He is not *me*, and with that recognition, *I* become *me*. That mindfulness of *me* as distinctive and different then reconfigures the subject's relation to the world. In this construction, instead of some core identity, persons are identified not as autonomous or insular, but rather as constituted in relation to society, nature, the divine, etc. Simply, relationship with an "other" defines the subject. In the conglomerate of identifications and interactions, a person is both identified (by others) and self-identified. An inner core in this formulation is simply eclipsed. This "relational" understanding of agency thus characterizes subjects living in and delineated by their relationships that define and ultimately frame their personhood (Tauber 2006). Then in the twentieth century, the Cartesian ego is further deconstructed by dispensing with that subject-object (*res cogito/res extensa*) structure altogether.[8] James easily fits into this story, not from examining the basis of selfhood as such, but by his attempt to overturn the dualistic metaphysics from which older formulations of personal identity had emerged.

In James's late philosophy, the self is deconstructed in terms of his radical empiricism that renders the conscious ego a second-order *sense* of identity which has only a *functional* role of connecting sensations, mental images, and feelings. Taken just as they appear, sensations are real concrete particulars, not mental representations, and thus do not represent anything beyond themselves. And because sensations are linked to external objects through perspectival causal relations and are directly perceived, no independent mental entity or even a stage or embedding medium is required for such phenomena to exist (Banks 2014, 9, 89). Accordingly, the unity of consciousness is simply the composite of levels of unconscious processing, in which mental contents become conscious by being functionally related to other contents in memory, time and space perception, judgment, and imagination. Recall that James defined radical empiricism as "the real particular relations between events" and thus

takes conjunctive relations at their face-value, holding them to be as real as the terms united by them. The world it represents as a collection, some parts of which are conjunctively and others disjunctively related. Two parts, themselves disjoined, may nevertheless hang together by intermediaries with which they are severally connected, and the whole world eventually may hang together similarly, inasmuch as some path of conjunctive transition by which to pass from one of its parts to another may always be discernible. . . . [Thus] the relations between things, conjunctive as well as disjunctive, are just as much matters of direct particular experience, neither more so nor less so, than the things themselves. The generalized conclusion is that therefore the parts of experience hold together from next to next by relations that are themselves parts of experience. The directly apprehended universe needs, in short, no extraneous trans-empirical connective support, but possesses in its own right a concatenated or continuous structure. The great obstacle to radical empiricism in the contemporary mind is the rooted rationalist belief that experience as immediately given is all disjunction and no conjunction, and that to make one world out of this separateness, a higher unifying agency must be there.

(James 1987d, 789, 826–7)

However, an ego delimiting mental from physical events simply does not exist beyond a collection of functions ultimately realized in the physiological activity of the brain. As Mach provocatively put it, "the ego cannot be saved" (*Das Ich ist unrettbar*) (Banks 2014, 9–10).

Because radical empiricism rests in the rejection of a representational model of the mind, perceptions are directly processed and thus omit indirect intermediary images or ideas. James thus sought to cut the Gordian knot in which

the whole philosophy of perception from Democritus's time downwards has been just one long wrangle over the paradox that what is evidently one reality should be in two places at once, both in outer space and in a person's mind. "Representative" theories of perception avoid the logical paradox, but on the other hand *they violate the reader's sense of life*, which knows no intervening mental image but seems to see the room and the book immediately just as they physically exist.

(James 1987a, 1145–6, emphasis added).

And James, as always, in rejecting artifice, sided with *life*, namely, the veracity and the vibrancy of experience.

Selfness, the sense of *me*, is radically personal, a product of one's own self-consciousness. From a third-party perspective, there is a discernable subject, with manifest behaviors whose composite array points to nebulous coherence from which identity emerges. And from the firsthand, self-reflexive vantage, the self serves as an integrating conception, an inclusiveness of being (perceiving, knowing, feeling, remembering) that is the *me* who must navigate the world and negotiate reality. However, self-discovery in terms of defining an ego is a vacuous exercise when conceived as looking for characterization of an entity, some *thing* with definition, boundaries, or any criteria applied to descriptions of a natural object. To examine the inner "me" and provide an accurate representation of motives, personal history, and character is to compose a self-image, the erstwhile *me*. For James, the self emerges in its life in the world and that life is self-crafted. Thus, the self would not be defined as such, but would reside as a testament to the process of its creation (Starobinski 1988). This is the Romantic legacy James inherited, and in his revival of its central tenet, he marched against a formidable resistance. After all, the ego was, and remains, ensconced in the Western mind. Descartes had refuted skepticism and built an epistemology based on the certainty of his own thought, and its repository, the knowing self. This is the foundation of modernist philosophy and has ramifications in every conceivable formulation of identity and agency. James unhinged those metaphysics. Indeed, as Davis observes, James's formulation of thinking

> is not under the control of a determining *I*, as thinker. James says that it is more like an *It* that thinks through the process: "If we could say in English 'it thinks,' as we say 'it rains' or 'it blows,'"—without having to know quite what "it" refers back to—then "we should be stating the fact most simply and with the minimum of assumption.
>
> (Davis 2022, 34, quoting James 1983, 220)

With this honest agnosticism, James defaults in postulating how the mind functions, having "grown up in ways of which at present we can give no account" (James 1983, 1280). The nature of the experienced *I* is also left as an open question, remaining as a description of an interactive process of that consciousness with the world.

Very early in his career, James recognized the irreducible subject-object structure of self-reflection. He carried this observation into his maturity, where it served to undercut his erstwhile attempts to establish a scientific introspection and, more broadly, it set the groundwork for deconstructing the presumptions of selfhood as a definable entity, as to *what* is me as a product of self-consciousness (James 1983, 290–1). So, when abandoning consciousness as the center of his ponderings, James required an alternate organizing concept. The "solution" to the failure of capturing experience in a first-order fashion by introspection was to collapse the distinction between consciousness and content into simple *experience*.

James was led to this revision by his underlying opposition to a duality in which the unity of consciousness is partitioned into a subject-object rendition of observation, a representative second-order description. In its place (as already discussed), he substituted *experience* as the most basic unit of the psyche, which he hoped would become the basis of analyzing what happens both within the mental realm (its qualities, including continuity) and outside in configuring its relations.

In conclusion, during his mature period, James makes two key modifications regarding the self that are most pertinent to our theme. First, his advocacy of experience placed the "individualized self" as active within a radically empirical and pluralistic field of consciousness, in which the primacy of the stream of consciousness, so dominant in *Principles of Psychology*, again frames his notion of personal identity as an orienting index of that experience, namely, experience as a sense of *mine* (McDermott 1976, xxxvii).

> The individualized self, which I believe to be the only thing properly called self, is a part of the content of the world experienced. The world experienced (otherwise called the "field of consciousness") comes at all times with our body as its centre, centre of vision, centre of action, centre of interest. Where the body is is "here"; when the body acts is "now"; what the body touches is "this"; all other things are "there" and "then" and "that." These words of emphasized position imply a systematization of things with reference to a focus of action and interest which lies in the body; and the systematization is now so instinctive (was it ever not so?) that no developed or active experience exists for us at all except in that ordered form. So far as "thoughts" and "feelings" can be active, their activity terminates in the activity of the body, and only through first arousing its activities can they begin to change those of the rest of the world. The body is the storm centre, the origin of co-ordinates, the constant place of stress in all that experience-train. Everything circles round it, and is felt from its point of view.
>
> (James 1987h, 803)[9]

Second, James finally acknowledged unconscious mentation, certainly not in the terms of Freud's conception, but as a more modest "subconscious" that leaves the self as some kind of undefined composite, sensed but uncharacterized (James 1987f, 193).

> The subconscious self is nowadays a well-accredited psychological entity; and I believe that in it we have exactly the mediating term required. Apart from all religious considerations, there is actually and literally more life in our total soul than we are at any time aware of. The exploration of the transmarginal field has hardly yet been seriously undertaken.
>
> (James 1987f, 457–8)

James does not further dwell on the matter of the self, for he has moved on to his larger project. Without the predicate structure of knowing, the dualism underlying the characterization of the self outlined in *The Principles of Psychology* was abandoned to the older metaphysics.[10] With radical empiricism, James had devised an approach that discarded mental/world dualism, the representational epistemology embedded in that metaphysical schema, and the *self* that held the entire construction together. Next, we consider how Freud dealt with the identity issue. Short answer: perhaps wisely, he didn't.

Who is the Freudian subject?

Freud's original ego/unconscious partition proved expendable. In his last formulation he described the mental as a continuum that begins with self-consciousness and extends into a shadowy area of preconscious thought and then to the unconscious domain (Freud 1923a).[11] The deep unconscious remains untapped and therefore utterly anonymous, while a second domain may serve as a reservoir of preconscious thought. In either case, this Other, residing at the depths of the psyche, cannot be directly known, leaving both the ego and the "id" with nebulous borders. Note that this revised psychic architecture did not change the fundamental character of the process by which the unconscious or preconscious becomes articulated.

Thus the (conscious) ego faces two forms of "the Other"—the unconscious (a repository of psychic trauma and unrequited desire) and the external universe of social and physical objects. In certain contexts, the ego is understood to possess rational autonomy and thus able to scrutinize unconscious motivations. With that authority, control might be asserted, and Freud conceived psychoanalysis to enhance that capability. However, he also maintained that the true mind is unconscious, and that the ego's consciousness may be construed as an epiphenomenon of the deepest psychic drives that are able to enlist the ego to attain their own goals. In this latter scenario, the ego is rendered largely impotent to the demands of unconscious desire, possessing only its "intellect," weak and largely ignorant of those forces it must control.

Freud thus presented conflicting visions of the ego. He entrusted the ego's rationality to serve as a bulwark against unconscious desire; however, he also adamantly rejected the equation of mind with consciousness, more specifically the ego's hold on reality and ability to thwart unconscious demands. He thus would dislodge "the arrogance of consciousness" (Freud 1910, 39) and assert how "it is essential to abandon the overvaluation of the property of being conscious before it becomes possible to form any correct view of the origin of what is mental" (Freud 1900, 612). Consciousness then becomes the evolutionary product of the unconscious mind and retains its linkage to that heritage, while reaching for its autonomy. How the architecture of the mind might be understood evolutionarily was well beyond Freud's interests. Indeed, ignoring the character of consciousness served his pedagogic strategy. While he recognized the necessity of some kind of exchange, a "dialogue" of sorts between conscious mentation and unconscious drives, his theoretical concerns were focused upon the dynamics and effects of the latter (Ogden 1992). This basic orientation consequently displaced consciousness and its attendant notions of the knowing agent as comprising *me*.

Freud's reiterated descriptions of repressed memory, the transitory nature of consciousness, the latency of pre-consciousness, and, most beguiling, the utterly different logic employed by the unconscious relative to conscious thought were all in service of highlighting the centrality of the unconscious in the psychoanalytic conception of the mind. Simply, for Freud, the unconscious *is* the mind, and psychoanalysis the means of revealing its true character (Freud 1900, 613). So, according to psychoanalytic theory, the unconscious, whether considered as an entity or as a locale of subconscious mental activity, is the bedrock of the psyche and the continuous source of the mental.

Perhaps the most jarring omission of Freud's theory is the assumed ego, who is left as an ill-defined functionary, a jockey struggling with the wild forces beneath her limited control.[12] Freud simply bypassed the philosophical status of the ego and assumed its analytic capacities within the strictures of unconscious repression, distorted memory, the allures of fantasy and the trappings of bias. After all, his target was the unconscious, not the ego. Through associations, transference, and other modes of disclosure, unconscious dynamics were to be explained, not by self-reflection as traditionally understood, but rather by an entirely new method of introspection. The first stage, based on the rational autonomy of the ego, employs an *analytical* approach modeled on a scientific philosophy to discern a natural object, the *inferred* unconscious (Tauber 2010, 62–7, 82–4, 238 n. 3). In this scheme, the *ego* with its critical capacities fulfills the requirements of Freud's epistemology, and the terminology is consistent with its historical use in philosophy. And then, in the second *therapeutic* stage, the conscious self-reflective ego functions are bypassed and the analysand is placed in direct confrontation with past emotional trauma.

The Other of the first analytic stage is a construction, a representation that attempts to "capture" the unconscious through symbols, slips of the tongue, jokes, dreams, etc., to objectify a psychic region heretofore hidden. In the second stage, the Other assumes a different character, one now subject to some degree of control as the conscious and unconscious centers recalibrate in the process of achieving improved emotional harmony. So, while psychoanalysis is the science of the unconscious, psychoanalytic therapy depends on the interpretive ability of the ego to draw insight and mediate the resolution of trauma on the one hand, and unrequited desire on the other. And as the psychic layers are uncovered, a key question looms: *who is the subject?*

In his writings, Freud addressed that agent of inquiry, the analysand, simply, as "*das Ich*" ("the I"). *Who* or *what* is *das Ich*? Freud was satisfied with the simple designation of "I"—unencumbered with the diverse constructions associated with *ego* or *self* so dominant in the philosophical literatures. He held no commitment to some totality of personal identity, and thus he remained satisfied with a commonsensical notion of personhood. Pragmatically, "the I" simply serves as a useful idiom that represents identity and the voice of the interior. But what is the relation between such a conscious voice and the inexpressible, a-rational mental interior? Or in the specifics of psychoanalytic (structural and economic) theory, where do repression and catharsis operate, and how are controls imposed? Chapter 1 outlined Freud's representational model of psychic dynamics, and here we delve into *who* is on the psychoanalytic couch, the cognitive agent as it were.

On the one hand, psychoanalysis provides the self-aware subject a means of autonomous interpretation, where rationality confers (some limited) authority over inner drives and desires. Such a subject possesses the ability to survey objects of her own intention, which, in the case of Freudian psychoanalysis, is the intimate other—the unconscious. From that understanding, the analysand putatively obtains various degrees of freedom from the a-rationality of libidinal drives. Here, the modernist model of an autonomous subject finds full expression (C. Taylor 1989; Seigel 2005; Thiel 2011), and when placing Freud in this philosophical setting, we clearly see that he struggled to find an interpretive analytic for his new psychiatry directed at personal liberation. Committed to the ideals of reason's power, the perfection of humankind, and, from the vantage of a physician, the therapeutic promise of analysis, Freud embraced a meliorism moderated by a powerful ambivalence (Whitebook 1995; Tauber 2012b).

On the other hand, that depiction is placed in opposition to the knowing subject with no such authority and (unless enlightened) ignorant of those unconscious despotic forces. The psychoanalytic design of the mind presents a reality organized by intentional desire (conscious and unconscious) mediated by a social-derived normative rationality. The line between fantasy and reality is no longer something like the difference between a mental event and a "real" event in some simple sense. Moreover, reason plays only one part among other contributing faculties to create the mental world in which one lives. With the status of self-knowing precariously lodged between desire and the demands of reality, skepticism finds its home. What can one know about his or her very own desire and motivations that rationalize choice and action? Given this dichotomy, *Who am I?* demands consideration of how unconscious forces define *agency* (the forces driving choices and actions) and impact the self-knowing, conscious *subject* (Moran 1993).

> The analysand is poised between scrutinizing her agency as some kind of "other" and then turning self-consciously to reflect on her own subjectivity arising from those psychic depths.
> *Das Ich* is not coincident with the subject and in fact it is precisely in the difference between the two that one begins to be able to discern the creation of a new conceptual entity: the psychoanalytic subject.
>
> (Ogden 1992, 572)[13]

Freudian theory thus splits the knowing (conscious) *subject* from the *agent*, the locus of psychic determinative control of thought, words, and deeds (Moran 1993). This division highlights an unresolved dilemma of Freudian theory: Who is the true *who*—the voice of the self-conscious subject or the psychic apparatus? Freud answered that the unconscious was the "true psychic reality" (Freud 1900, 613).[14] And his choice of vocabulary, the unassuming *das Ich*, offers a deflationary designation of the subject, one dramatically different from the Cartesian ego, who asserts his very existence based upon the certainty of his own thinking—a thinking *thing* (Descartes 1985, 127). In the psychoanalytic scenario, *das Ich* is *not* that sense of self (Tauber 2023).

The psychoanalytic mantra insists that *I* am not what I think I am—both in terms of self-knowledge and in regard to the exercise of choice in decision-making. Freud repeatedly asserts that free will is an illusion, that humans are directed by deterministic unconscious forces, and the "true" *Ich* is *Es* ("it"), the id. So again, *who* is the subject Freud cites—*me* (as colloquially understood) or some combination of *das Ich/das Es* arising from the melding of ego-id dynamics? The conglomerate seems the best designation, considering the dual agenda of psychoanalysis: the analyst addresses the conscious, reflective *I* and at the same time seeks to uncover the disguised manifestations of the unconscious and elucidating its impact on the ego. When stated as an unadorned opposition, a synthesis beckons, for psychoanalysis does, in fact, regard the subject in both ways, and from that construction the unyielding problematics of psychoanalysis take root. What is the role of conscious awareness within the context of unconscious psychic dynamics? How are a-rational forces linked to the self-reflective individual? How is rational insight transmuted into analytic cure? What, indeed, is the proper balance between the two domains of mental life, between erotic desire and social reality (e.g., Horkheimer and Adorno 1993 [1947]; Marcuse 1955; Brown 1959)?

Although these questions remain unsettled, the success of psychoanalysis rests on the underlying premise that emotional recognition coupled with rational insight leads to personal freedom. In that schema, self-consciousness is the lynchpin of psychological and existential health. Because Freud does not explicitly consider the character of self-consciousness—the "relation of oneself to oneself"—he ironically left the introspective subject uncharacterized. Although he admits that self-consciousness is an "accomplishment" of sorts (Tugendhat 1986, 127), Freud dismissed the need to probe the nature of consciousness, took it as given, and thus assumed its immediacy—and reality (Freud 1933, 70). However, if psychoanalysis is the science of the unconscious mind, what is consciousness that would *know* it? Freud, at best, was agnostic and assumed a skeletal notion of the self-aware, intelligent subject. In that choice, he uncritically drew upon a philosophical tradition that had employed the reflexivity of a subject examining its intimate other—a split *I* regarding its own selfhood. Simply put, Freud adopted the same introspective predication of the Cartesian ego, and we have reviewed in several contexts the problematic status of such inquiry.

Freud skirted the identity question by using the neutral, *das Ich* instead of *ego*. That decision is fraught with controversy (Tauber 2023). The English *Standard Edition* of Freud's works introduced translations that have purportedly altered basic understanding of psychoanalytic theory. Most prominent among the disputed meanings concerns the construal of Freud's use of *das Ich*—"the I." Some have maintained that translating "the I" as "the ego" introduces a semantic distortion with a host of issues embedding ambiguities in discerning Freud's intent and the development of his thought (Wilson 1987; Gilman 1991; Kobrin 1993; Hawkins 2018). Critics hold, noting Freud's meticulous use of language, that his word choice of *das Ich* is deliberate. He might have used *ego*, inasmuch as it was introduced in the mid-nineteenth century in psychology and was explicitly used in the literature on hysteria before publication of *Interpretation of Dreams* in 1900 (Clarke 1894, 130).[15] However, from his earliest clinical writings to his last summary statements, Freud conspicuously omits *ego* or *Selbst* (self) to designate the subject. Freud used *Selbst* only once in his writings (fourth paragraph of *Civilization and Its Discontents* [1930].) He freely uses *das Ich* as opposed to *Selbst*, but the Freudian *das Ich* does not equate with "the self," although some commentators assume that an implicit understanding suffices (e.g., Dilman 1984, 106; McIntosh 1986).[16] Moreover, when *self* occasionally appears in the English *Standard Edition*, it is misappropriated. Indeed, selfhood considered in any formal sense escaped Freud's explicit interest.

Without defining the ego as some natural entity, Freud accepts that the mind integrates disparate forms of human consciousness as a fundamental condition of coherent human cognition. This is basically a transcendental depiction, one restricted to portraying the conditions for cognition. By dispensing with "a thinking thing" (an entity), he was satisfied with a structure for the "coordinated organization of mental processes" (Freud 1923a, 17; see Longuenesse 2017). In that formulation, Freud sought no further delineation of *das Ich* and left *me* in the I's radical subjectivity of self-consciousness. Indeed, the subjective ego never found its conceptual traction in his oeuvre, and perhaps that is why James Strachey (the editor of the English *Standard Edition* of Freud's works) accepted a vocabulary that would support a scientific orientation articulated with a specialized terminology.

Comment

Freud did not critically evaluate self-reflection as a reliable means to his ends. As for his interpretive method, he accepted the standing of reason, and regarding the "text" to be interpreted, he relied on the analysand's memory (albeit screened, repressed, and thus contorted), at least to the extent that it offered the basis for analysis.[17] For Freud, at least, remembrance *as given*—whether "true" or not—was sufficient for his purposes. And, in bypassing self-consciousness as a warrant of interest, he abdicated efforts to seriously examine the modes of self-identification and self-reflection that characterize the analysand's *das Ich*, or sense of self. This is an ironic move. After all, the analysand's subjectivity is the substrate for the work of psychoanalysis, but only in the aftermath of orthodox Freudianism did ego and self-psychologies directly address *me* as the object of clinical intervention.[18]

In Freud's mature thought, *das Ich* is characterized not by a sense of self, but as a locus of three functions: (1) a coherent organization of mental processes; (2) an assembly of defenses that mediate the competing demands of unconscious desire and social reality; and (3) the construction of multiple identifications (Freud 1923a).[19] This is a structural-functional psychological model that eschews, in its theoretical description, what may be captured as the sense of *me*. Simply put, Freud's focus on the agency of the unconscious (the drives, primary processes) left the self-conscious subject in abeyance. Moreover, because the analysand carries only a phenomenological identity, unencumbered by implicit notions about personal identity, the schematized *ego* is a designation of a technical terminology with specific categorical meanings.

The basic schism of agency embedded in Freud's theory already appears clearly in *Interpretation of Dreams* (1900), where the psychic processes he described are "devoid of a subject; they simply operate within the subject," thus leaving an unaccounted gap between *das Ich* and the unconscious domain (Moran 1993, 48–50). In his later writings, best developed in *The Ego and Id* (1923a), Freud blurs the boundaries between the conscious and unconscious domains by placing *das Ich* straddling the boundaries and engaged in a repressed/repressing dynamic. And with *Civilization and Its Discontents* (1930), Freud makes one last stab at finding the missing connections between the conscious subject and the agency of the unconscious:

> Normally, there is nothing of which we are more certain than the feeling of our self [*Selbst!*], of our own ego [*das Ich*]. This ego [*das Ich*] appears to us as something autonomous and unitary, marked off distinctly from everything else. That such an appearance is deceptive, and that on the contrary the ego [*das Ich*] is continued inwards, without any sharp delimitation, into an unconscious mental entity which we designate as the id [*Es*] and for which it serves as a kind of façade—this was a discovery first made by psycho-analytic research, which should still have much more to tell us about the relation of the ego [*das Ich*] to the id [*Es*].
> (Freud 1930, 65–6)

This passage reveals Freud's own appreciation of the split subject: The first two sentences assert the reality and immediacy of the sense of one's own self, one's intimate subjectivity. He then shifts to objectifying this *I* in asserting the relationship of this conscious subjectivity with its unconscious components. Note that *das Ich* is used in both discourses—subjective and objective—and thus Freud embeds two meanings in the same terminology. When the analysand lays upon the couch, the subjective *me* becomes an object of analysis, an "ego" defined by psychoanalytic theory. A distinguishing terminology would make these two points of view explicit and thereby clarify the character of the subject. Indeed, the duality points to a larger philosophical conundrum opened for inspection.

Despite confident assertions, Freud's program operates in ambiguity: given that the self-conscious, rational ego functions autonomously, what grounds that function, and by what authority does Reason achieve its adjudicating role? *What* is this ego, this agent, this me, she, or he? And more to the point, the philosophical character of Reason and its active personification were also left nebulous, and possibly incoherent, throughout Freud's various characterizations (dating from the early 1890s to the topographical definition described in *The Ego and the Id* [1923a]). Simply put, the ego (the *Standard Edition* translation of *das Ich*) swings between the Cartesian indubitable self and the Kantian noumenon, fundamentally unknowable given its complex conscious/unconscious structure (Laplanche and Pontalis 1973, 130–43). So, again, what is this rational faculty enlisted into the deliberations of consciousness? These questions are, of course, central to a critical assessment of psychoanalysis, but Freud himself offered little guidance, largely because this issue eclipsed his interests. In short, he took reason as a given, and just as a carpenter uses a hammer, so Freud applied an interpretive rationality to reveal the psyche.

As noted, in Freud's mature writings, the ego became a complex composite of conscious and unconscious domains, with the latter in dynamic intercourse with the id and superego. The ego as part of the mental triad increasingly attracted his attention as he pondered the mystery of an introspective faculty surveying and judging other domains of the mind. He explained this ability in almost an offhand gesture in his 1933 lecture, "The Dissection of the Psychical Personality":

> We wish to make the ego the matter of our enquiry, our very own ego. But is that possible? After all, the ego is in its very essence a subject; how can it be made into an object? Well, there is no doubt that it can be. The ego can take itself as an object, can treat itself like other objects, can observe itself, criticize itself, and do Heaven knows what with itself.
>
> (Freud 1933, 58)

Freud might have then further developed this presumption, but he did not, and instead he observes how consciousness becomes self-consciousness:

> In this, one part of the ego is splitting itself over against the rest. So the ego can be split; it splits itself during a number of its functions—temporarily at least. Its parts can come together again afterwards. That is not exactly a novelty, though it may be putting an unusual emphasis on what is generally known.
>
> (Freud 1933)

Agreed, and in this wave of the hand, Freud skirts the philosophical status of consciousness and the hermeneutics upon which his entire enterprise rests.

Although Freud entrusted the analysand's rationality (albeit weak and fallible) to serve as a bulwark against unconscious forces, he also adamantly rejected the equation of mind with consciousness. He thus would dislodge "the arrogance of consciousness" and asserted how "it is essential to abandon the overvaluation of the property of being conscious before it becomes possible to form any correct view of the origin of what is mental" (Freud 1910, 39). In his five lectures at Clark University, Freud highlighted the mind/consciousness distinction, which, superficially at least, resonated with James's demotion of consciousness, albeit for radically different reasons. If *that* was the topic of their discussion on their walk to the train, then they would have quickly discovered how the basis of their respective conclusions drastically differed. For Freud, at the level of discourse where psychic data emerges and analysis begins, the standing of consciousness is unsteady in terms of the veracity of its conjured memory, the meaning of its associations, and the rational conclusions of its explanations. After all, given the limits of the knowing conscious subject, analysis lacks a firm epistemological foundation and, correspondingly, no "gold standard" of judgment. Accordingly, psychoanalysis is interpretation all the way down and thus open to severe criticism as a scientific enterprise. In this latter context, much is at stake, for if autonomy has been so severely compromised, how can *I* function with the limited authority Freud assigns *me*? Here, an unguarded theoretical flank has been exposed. Indeed, this assault on free will and self-knowledge became a critical factor in the ego's requiem during the postmodern appraisal of the subject (Tauber 2013a).

And so we again arrive at the conundrum of representationalism. When Freud presents the realization of a wish as something divorced from some distinct social reality, and the ego becomes the agent that creates and presents those series of representations that would mediate the wish, it becomes a "generator" of the endless reproduction of those representations to address unfulfilled desire, and the "ego must now be sought in the forest of signs and illusions" (Henry 1993, 303). Given our previous discussion, suffice to note here that if this is the residual basis of selfhood, a function that translates a deeper psyche through representations, then Freud justly leaves the issue, for he has only assumed the evidentiary basis of his representational construct and left unexamined the rationality in which the ego discerns its own experience.

Moreover, Freud abdicated a coherent philosophy of personal identity and the ethical structure upon which it might rest (Tauber 2010, chapter 6). Yes, Freud held to the ego's authority to mediate a moral position, but not one necessarily consistent with his psychological depiction of psychic dynamics. To internalize social mores and strictures within the superego hardly suffices to designate greater agency as generally understood. For him, the unconscious dominates the psychic economy, and the ego is depicted as a jockey atop a blinkered horse (1923a, 25; see note #12). The rider, astride his unconscious Other, may think he directs it, but that control is largely illusory. Watching the ongoing dynamic of horse and rider, we may well ask, who is the Subject and who is the Other, for the unconscious constitutes the psyche's center, and the relationship between consciousness, with its armory of rationality, resides in both a conceptual and psychological no-man's-land.

Within psychoanalytic theory, *"Who is the subject?"* remains an outstanding question (e.g., Borch-Jacobsen 1988; Lacan 1991; Ogden 1992; Moran 1993; Cavell 2006). *Das Ich* skirts the issue. Like Kant before him, Freud sought only to define the conditions from which the subject took form in actions and behavior (Longuenesse 2017), for he was not interested in issues framing personal identity or modeling conscious agency. As a psychologist focused on unconscious processes, the philosophical questions underlying conceptions of the self-aware subject were thereby eclipsed by other theoretical concerns. Indeed, the ego of Descartes's *Ego Cogito Cogitatum* is nowhere to be found in Freud's theory. He makes no inquiry

> about the existential and thinking subject . . . the question of the *I think, I am.* The *Cogito* does not and cannot figure in a topographic and economic theory of systems or agencies; it cannot possibly be objectified in a psychical locality or a role; it denotes something altogether different from what could be spelled out in a theory of instincts and their vicissitudes. Hence it is the very factor that escapes analytic conceptualization.
> (Ricoeur 1970, 420)

Here, at the nexus of philosophical questions about the self-conscious ego, Freud employs *das Ich*, a nomenclature that makes no further *philosophical* claims about identity beyond standing for the analysand's own grossly configured identity, subjectivity, and intellectual discernments. Freud remained satisfied with the voice of *the I*, whose associations, dreams, and parapraxis offered an interpretive "royal road" to the unconscious (Freud 1900, 608).

In sum, Freud does not explicitly consider the character of self-consciousness—the "relation of oneself to oneself"—that serves as the lynchpin of his entire enterprise. Nor did he critically consider the status of reason in its instrumental use despite its problematic status. For Freud, further discernment apparently was not necessary for his purposes, and he left the knowing ego (ironically) uncharacterized (Freud 1933, 70). Indeed, he never gave "the self" a passing nod. *Das Ich* in the Freudian context has a specific *psychological* structural and economic character; its functions are specified. That is not to deny that a *latent* conception of the self—construed as a sense of "me," i.e., an integrated purposeful person—ultimately orders the narrative story that emerges in analysis (Dilman 1984, 106). Even though such an *implicit* identity never appears as a governing status in Freud's writings, the analysand does adopt some version of self-identification along these lines. Yet from a formal point of view, the analysand is not construed beyond the ordinary pronominal agent.

So again, we might fairly ask, *who* is this agent of inquiry? Freud offers a deafening silence: *Ich* is simply *I* or *me*, a self-reflexive, self-conscious, interpreting *person*. This is a phenomenological identity; the self as some essential or totalizing entity may be assumed, even implicit, but *Selbst* (self) simply vanishes upon any attempt to define such an entity. Yet, Mr. Analysand lays on the couch, pays his bill, and asserts his "I-ness" freely. On this pragmatic view, the "I" serves as a useful point of reference, but no more. With only an implicit understanding of agency (Dilman 1984, 106), Freud invoked the authority of individuals to probe their inner-emotion and thought, and, as a result of this introspection, a new interpretation of that experience conferred the possibility of a therapeutic outcome and per-haps even a revised sense of personal history and identity through a pro-cess that putatively generates options and choices arising from insight and reconstruction.

Freud was undoubtedly correct in specifying that psychoanalysis is about elucidating "mental organization," for his *scientific* interest focused on dis-secting the mind and discerning its functions. And with that motivation, the subject *qua* the subjective becomes a secondary matter. Of course, *Dr. Freud*, the physician, was oriented by his patient's suffering and an implicit sense of I-ness the analysand experiences. As discussed, the feelings of the analysand fall into the clinical category of transference, residing beyond the *analytics* of the consultation. Here, humanistic elements must come into play. However, *Prof. Freud*, the scientist, developed his theory without con-founding issues about consciousness and accompanying subjective states. So the terminology debate is more than a semantic squabble, for it exposes the tension between two different frames of reference—Freud's scientific interests and the subjectivity of his patient. For Freud's interpretive method, the subjective becomes a tool to dissect the psyche, a portal into the depths of the unconscious. The subjective "surface" would be pierced by an analy-sis to reveal unrecognized feelings, self-awareness, and conflict. *Das Ich* is thus objectified; but then, where am *I*?

Ludwig Binswanger, and Freud's own daughter, Anna, were among those early analysts who shifted the psychoanalytic target from the unconscious to other foci, i.e., "ego psychology" and "object relations," which then fanned out into myriad "person" centered orientations (Tauber 2010, 268–70; Schneider and Krug 2017). That general movement reflects profound cultural undercurrents that lie well beyond this study, but it seems reasonable to infer that a fundamental shift to the "person" reflected a de-emphasis on the scientific mission with a replaced new-found humanist focus on *me* (further discussed in the Conclusion).

Freud's scientism was hardly unorthodox in the context of the excitement about the birth of academic psychology. Indeed, his intellectual affinities reflect the philosophical assumptions and commitments he had made in the context of joining the new sciences of the mind. The ramifications of his seminal revision of Western notions of personal identity, framed by a deep skepticism about self-knowledge, can hardly be overstated. However, the success of psychoanalysis is not based on its scientific standing (Grünbaum 1984; Eysenck 1985; Webster 1995; Macmillan 1997; Cioffi 1998; Crews 2017). Eschewing discussion of the benefits derived from its practice, the *science* Freud invented proved fallible due to philosophical weaknesses inherent in the assumptions that a self-divided ego can faithfully scrutinize itself with objective tools adopted from physics. That Freud might have held a more circumspect view of his methods required a heightened self-critical attitude he did not possess. Indeed, such scrutiny would have undermined his project. In contrast, James suffered no such illusions and instead embraced a humanism centered on experience that employed a plurality of methods which enabled him to present a psychology where subjectivity resided *sui generis*. These differences are clearly projected in their respective depictions of moral agency, as discussed in the next chapter.

Notes

1 The autonomous (even insular) concept of selfhood had been devised during the early modern period as political philosophers, most notably Locke, endeavored to define new political identities, and philosophers seeking to establish the scientific basis of objectivity required an agent who could stand back out of the world and observe it. Indeed, Locke extended Descartes's construction for a full-fledged philosophy of the self as a neutral, rational, independent "knowing agent." That description in turn derived from an ideal of objectified science. Such a detached witness might study nature dispassionately and thereby obtain scientific truth. This atomistic (or core) self was part of the early modern scientific theory, which held that objectivity required separation of the knowing agent from the world he inspected. Indeed, the Lockean observer assumes the power to view the world neutrally, and thereby distance the mind "from all the particular features which are objects of potential change" (C. Taylor 1989, 171; Thiel 2011).

2 When *I* am reduced to a thing, *me* is transformed into something else, an inauthentic self, when *me* becomes an *it*. "Inauthenticity" (what Sartre calls *mauvaise foie* or "bad faith") in the Kierkegaardian tradition refers to the assumption of a false identity that subverts one's freedom. By identifying and resisting external identifications (incumbent expectations), the existentialist recognizes counterfeit identity and countermands it by asserting independence of choice and action. The more skeptical view (e.g., Freud and Foucault) contends that the "'liturgy of inwardness' is founded on the flawed idea of a self-transparent individual who is capable of choosing herself" (Schacht 1970; Adorno 1973, 70; quoted by Varga and Guignon 2017).

3 Hume was concerned only with what might be understood about the mind *empirically* and thus "concerned not with the mind's real nature but only with its introspectively accessible features" (Thiel 2011, 421). Hume does not deny the existence of a persisting self beyond the perceptions, nor the inner sense of *me*, just the empirical basis for such a sentiment, which leaves the issue of personal identity's coherence unsettled (Thiel 2011, 383–430).

4 The following discussion offers an overview framed by the dualist thematic concerns of this study that may be usefully supplemented by Myers 1986, 348–62; Bordogna 2007; Inukai 2012; Leary 2018; Magri 2022; Rovane 2022.

5 James admits that "between what a man calls *me* and what he simply calls *mine* . . . is difficult to draw" (1983, 279). Nevertheless, instead of dwelling on this irascible issue, he discusses the modalities of selfhood as: (1) the material (the body); (2) the social, the relational basis of identity; and (3) the spiritual, the inner subjective being, psychic dispositions. After summarizing those well-rehearsed formulations, he avoids the terms of traditional philosophical discourse and works his way into selfhood with firsthand principles that draw from the common experience of his readers (1983, 279–352). In the process, he dispensed with his classical predecessors.

6 As discussed later in this chapter, Freud essentially abdicated any interest in characterizing consciousness and, ironically, the ego as well. Yet, in a sense, one might construe psychoanalysis as a method of discerning intention, unconscious, and the a-rational, so using a phenomenological framework, the psychodynamics depicted in the Freudian universe may be configured as following integrative intentional behaviors, now organized to fulfill fantasy and desire. I have discussed in detail the undeclared influence of Brentano on Freud's intellectual development (Tauber 2010, 6, 29–30, 40–53). Such a parallel might profitably be followed to illuminate the underlying conceptual structure of psychoanalysis within the same general framework James adopted (Merleau-Ponty 1982–83; Nissim-Sabat 1986; D'Agostino, Mancini, and Monti 2019).

7 As Sartre writes (reiterating the split identity construction already discussed [Chiesa 2007; Neill 2011]):

> it must be remembered that all writers who have described the Cogito have dealt with it as a reflexive operation . . . a consciousness which takes consciousness as an object . . . . But the fact remains that we are in the presence of two consciousnesses, one of which is conscious *of* the other . . . Thus the consciousness which says I *think* is precisely not the consciousness which thinks.
>
> (Sartre 1957, 44–5, emphasis in original)

8 Most prominently, Heidegger proposed Dasein, while Wittgenstein and many others critiqued fundamental notions of subjectivity, agency, and the self based on self-knowledge, introspection, and self-consciousness as qualified knowledge (Heidegger 1962; Wittgenstein 1960, 66; 1979, 80e; Jopling 2000, 13; reviewed in Tauber 2013a).

9 James goes on to observe that

> the word "I," then, is primarily a noun of position, just like "this" and "here." Activities attached to "this" position have prerogative emphasis, and, if activities have feelings, must be felt in a peculiar way. The word "my" designates the kind of emphasis. I see no inconsistency whatever in defending, on the one hand, "my" activities as unique and opposed to those of outer nature, and, on the other hand, in affirming, after introspection, that they consist in movements in the head. The "my" of them is the emphasis, the feeling of perspective-interest in which they are dyed.
>
> (James 1987h, 803)

10 Dewey argued that James had not gone far enough, and that psychology was still plagued by the dualism James had discarded (Dewey 1940).

11 The status of "*the Unconscious*" (a separate entity) and how it may function in Freudian depictions underwent modification. That the "unconscious" may be an adjective or a noun has long been the subject of philosophical discussion, and commentators have noted the significant shift in *The Interpretation of Dreams* (1900), when the unconscious first appears as a "system" (MacIntyre 1958). During the meta-psychology phase of theorizing, Freud elaborates the description to include "topographic, economic, and dynamic" aspects, and in *The Ego and the Id* another shift occurs, where the unconscious overflows its original boundaries to include parts of the ego, and thus the dichotomy is compromised (Laplanche and Pontalis 1973, 127–30, 449–53). So, the structural model's last iteration allowed the ego to possess both conscious and unconscious characteristics: perception and motor control are conscious, while dream censorship and repression were placed in the unconscious portions of the ego (Freud 1923a, 24). Thus, the Cartesian divide, where the faculty of reason and self-consciousness—*me*—is set in an autonomous realm against the other, das Es, could not be sustained.

12 Acknowledging the limits of self-consciousness, the inability to "reason" with the unconscious, and the creation of psychic reality from the throes of unrequited desire, Freud portrayed the human subject much as Plato had in the *Phaedrus* (246a–254e)—like a charioteer holding in check two steeds, each vying to go his own way. Whereas Plato had divided the soul into three characters, two horses and a charioteer, to control their opposing natures, Freud wrote:

> In its relation to the id it is like a man on horseback, who has to hold in check the superior strength of the horse: with the difference that the rider tries to do so with his own strength while the ego uses borrowed forces. The analogy may be carried a little further. Often a rider if he is not to be parted from his horse, is obliged to guide it where it wants to go; so the same way the ego is in the habit of transforming the id's will into action as if it were its own. The ego represents what may be called reason and common sense, in contrast to

the id, which contains passions. All this falls in line with the popular distinction which we are all familiar with.

(Freud 1923a, 25).

13 Moran (1993) makes the same point by what she calls "structuring," in which structure and agency form an interdependent recursive process.

14 Yes, perhaps as a source of psychic dynamics, but human life is configured by the complexity of how unconscious desire finds expression amid the exercise of defenses and repression required for the psychic house to remain in order. Perhaps this myopia accounts for Freud's neglect of the ego and its complexities, a topic left for his heirs (Tauber 2010, 268–70; Schneider and Krug 2017).

15 According to the *Oxford English Dictionary* ("Ego"), the use of *ego* in English psychology appeared by 1830: "In every act of consciousness we distinguish a self or ego" (*Edinburgh Review* 50:200, 1829; for general overview, see R. Smith 1997b).

16 Such assumed confidence takes little account of the semantic evolution of *Selbst* and *das Ich* in the German philosophical tradition, a literature Freud knew quite well (Tauber 2010). While Fichte based his entire philosophy on *das Ich*, with Hegel, *Selbst* makes its formal entry into the German canon. And with Nietzsche, *das Ich* "has become a fable, a fiction, a play on words" (Nietzsche 2005, 178). Of the vast commentary on this topic see Ameriks and Sturma (1995); Klemm and Zoller (1997); Beiser (2002); Pinkard (2002).

17 The disputes centering on the interpretation of retrieved memory date from the earliest presentation of psychoanalysis and renewed in the 1990s during the "memory wars," when the métier of psychoanalysis again become the focus of controversy (Crews 1995, 2017; Loftus and Ketchum 1994; Shaw 2017).

18 While early post-Freudians introduced ego psychology, only with Heinz Kohut's object relations theory in the 1970s was an explicit "psychology of the self" expounded. Although Kohut failed to provide a definition of the self that sat at the center of his theory (Kohut 1977, 310–11), the ordinary meanings of *ego* and *self* became operative in the psychoanalytic literature as analysts turned to the broad concerns of development and adaptation of the individual. And here we find the tension that lies at the base of the *das Ich*/ego controversy: Despite Freud skirting the psychology of what came to be called "the ego," his followers could not relinquish the search for a latent conception of one's selfhood that *they* thought lies at the base of his theory. Note that, in 1900, the year Freud published *Interpretation of Dreams*, Mary Calkins had written a paper that would serve as the Ur-text of what she called, "self psychology" (Calkins 1930). The article defended a "personalist psychology" as opposed to "atomistic psychology" that "treat contents-of-consciousness as such . . . without reference to any self" (Calkins 1900, 490).

19 I am indebted to Béatrice Longuenesse for noting the distinctive difference of *das Ich* as a "metapsychological" concept and the emphasis I place on the subjectivity of the *I* (private correspondence; see Longuenesse 2017). In regard to the various uses of *das Ich* Freud employs, she further notes that Freud left unresolved how the various notions of *das Ich* relate to one another—i.e., are these three different concepts, or are they three different functions of one and the same structure?

Chapter 6

On agency

Although the major conceptual differences separating our protagonists have been highlighted, at a deeper level they shared a humane ground in which each sought ways of dealing with the trials of the modernist subject, a construct that later would suffer debilitating postmodern attacks. In several respects, they fought a rear-guard action in defense of the self-assertive individual. Discerning their positions, conflicted yet closely aligned in a larger cause, illumines the identity conundrum of our own age, in which moral agency has seemingly lost its traditional footing and uncertainty has raised its hoary head (Tauber 2022, 293ff.).

Moral refers to the entire panoply of human life existing within a stratification of values. Actions, choices, relationships, and self-understanding fall upon the coordinates of importance, worthiness, costs, and consequences. And *value* is the métier of the moral universe. Charles Taylor asserts (in the form of a question) the key point: "Is there a sense in which the human agent is responsible for himself which is part of our very conception of the self?" (C. Taylor 1976, 281–2). Yes. Why? And here James and Freud converge, for

> the human subject is such that the question arises inescapably, which kind of being he is going to realize. He is not just de facto a certain kind of being, with certain desires, but it is somehow "up to" him what kind of being he is going to be . . . [W]e have the notion that human subjects are capable of evaluating what they are, and to the extent that they can shape themselves on this evaluation, are responsible for what they are in a way that other subjects of action and desire (higher animals for instance) cannot be said to be. It is this kind of evaluation/responsibility which many believe to be essential to our notion of the self.
>
> (C. Taylor 1976)

DOI: 10.4324/9781003565413-6

Taylor is building on a long line of existential thinkers (Kierkeg-aard, Nietzsche, Sartre, Camus), who have made human choice—the whom-I-want-to-be—the central characteristic of one's humanity. For them, the individual viewed through the moral prism is irreducible.

Whether one is free to act so is another question. However, the assertion that one *might* act by choice is the freedom that already sets the course of the road one must travel. And on that basis the key component of the identity issue appears: The challenge for one who makes choices, whether "free" or only imagined as independent, becomes the determinative element setting one's life-course. Simply, those selections establish one's identity. And the result of that line of reasoning resets the anchor of identity.

What one cares about and identifies with, what values are embraced, which choices are made, and which behaviors are enacted, define *me*. *Who-am-I?* embeds identity as an agent of responsibility, whose constancy in relationships and character traits determines expectations and reciprocity and thus constitute the practical aspects of interpersonal ethics. Here, moral inquiry is considered in the most general sense of identifying *who-I-am* in the context of the fallibilities of self-knowledge. It is in this context that the comparisons of our protagonists assume their most striking contrasts, not in terms of the priority of viewing their subjects humanely, but how their respective moral prisms differed and why.

Freud, the moralist

Freud introduced a profound insecurity about individual autonomy and self-knowledge. Instead of accepting the expectations of Reason's role to know the world, govern the social, and attain self-knowledge, a judicious circumspection has taken hold, where a cautious, aspirational certitude once resided. Repression, conflict, and anxiety displaced the "given" character of personal identity and moral autonomy. Worse, Freud asserted how little control one has over *whom-I-am-to be*. While he relied on the quiet voice of the intellect to counter the disruptive unconscious, he also undercut Reason's authority in his presentation of psychic life as fraught with fantasy, distortion, and emotional vulnerabilities. He argued that individuals function according to rules well beyond rational self-understanding. And given the autonomy and dominance of the unconscious, Freud's *das Ich*—limited by distorted rationality and restricted insight—has compromised (if not forfeited) its free will, the underlying tenet of the Enlightenment's conception of agency. Accordingly, the authority of self-knowledge and rational deliberation guiding moral decision-making that traditionally grounded ethics has been displaced.

Uncertainty reigns, for beyond the limits of articulation and the distortion of memory, the psychoanalytic report is plagued by persistent insecurity about self-knowledge (Tauber 2022, chapter 14). After all, if one's deepest motivations are not objectively discerned, then sovereign agency is always in doubt. And precisely because the psyche is immune to neutral appraisal, objective knowledge is limited, leaving the constraints of hermeneutics to do as best it can. Psychoanalysis is not science, but rather a way of understanding human subjectivity. One "knows" oneself better, in a particular way, but without the assurances of objectivity, the uncertainty generated by even this most intimate analysis has placed moral psychology in the spotlight. If I do not know *who-I-am*, then how can *I* be responsible? Practical demands impose moral imperatives, but the uncertainty is not thereby resolved. Here we find the heart of Freud's humanist conception of human potential and the full ethical dimension of psychoanalysis: despite the determinism in which humans are locked by unconscious drives, we must be free or, at least struggle against psychic demons, in which the evolution from patient to liberated soul constitutes both a psychological project and an ethical venture (Tauber 2010). At this juncture, a contrast with James's own views highlights the challenges raised by Freud's legacy.

In that enigmatic space separating the subject from her alien Other, Freud addressed the beguiling problem of how the ego, with its privileged yet flawed rationality, might understand and thus control psychic forces. He heavily relied on Reason in service to the ego to fulfill that mission and thereby act as a responsible moral agent, one who might discern psychic reality that would differentiate fantasy from reality and make choices adherent to the social order (Tauber 2009c, 2010, 2025). As already discussed, a tension exists within Freudian theory: psychoanalysis valorizes the ego's rationality and autonomy, despite all the evidence Freud himself marshals against such an understanding (Freud 1927a). Indeed, for him, while insight might ostensibly lead to human choice, humans lack free will and ultimately are subject to the determinism evident in nature. He consistently followed the scientific mandate of seeking natural causes, and in this respect, discounting his maligned efforts, he must be credited with at least pursuing that agenda to its logical conclusion. By accepting the material metaphysics of physics and chemistry, Freud's theories directly followed those philosophical commitments. After all, as animals, humans are fundamentally part of the natural world and thus subject to natural law (Sulloway 1979). And from his point of view, that law, applicable to all that is human—"all too human"—is deterministic.

Freud was pushing against the melioristic sentiments of liberal democracy, as he repeatedly admonished any resistance to accepting the reality of psychic determinism (Tauber 2012b). Indeed, that claim lay at the very foundations of psychoanalysis: "You nourish the illusion of there being such a thing as psychical freedom, and you will not give it up. I am sorry to say I disagree with you categorically over this" (Freud 1933, 49). Obviously, he did not advocate a simple mechanical linearity, but he nevertheless held to the basic principle of psychic determinism while never losing sight of the counterpoise of freedom.[1]

The exercise of freedom, even severely limited, represents the critical inflection of the psychoanalytic project, first in terms of suspending its naturalism and deterministic metaphysics, and then, reflecting that switch, moving from an epistemological method to describing an ethical procedure. Through insight and reason, humans must attempt to exercise choice and act ethically in the face of natural, deterministic psychic forces organized to fulfill fantasy and desire. This psychic calculus leaves an unresolved paradox: humans are determined, yet they must exercise freedom of choice to enact their moral agency. Indeed, psychoanalysis was designed to liberate the individual from the tyranny of her emotional trauma and misalignments by shifting the psychic oscillations towards free will. As Freud repeatedly observed, psychoanalysis *requires* the "illusion" of freedom irrespective of contradicting the naturalist commitments. Despite the obstacles for emotional liberation from repression, the "talking therapy" provides a schema in which to undertake the search for self-knowledge. In the province of consciousness—where recognition, reflection, reason, and resolution all reside—choice has the potential of being exercised.

According to Kant, free will and natural cause are understood with different forms of Reason—the former he called "practical reason" and the latter "pure reason." Freud, like Kant, accepted that the moral and natural universes coexist according to their own laws, and their rationalities were not reconciled other than by admitting their respective authority. Putting aside philosophical consistency, moral decision-making is then exercised, but unlike Kant, Freud recognized the weakness of rationality; how rationalization may work as a defense mechanism; how illusion nurtures fantasy; how denial obscures psychic realities, and so on. He understood that emotivism lies at the base of moral actions, not logic. Not only is rationality often revealed as flawed, but to even believe that ethical actions are reducible to one's rationality ignores the complex array of social, existential, historical, and emotional factors that go into play in any reasoned decision. And the final complication of this calculus concerns the psychoanalytic basis of the moral psychology that governs the subject's sense of right and wrong. Freud assigned the "superego" the role of judgement that functions through unconscious dynamics to exert its own determinism to the complex interplay of id-derived desire pitted against internalized normative standards of the ego facing her reality principle (Freud 1923a; Laplanche and Pontalis 1973, 379–85, 435–8). So, the subject must struggle not only against unrealized fantasy, but also the power of emotional strictures imposed by parental and social authorities, another component of the maelstrom characterizing moral behavior in the Freudian universe.

Hume, long preceding Freud, argued that ethics are grounded in human need, emotion, and caprice that are rationalized into moral justifications (Hume 1978, 413), and reason can only help direct our choice (Lindley 1986, 30; Schroeder 2008). Furthermore, not everyone has to reason in the same way; consequently, individuals might arrive at divergent choices, each of which may be reasonable within their own frame of reference. Arguments based on austere logic do not necessarily coincide with a rationality fed by diverse mores and values. In other words, something more than *reason* is "rational" (Kahneman and Tversky 2000; Gilovich, Griffin, and Kahneman 2002; Hanna 2006; Tauber 2014). Admitting the foibles of Reason and relinquishing consistency, Freud still endorsed the exercise of reason as the sole resource to explicate emotional dysfunctions and thereby enable the individual to exercise choices freed of psychic determinants. And herein lies the central free will/determinism paradox at the heart of psychoanalysis. In short, the voice of reason is quiet, but it is all humans possess to assess themselves and assert ethical behavior. As Freud famously pronounced:

> The voice of the intellect is a soft one, but it does not rest till it has gained a hearing. Finally, after a countless succession of rebuffs, it succeeds. This is one of the few points on which one may be optimistic about the future of mankind, but it is in itself a point of no small importance. And from it one can derive yet other hopes.
>
> (Freud 1927a, 53)

So, despite the distrust of self-knowledge and its conceits, Freud rightfully claims the title (humbled) Defender of Reason, by insisting on the exercise of self-analysis and self-correction guided by reasoned interpretation. And irrespective of the success of achieving some idealized psychic balance as a result of such analysis, the exercise itself constitutes the basis of moral agency.

The bridge from natural causation to freedom of the will has had numerous explanations, but none truly elucidate this enigmatic passage. The judgments of seemingly endless commentary on this matter are not our concern other than to note that one need not endorse Freudianism in any of its particulars to accept its cardinal message: Exploring the deeper reaches of motivations and desires excavates one's own identity—by whatever means (Tauber 2013b). As strangers to ourselves, the *who-am-I?* question constitutes the initial step in moral cognizance (MacIntyre 2007). Once posed, the process of inquiry continues because self-reflection is, by its very nature, ceaseless. The Sisyphusian inquiry then becomes the basis of moral agency.

As discussed, Freud refrained from defining personal agency with explicit coordinates or foundations, yet psychoanalysis nevertheless serves *das Ich*, who (with guided interpretations) effectively introspects to exercise rational self-responsibility and thus assert moral authority. Despite postmodern dismissals, Freud's staunch adherence to this ethical venture remains salutary. He attempted to renew the humanist project, and despite the powerful critiques leveled against him, his efforts to assert personal responsibility remain an enduring contribution. As for the truth claims he made, well, that is another story. Nevertheless, Freud's principal message holds: Following his own pervasive pessimism, we must still employ a rationality whose weaknesses have been revealed in full embarrassment. As social, moral subjects, we have no other option than to relentlessly scrutinize our own motivations, then hope that rational analysis provides the basis of making ethical decisions, and finally that we follow our conclusions as best we can.

However, the psychoanalytic imbroglio lies at a deeper stratum than the authority of reason. Freud remained steadfastly reliant on fallible reason despite the obvious effects of biased judgment and rationalized emotion, because his larger agenda required a normative basis for moral choice. While his epistemology failed to establish a science of the mind based on his interpretive methods, his defense (viewed from the ethical perspective) originates with the underlying search for a way of saving psychoanalysis for its most profound mission, namely, self-knowledge in service to a therapy. By following a modernist (Kantian) ideal, the analysand invests the authority of reason to struggle against unbridled desire. In that battle, a new form of moral authority emerges. Although left bereft of self-determination, psychoanalysis (putatively) leads to a deepened and strengthened self-knowing despite its concluding contradiction that we are determined yet free. So, in the end, Freud appears as an ethicist whose profound influence in offering a new identity narrative remains his abiding contribution.

Concerning identity

As discussed in the preceding chapter, choosing to bypass elucidation of *the self*, Freud shrewdly protected his conception of the psyche. The self "existed" only when invoked by a third party (e.g., the philosopher referring to agency or "the knowing subject"). The interlocutor could be another or the inner voice of self-consciousness—it made no substantive difference. And, perhaps more saliently, in "real life" one lives in the world essentially unaware of such a conception as *selfhood*. Persons evidently *are* and simply *do*. One defines the self as an entity by a process of self-reflection that yields an objectified construct—a subject construing an object (albeit itself). Certainly, constructs are useful, but there is no homunculus, a core ego, an essence of some sort. Such a conception perhaps serves the autobiographies one tells to order emotional lives and to create useful coherence, which is, of course, no small task and certainly a worthy one for psychological health. However, the circumspective philosophical dissection leaves even the storytelling suspect. Taking various forms, such narratives characterize *me* or *I* as a projection of what seems self-justifying to oneself and explanatory to others. These tales are crucial for grounding behavior by establishing goals, conferring responsibility, and bestowing reasons for choices and actions. However, their consistency, comprehensiveness, and veracity are always tentative and never settled (Tauber 2022, 158–9, 294–7, 314–18). How does one accurately represent an inner state, an emotion, a memory? Obviously, we represent ourselves to ourselves, but capturing such subjectivity is only an approximation. After all, it is only a *re*-presentation with inescapable distortions and lacunae.

Yet a story is told—indeed, must be told. Out of the complexities and noise of the everyday and the chaos of the disruptive, one imposes sequences and linkages to build the contours of personhood. And then from that ordering, given the selection and partial recall, how is the exposition to be judged?

> The stories others tell about you and the stories you tell about yourself: which ones come closer to the truth? . . . But, actually, that is not the question on my mind. The true question is: In such stories—is there, as a matter of fact, a difference between true and false? . . . Is the soul a place of facts? Or are the alleged facts only the deceptive shadows of our stories?
>
> (Mercier 2008, 142)

A most reasonable question, for within the domain of the personal, truth assumes varying "valences." Indeed, we allow latitude for the subjective account, and so one can only claim best intentions to capture that which is now gone. In the end, although Freud sought to free the conscious *I* from the shackles of the unconscious, the question of identifying the true *me* can never be resolved, because it is not a question of *fact*. Here, Freud's seminal contribution to characterizing the postmodern subject appears in full relief: We are strangers to ourselves. But more, the entire attempt to discern our inner life as an objectification is futile. Identity (following Charles Taylor [1976] and Alasdair MacIntyre [2007]) is best understood in terms of moral choice, and enactment is key to Western notions of personal identity. And upon that platform, Freud and James stand together, although radically separated by their respective views of agency that must configure ethics and the means by which subjects act in their social universe.

Freud's suspicions about self-understanding and, correspondingly, personal identity effectively challenged the autonomous model he himself helped disassemble. From a reassessment of self-determination, postmodernists have directed their critiques of falsely imagined individuality. Instead of the sovereign subject described by Kant, they depict the self-knowing ego as conflicted, often self-deluded, fundamentally opaque, and directed by archaic drives and desires of which one is unaware and consequently cannot control. These forces may be intra-psychic (Freud); social, i.e., persons constituted within and by regimes, discourses, and power of which they have little knowledge or control (Foucault); or historically specified cultural ideals that masquerade as universal norms (Tauber 2022, 158–9, 295–7).

Postmodernists (more specifically, poststructuralists) highlighted the contingency of the self's construction, whose lack of a reference point precludes order or structure, features required for characterizing a *thing* (Tauber 2022, 295–6). Since no transcendental significance to limit meanings exist, they refer to the self's "indeterminacy"—a decentered subject, no longer an origin or a source, but rather the product of multiple historical, social, and psychological forces. From this perspective, no claims might be made regarding the natural state of cultural structures (e.g., language, kinship systems, social and economic hierarchies, sexual norms, religious beliefs) that would define the self. Complementing these views, a rich anthropological literature has revealed the idiosyncratic character of the prevailing notions of Western identity and the self-consciousness that characterizes it (e.g., Roland 1988; Morris 1994; Reiss 2002; Li 2024).

With such ambiguities, the status of the self effectively focuses the larger cultural and philosophical divisions that have placed identity politics at the center of postmodernity, a debate that draws from both the a-rationality stream fed by Freudianism and the potentialities originating in James's pluralism. Those lamenting the challenged, if not lost Enlightenment ego ideal are countered by those who claim that the indeterminacy of personal identity exchanges preconceived and restrictive notions for an expansive construct by breaking limiting identity categories and modes of thinking. So, while some see incoherence amid threatened self-knowledge, postmodernists celebrate the plasticity and promises of an "opened" identity (Deleuze and Guattari 1977). Whether viewed favorably or with alarm, each appraisal tracks back to Freud, who articulated (and bequeathed) the profound challenge of self-determination in the face of irresolvable uncertainty. And not surprisingly, contemporary theoreticians have taken note that the ego psychologies built upon the Freudian foundation must now be re-assessed in light of postmodern critiques (Barratt 1993; Elliot 1999; Fairfield, Layton, and Stack 2002; Civitarese, Katz, and Tubert-Oklander 2015; Elliott and Spezzano 2019).

On balance, despite dislodging the ego from its rational, self-knowing perch, Freud would not have found a comfortable home in the postmodern camp. That appraisal does not gainsay how his critique of reason and the limits of self-knowledge laid the groundwork for later postmodern a-rationalists. Yet, his commitment to rationality separates him from what followed. He was, in fact, a social philosopher, a cautious utopian thinker who ultimately embraced human freedom or choice, which, despite the force of posthumanist criticism and the shredding of its scientific conceits, remains at the core of his vision, one from which we continue to develop (Tauber 2012b, 2025).[2]

Comment

Although post-Freudian orthodox practice dwindled after its peak popularity in the 1950s, *hundreds* of distinctive psychotherapies ("talking cures"), most untethered from Freudian principles, are currently exercised, even some inspired by James (Beichman 2020; Kaag 2020; Yeung 2021).[3] That social fact states a simple conclusion: *analysis* yields insight—or at least, that is a widely held truism. More specifically, insight seems to have displaced the anxiety about determinism. At this juncture, the need to believe, what James preached as "the will to believe," brings the philosopher and psychoanalyst into closer alignment.

The very fact that analytic therapy is sought testifies to the need for clarification or even explanation placed within a narrative that one can endorse. Any attempt to objectify experience through some investigative process constitutes a therapeutic paradigm highly respected and practiced in contemporary society. In this regard, Freud's essential claim has prevailed. The psyche may be studied according to some objectifying criteria and thereby address human emotional imbalance through insight. At some point, if effective, truth of the investigation is assumed by *Jamesian* pragmatic criteria: it (putatively) works, because people report improved well-being (Zarbo et al. 2015). Despite the philosophical weaknesses detailed in previous chapters, (psycho)*analysis* has survived, albeit in diverse formats, some far-removed from the original theory and practice. And in terms of his standing, Freud is one of the most cited figures in history and among the most eminent psychologists of the twentieth century (Haggbloom et al. 2002).[4]

Freud holds this prominent position by straddling two modalities: the first, as a putative scientist who probed the dynamics of the mind; and second, as a moralist (Rieff 1959), whose inquiries were framed by the Western precept of "know thyself." The latter persona clearly prevails. Freud effectively evoked the underlying emotions of Westerners' psychic life, affections we *feel* but may not *know*.

> In the final analysis, in its transcendent constructions and its best phenomenological texts, Freudianism holds deep within it what our era most lacks. That is undoubtedly the reason—despite its theoretical uncertainties, contradictions, even absurdities—for its strange success. Psychoanalysis therefore does not belong to the body of the sciences of man to which it is now attached . . . It is rather, the antithesis of those sciences.
>
> (Henry 1993, 7)

On this view, Freud's project, masquerading under the positivist's allure, might best be appreciated as a powerful means by which a narrative, a coherent portrayal of one's life, assumes meaning. He followed the ancient Greek tragedians, who presented the drama of the human being on a mythic stage. His métier was "science," but the psychoanalytic "play" emerges from a creative amalgamation of fact and fancy; history and memory; knowledge and imagination, which in coordination Freud hoped would capture the key features of human nature in a mythological expression. Analysands tell a tragic story: destined to know their past and having lived the fate of their experience, they come, like Oedipus, to understand the true character and deeper meanings of that experience. Psychoanalysis thus endeavors to fulfill the tragic criteria of self-knowledge, accompanied by acknowledgement, acceptance, and then transformation.

On this view, self-appraisal leads to personal emancipation, not a final escape from one's fate (as determined by personality and past experiences), but in strengthening the sense of establishing a point of view for expressing *the* fundamental moral question, *who-am-I?* The insights of psychoanalysis are "true" in the ways myths are true, namely, as depictions of one's own self-image or, at least, its idealization. This is an ironic conclusion given the scientific objectivity Freud claimed for psychoanalysis and its further development promoted by his followers.[5] However (as discussed in previous chapters), such objectification cannot be *true* in the ways we judge claims about ordinary encounters or objective accounts of both everyday reality and the pictures offered by laboratory investigation.

In the pursuit of self-knowledge, Freud tapped into the wellspring of Western philosophy, the divine Delphic command—*gnothi seauton* ("Know thyself"), a dictum originating in philosophy's earliest Socratic stirrings.[6] What that means today differs from the expectations of the ancient Greeks, but across the millennia, the imperative of self-inquiry remains intact as an ethical dictate. It is in this second self-inquiring moral persona that Freud tapped into the ancient philosophical dictum of uncovering what is hidden (and perhaps) repressed. That becomes the key step in liberating oneself from alienation, from the estrangement of the stranger within. While Freud's "science of the mind" has suffered grievous insult, his mythical pursuit buried beneath those analytics has endured. Indeed, the power of that myth has had a dominate impact on contemporary notions of personal identity. And here Freud, the humanist, appears, one who employed a scientific ideal to promote a humane endeavor with a new dramatic form in which to configure human experience and agency.

The science-mythic partnership highlights the tensions that lie at the base of psychoanalysis. Freud struggled with fitting the objective mode of knowing within the broader therapeutic agenda he set himself, one that required a deeply *interpretive* account of human living. For him, science did not function solely as some kind of separate intellectual or technical activity to study the natural world, but rather was an instrument to help define human realities in the humane quest of self-knowledge. That humanism was based on acknowledging the primacy of the subjective. In a remarkable conversation in 1927 reported by Binswanger, Freud, unrestrained by the defensive scientism of his public persona, offered a forceful confirmation of this deepest understanding:

> I could scarcely believe my ears when I heard him say, "Yes, the spirit is everything," even though I was inclined to surmise that by 'spirit' he meant in this case something like intelligence. But then Freud continued: "Mankind has always known that it possesses spirit; I had to show it that there are also instincts." (Binswanger 1957, 81)

In other words, Freud's naturalism would not, could not, displace the primacy of the subjective *me*. His positivist gaze was but part of a bifocal vision that presented humans as primitively willed but more fundamentally constituted by "spirit," which, although left undefined, draws from the German metaphysical tradition of *Geist* – the essential core of human spiritual identity that is placed in opposition to the "alien" (natural, animal) *Trieb*. Those inner forces, albeit mine but, most emphatically, are not *me*. From this point of view, psychoanalysis was developed to better understand (even control) that *other* in defense of the soul. Drawing together these threads of his thought, Freud exemplifies the "natural philosopher" in the broadest and most noble tradition: to know nature; to define ourselves within nature; to control nature in order to direct human destiny. To ignore this humanist orientation (and commitment) is to distort Freud's larger moral mission (Tauber 2009c; 2010). And as we place James and Freud in juxtaposition, we find them joined in a common humanist agenda, albeit the means to achieve their shared vision radically differed.

Asserting the freedom of the will

Whether formalized in psychoanalysis or conducted *ad hoc*, deliberate self-reflection is the beginning of asserting personal responsibility constitutive to moral agency. And in this calculus, Freud dramatically set the stage of the modern conundrum: ethical freedom, deeply compromised, originates in self-knowledge, albeit flawed, incomplete, and confused by unconscious desire. Freud thus left the subject pressed between the imperative of freedom of the will to exercise moral choice and the deterministic psychic forces operating for their own self-fulfillment. As already discussed, he chided his reader that

> you nourish a deeply rooted faith in undetermined psychical events and in free will, but that is quite unscientific and must yield to the demand of a determinism whose rule extends over mental life. I beg you to respect it as a fact. . . . I am not opposing one faith with another. It can be proved.
>
> (Freud 1933, 106)

In the starkest terms, he embedded determinism in the foundations of his theory, which in turn limited the very freedom required for assuming individual responsibility and full moral agency (at least as understood in Kantian terms). Yet Freud held to the paradox with which he could not escape, the Spinozist conclusion that we are determined yet free. As already explained, that freedom resides in the power of recognizing our psychic predicaments and facing them forthrightly with the sole means of response, Reason. This vision is not readily mortgaged, much less forsaken. On this view, the lasting influence of Freud's work rests squarely on the meliorism derived from the attempt to achieve insight, explanation, and a new equilibrium. And that position James would have readily supported. However, their shared sentiments belie striking differences in their respective philosophies, and, more specifically, in how they viewed causation.

In the face of advocating psychological determinism, Freud was left with reconciling the naturalism he embraced with the exercise of free will required for moral deliberation and action. Extrapolating those laws of physics to the psyche was premature. He could have kept his naturalism, if he appreciated that the Newtonian metaphysics he had adapted distorted human experience and an alternate was available. Ironically, just as he published *Interpretation of Dreams* in 1900, Max Planck announced his epic discoveries of the quantum. Indeed, well before he died in 1939, Freud might have revised his physics to embrace tychism, *chance* and *spontaneity* as did James, who did so not on the basis of extrapolating from scientific knowledge, but rather through a philosophical examination. He intuited a universe of dynamic "processes" with uncertain probabilities as opposed to "things" interacting as billiard balls in physics. In such a universe, probabilities rules (Tauber 2022, 124–37).[7]

James asserted free will and did so by enjoining chance in his dynamic view of human choice and freedom. Whereas the Ancients thought of chance as reasonless accidents that insulted intelligence, harmony, and order, he countered with a re-conception. In the "Dilemma od Determinism," James observed,

> The sting of the word "chance" seems to lie in the assumption that . . . if anything happens by chance, it must needs be something of an intrinsically irrational and preposterous sort. Now chance means nothing of the kind. It is a purely negative and relative term, giving us no information about that of which it is predicated, except that it happens to be disconnected with something else not controlled, secured, or necessitated by other things in advance of its own actual presence.
>
> (James 1992h, 572)

In fact, for James, *chance* represents the open possibilities of "unconditional properties" and, more broadly, *chance* was another word for *freedom*— freedom of will, freedom of choice. While "chance begets order," that order, as exemplified by statistical mechanics of gases, is a depiction of the disorder and the chance interactions of myriad particles (Peirce 1992, 358).

James developed the notion of chance as the conduit to his central dogma, the "will to believe" (James 1992h), whose genealogy dates to an existential watershed, when he suffered severe depression upon graduating from medical school in 1869 (at age 28). As evidenced by letters and diaries, intransigent back pain led to a preoccupation with suicide.[8] It is in this context that James's famous decision to exercise free will was declared, based not on intellectual grounds but on what he later called a "passional" basis (James 1992h; see R. A. Putnam 2017, 351–3). He recovered, he said, only by exercising a "vigor of will" (Perry 1935, I:323). In February 1870, he recorded in his diary,

> Today I about touched bottom, and perceive plainly that I must face the choice with open eyes: shall I *frankly* throw the moral business overboard, as one unsuited to my innate aptitudes, or shall I follow it, and it alone, making everything else merely stuff for it? I will give the latter alternative a fair trial. Who knows but the moral interest may become developed. . . . Hitherto I have tried to fire myself with the moral interest, as an aid in the accomplishing of certain utilitarian ends.
>
> (quoted by Perry 1935, 1:322, emphasis in original)

James regarded his crisis as a *moral* one, and two months later he recorded a philosophical inflection, a resolution that affirmed his freedom of choice. Having read Charles Renouvier, James reported that

> I think that yesterday was a crisis in my life. I finished the first part of Renouvier's second *Essais* and see no reason why his definition of free will—"the sustaining of a thought *because I choose to* when I might have other thoughts"—need be the definition of an illusion. At any rate, I will assume for the present—until next year—that it is no illusion. My first act of free will shall be to believe in freewill. . . . Hitherto, when I have felt like taking a free initiative, like daring to act originally without carefully waiting for contemplation of the external world to determine all for me, Suicide seemed the most manly form to put my daring into; Now, I will go a step further with my will, not only act with it, but believe as well; believe in my individual reality and creative power. My belief to be sure can't be optimistic—but I will posit life (the real, the good) in the self governing resistance of the ego to the world . . .
>
> (quoted by Myers 1986, 388–9, emphasis in original)

And Renouvier's adage, "Properly speaking there is no certitude; all there is men who are certain" (quoted by Richardson 2006, 177), leads directly to our theme, for from that position,

> rather than see doubt and uncertainty as troublesome or negative, Renouvier, with James right behind, recognizes that what we call freedom in human affairs rests on and grows out of what in physics is called chance—that is, not determinism. Just as the possibility of there being such a thing as a chance occurrence is what we mean by the word "freedom," so doubt, instead of meaning a lamentable loss of certainty, meant for James, the positive possibility of certainty.
>
> (Richardson 2006, 177)

In this sense, from the limits of certainty, the boundaries of the uncertain may be derived. And in uncertainty, lies freedom.

The biographers all agree that the 1870 cathartic moment in which James overcame his depression framed his later philosophy.[9] At that point, he grounded himself in himself, in his own "will to believe" that legitimates the spiritual and all that lies outside scientific investigation. And following another tack, that same independence bestows the freedom of choice required for assuming responsibility that grounds moral agency. *Freedom* is not necessarily a spiritual leap à la Kierkegaard, but rather the dimension in which one fulfills the moral imperative of accepting responsibility for making choices. For James, this is an act of Will, not Reason, because the strictures of self-knowing leave, in principle, no lines of causation by which one can track with confidence the basis for making an ethical decision. Accordingly, ethical questions could be addressed only by making a decision and *then* fortifying that decision with persuasive, reasoned justification.

> The decision [comes] first and its reasons secondary. In ethics and metaphysics, as James conceived them, the issues are eternally debatable and can never be resolved either argumentatively or experimentally; it is by a decision, which then gathers reasons around itself, that we are motivated to choose one belief instead of another. When we understand that competing reasons are at a standoff, we realize that no reason activates a choice; our decision must be hoisted under its own strength. . . . According to the Jamesian perspective, arguments and theories in ethics and metaphysics serve personalities and their choices rather than vice versa.
>
> (Myers 1986, 391)[10]

Note that during his emotional crisis, James sought a philosophical solution, but he could not resolve competing opinions about the standing of free will versus determinism within those debates. Simply put, he resolved his depression by assertion of will, not argument.

This pivotal moment focused his attitude on the pessimism of being subject to deterministic forces beyond his control. Pessimism

> can be avoided, James thought, if one's moral interests are real rather than illusory; but they cannot be real if there is no free will, because there is no sense in holding that we ought to do what we cannot do.
>
> (Myers 1986, 46)

Accordingly, if a person could summon the requisite willpower, disability would be overcome. Years later, in a letter to his wife, James wrote,

> I have achieved a moral victory over my low spirits and tendency to complain. . . . I have actually by steady force of will kept it down and at last got it under for a while and mean to fight it out on that line for the rest of my life, for I see that is my particular mission in the world.
>
> (quoted by Myers 1986, 388)

In short, James regarded his predicament as a moral challenge for which he assumed responsibility and proclaimed the imperative of choice. Indeed, *choosing* freedom was an act of moral courage.

That James understood that the dilemma of free will pitted against determinism could not be analytically decided was a philosophical conclusion. Beyond exemplifying a cardinal feature of James's character, this episode illustrates James's attitude about philosophy, more specifically, analyticity. He adopted a more inclusive understanding of rationality than what the customary logic of analytics can offer, one that factors the emotions and everyday experience. On this view, the subjective and the objective reside on a continuum of different kinds of knowing (Nussbaum 2001; Tappolet 2016, 2022).[11] Moreover, emotional elements must be accounted to explain the origin, pursuit, and, finally, resolution of the philosophical questions posed. On this general view, James's engagement with philosophy becomes a story of his own trials and emotional responses refracted through a powerful intellect. As he himself admitted, James resolved his own depressions through an act of *will* to believe that in turn was based on his own self-reliance and moral rectitude, a choice that may be readily understood in terms of his moral psychology (Leary 2022; Madelrieux 2022; Gunnarsson 2022; Sutton 2023).

In sum, James *chose* free choice and a metaphysics of indeterminacy, not by argument—no syllogism sufficed to solve the issue—but by selecting what seemed right as a basis for his own ethics. For him, a moral universe without freedom of choice was incoherent and hopelessly illogical. This position was consistent with his psychological views, which, as detailed in previous chapters, highlighted pluralistic knowledge and ways of thinking. He held agnostic views on mental causation. and while (like Freud) he tracked complex human motivation to ill-defined instinctual behaviors, those pathways were overdetermined and thus largely undefinable. In this regard, a striking contrast with Freud appears.

The psychoanalyst sought to trace mental causation through a mechanically designed psychic apparatus, while James engaged in a descriptive psychology that made no attempt at establishing explanations of complex behavior. So, although James and Freud agreed that linking mental phenomena to brain states was impossible with methods available to them, Freud nevertheless still postulated mechanisms that might mimic such physiology. James did not and argued instead that consciousness and all its attendant functions were different aspects of experience (a view that has gained traction in contemporary biology [Mitchell 2023]). On this view, James had very different ambitions from those pursued by Freud, not just in terms of therapy but more broadly in terms of describing mental life. We have outlined their philosophical oppositions, which obviously have strong intellectual basis for their respective positions; but underlying their conflicting ideas about science, the character of the mind, and the metaphysical foundations grounding their divergent views, the prevailing influence of temperament still must be accounted and from there, an appraisal of how they each regarded philosophy is clarified.

Humanism redux

If James had written a critique of psychoanalysis, he would not have abided the conclusions Freud derived from his *scientific* appraisal of the mind. For James, to characterize subjectivity and its associated domains (ethics, spirituality, aesthetics) that are governed by values, meaning, and affects with the same forms of reason applied to objectifying nature conflates two ways of knowing. The distinction is crucial, and James would have indicted Freud for committing the "sin of scientism" in the search for a "new science of the mind." There could be no argument based on some disputed singular point, for they conflicted at the deepest foundations of their respective thought. Freud held an overriding philosophy that he believed would establish the very basis of reality, namely, a positivism affirming that "scientific work is the only road which can lead us to a knowledge of reality outside ourselves" (Freud 1927a, 31). James demurred. For him, a positivist depiction of the world is only one picture, but more to the point, it must contort phenomena to fit its mode of understanding. The underlying epistemological structure of predicate-structured knowing *requires* a representational epistemology to mediate between the knower and the world that she surveys. For some phenomena, the method is highly successful; for others, not.

These attitudes ramified into our protagonists' respective views of moral agency. While Freud placed moral sensibilities in the superego (another deterministic unconscious locale), James affirmed a diversity of options, the pluralism of means of choice and underlying belief systems, and the pragmatic enactment of individual responsibility as he himself promoted in both his public pronouncements and private musings.[12] These positions were (1) grounded in a metaphysics of indeterminacy that led to (2) the potentials offered in emergence and mental creativity, which in turn resulted in (3) the jettisoning of the implicit reductionism embedded in psychoanalytic theory. James's revised "principles of psychology" (i.e., the radical empiricism of 1897–1905) thus contradict all of Freud's characterizations of the mind and the determinism that accompanied the naturalism on which it was based. The radical empiricist was content to deal with experience alone, the subjectivity in which he entrusted his moral sensibilities. And the key James found to proceed along that pathway was philosophy, the very discipline Freud abhorred.

In psychoanalysis, uncertainty governs the most intimate sense of human being, but not in the ways James saw human potential and growth. Where James saw the vibrancy embedded in the indeterminant character of the mind's emergent functions, Freud saw uncertain self-knowledge as a deterrent to human self-fulfillment. By profoundly challenging individual autonomy and human authority, Freud argued that human actions have motivations alien to conscious intention. Instead of individual choice, the repression required for successful social interactions belittles self-determination. He thus maintained that we are strangers to ourselves and, in so doing, he left an abiding skepticism about human choice and the moral structure of human motivations.

James offered a strikingly different portrait of moral agency, one framed by a humanism that grappled with how ethics is placed within what Thomas Huxley called, "cosmic processes" (1894). The application of scientific knowledge for characterizing human nature was hotly debated, as the balanced relationship between science and humanist ideals had been upended by Herbert Spenser's advocacy for uncovering the "laws" of morality. Spenser based his social philosophy on evolutionary theory and extrapolated such derived naturalistic principles to support social Darwinism. That orientation was wildly popular by the 1880s, and the "universal solvent" of Darwinism has continued into our own era (e.g., Dennett 1996). Scientific explanation of various human beliefs and complex human behavior (e.g., morality, religion, and social organization) have been fitted into a modern consilience program (e.g., evolutionary psychology) from which judgments about human nature have been drawn (E. O. Wilson 1998; Dennett 1996; Joyce 2005; Hunter and Nedelisky 2018; Buss 2019; Wilkinson 2024).

Assuming a Jamesian position is not to gainsay the importance of furthering human knowledge, but to recognize that applications of such scientific knowledge are always value laden. His pluralism undergirds the legitimacy of different ways of thinking and, more specifically, placing in balance scientistic thinking within the context of other modes of interpretation and knowing. James's humanism prunes scientific constructs overextended beyond their epistemological limits and judges their social applications fully aware of ideological or politically motivated extrapolations (e.g., Tauber 2009a).[13] That awareness has led to citizen activism and informed public policy debates ranging from assessing global warming to the status of the fetus.

A second aspect of James's humanism is firmly set in the Romantic lament, namely, the loss of humane, personal elements at the expense of the scientific view.[14] Beyond technical mastery and exploitation of scientific gains, a humane component remains to absorb the evidence and place it within social realities and personal needs. What do facts mean in terms of all the dimensions of human industry, personal understanding, and existential standing? To portray a "disenchanted" universe as the inevitable product of scientific inquiry is misguided. This indictment, dropped at the doorstep of the laboratory, is better understood as part of the larger secularism that has taken hold in the postindustrial West, which is not to gainsay the explicative role of philosophy and its mission to formulate a response to what Heidegger called the "world picture" bestowed by science (Heidegger 1977a, 1977b; see Tauber 2009a, 30–1, 68–70, 182–4). And most intimately, viewing that inner domain of the personal requires a philosophy of the subjective that bridges the gap between objective knowledge and subjective feeling. In response to that challenge, Dewey, James's protégé, called for redirecting philosophy to its humane directives:

The problem of restoring integration and cooperation between man's beliefs about the world in which he lives and his beliefs about the values and purposes that should direct his conduct is the deepest problem of modern life. It is the problem of any philosophy that is not isolated from that life.

(Dewey 1984, 284)

Dewey, building upon James's platform, underscored the need for pursuing an integrative approach to the fragmentation of modern life and the displacement of the privileged *I* that had so dominated Romantic thinking (Tauber 2001, 195ff.). Dewey, like Husserl, wanted a philosophy to bridge subjective and objective ways of knowing (see Chapter 1, note #3). Pragmatists sought to envelop all experience, from esoteric frontline science to the full personal appreciation of a world so depicted. Such a project would draw from diverse cognitive and emotional faculties and harness them into some coherence. In short, an integrative description of the world and one's experience of it envelops science in its broadest humane context (Tauber 2001, 2009a, 182–4). That integration could occur only within a renewed humanism. James revitalized that mission and its further development.

James's challenge to positivism had an auspicious future. Dewey, and an entire group of twentieth-century philosophers (e.g., Heidegger, Husserl, Jean Paul Sartre, Herbert Marcuse, Jürgen Habermas) regarded positivism as a symptom of a malady, not of itself, but as an epiphenomenon of a deeper metaphysical crisis originating with the partition of the world between *self* and *other*. Their revolt, broadly understood, essentially sought ways to reestablish one's own constitutive place in the known world. The sciences, then, must be broadly construed as

part of disciplined moral knowledge so far as they enable us to understand the conditions and agencies through which man lives. . . . Moral science is not something with a separate province, for physical, biological and historic knowledge must be placed in a human context where it will illuminate and guide the activities of men.

(Dewey 2002, 296)

Accordingly, no firm demarcation between moral judgments and other kinds are possible, for "every and any act is within the scope of morals, being a candidate for possible judgment with respect to its better-or-worse quality" (Dewey 2002, 279). With that avowal, Dewey widened the scope of "morals" to value judgments writ large: "morals has to do with all activity into which alternative possibilities enter. For wherever they enter a difference between better and worse arises" (Dewey 2002, 278). He was following James's lead, who maintained that the values through which we know the world and frame our own experience are constitutive to the reality in which humans live. On that basis, James revamped *Truth*, the epistemological criterion that offers moral philosophy its basis of judgment. And when truth, based on experience, is understood in this context, all components of James's "non-systematic" philosophy finally fit together.

Natural realism

As already discussed, the basis of reason's autonomy rests on the metaphysical placement of the subject separate from the world. This Cartesian *cogito* orders experience and surveys nature, and itself, with the authority of a mind distinct from the object of its scrutiny, and it does so through representations of the world it encounters as an adaptation of a correspondence theory of truth (see Chapter 2; Chapter 3, note #6). As discussed in Chapter 1, the key weakness of the representational view of the mind is to account for how representations link the world to the knowing subject (Rorty 1979). How the gap between knower and the known—the gap representations must bridge—is regarded, which, in turn, becomes dependent on antecedent metaphysics: do representations, in fact, depict "the real," or serve only as a mediation entrapped in a hermeneutical reconstruction of reality? Crudely put, are representations good enough?

For Freud (and positivists more generally), representations are the métier of depicting reality, if not directly, at least with verisimilitude. Knowledge then follows a "correspondence theory of truth," in which what we perceive in some contexts by direct sensory perception and, in second-order scenarios through the processing of reliable representations to derive *facts*, offers "true" mirrored descriptions of the natural world. That epistemology underwrites scientific practice and as such was adopted by Freud. James, on the contrary, regarded truth as a

> relation, not of our ideas to non-human realities, but of conceptual parts of our experience to sensational parts. Those thoughts are true which guide us to *beneficial interaction* with sensible particulars as they occur, whether they copy these in advance or not.
>
> (James 1987b, 871, emphasis in original).

While critics insisted on the autonomy of truth and its rational (logical) basis, James argued for what he called an "ambulatory" account of "knowing as it [truth] exists concretely" (Bordogna 2008, 171–4). Accordingly, for him, truth was embedded in the experience of the knower and consequently lodged firmly in its use and thereby serving as the basis for belief. His critics would leave truth in its own independent domicile; how it was employed was another matter, altogether.

James was roundly criticized for his pragmatic definition of truth, and he went to great lengths in clarifying his position, which hinged on refuting the charges that he was ignoring or denying the reality of the natural world. In a letter to Dickinson S. Miller in 1907, James clearly asserted his effort to produce a metaphysics and epistemology close to the natural realism of ordinary experience in which reality is framed by human interest and the values inherent in any cognitive appraisal.

> I am a natural realist. The world *per se* may be likened to a cast of beans on a table. By themselves they spell nothing. An onlooker may group them as he likes. He may simply count them all and map them he may select groups and name these capriciously, or name them to suit certain extrinsic purposes of his. Whatever he does so long as he *takes account of them* his account, is neither false nor irrelevant. If neither, why not call it true? It *fits* the beans-*minus*-him, and expresses the *total* fact of beans-*plus*-him. Truth in this total sense is partially ambiguous, then. If he simply counts or maps, he obeys a subjective interest as much as if he traces figures. Let that stand for pure "intellectual" treatment of the beans, while grouping them variously stands for non-intellectual interests. All that . . . I contend for is that there is *no* "truth" without *some* interest and, that non-intellectual interests play a part as well as the intellectual ones. Whereupon we all are accused of denying the beans, or denying being in any way constrained by them! It's too silly!
>
> (James, letter to Dickinson S. Miller, 1907 quoted by
> Putnam and Putnam 1996, 14, emphasis in original)

James redefined truth in terms of everyday life and in the process unwound the philosophical tradition that "interposed certain types of private entities ('ideas' or 'impressions' or 'sense data') between the perceiver" and the public world, which then reconstructs what James called a "congeries of solipsisms" (Putnam and Putnam 1996)

James's pragmatic conception of truth (1909) builds from the basic precepts of radical empiricism (already detailed in Chapter 2):

> The postulate is that the only things that shall be debatable among philosophers shall be things definable in terms drawn from experience . . .
> In the prevalent idealism this agency is represented as the absolute

all-witness which "relates" things together by throwing "categories" over them like a net. The most peculiar and unique, perhaps, of all these categories is supposed to be the truth-relation, which connects parts of reality in pairs, making of one of them a knower, and of the other a thing known, yet which is itself contentless experientially, neither describable, explicable, nor reduceable to lower terms, and denotable only by uttering the name "truth."

The pragmatist view, on the contrary, of the truth-relation is that it has a definite content, and that everything in it is experienceable. Its whole nature can be told in positive terms. The "workableness" which ideas must have, in order to be true, means particular workings, physical or intellectual, actual or possible, which they may set up from next to next inside of concrete experience. Were this pragmatic contention admitted, one great point in the victory of radical empiricism would also be scored, for the relation between an object and the idea that truly knows it, is held by rationalists to be nothing of this describable sort, but to stand outside of all possible temporal experience; and on the relation, so interpreted, rationalism is wonted to make its last most obdurate rally.

(James 1987b, 826–7)

So, by asserting the primacy of experience, James places "reality" *within* experience and not in an extra-experiential realm, and that reality is firmly lodged in the individual: "reality is an accumulation of our own intellectual inventions, and the struggle for 'truth' in our progressive dealings with it is always a struggle to work in new nouns and adjectives while altering as little as possible the old" (James 1987b, 863). James thereby adopts what he calls a "humanist" perspective in which truth sits firmly within human-centered, human-mediated experience.

In sum, for James, *truth* resides firmly *within* individual judgment and that ruling is centered on personal experience. In other words, *truth* is not some Platonic ideal hovering in a universe of abstract Forms but *lives* directly within human experience where only humans might appraise and apply its mandates.

Truth thus means, according to humanism, the relation of less fixed parts of experience (predicates) to other relatively more fixed parts (subjects); and we are not required to seek it in a relation of experience as such to anything beyond itself.

(James 1987b, 865)

What could be more alien to Freud's way of thinking? James undercuts Freud's philosophy of mind at the very heart of the psychoanalytic enterprise with an anti-representational philosophy in which "nothing *happens* in the realm of concepts" and only perception, not conception (representation), can give insight into moving life (James 1987d, 743, emphasis in original).[15]

Addressing a Boston audience in 1906, James clearly presented these views as a central aspect of his pragmatic position:

> Metaphysics has usually followed a very primitive kind of quest . . . Solomon knew the names of all the spirits, and having their names, he held them subject to his will. So the universe has always appeared to the natural mind as a kind of enigma, of which the key must be sought in the shape of some illuminating or power-bringing word or name. That word names the universe's principle, and to possess it is after a fashion to possess the universe itself. "God," "Matter," "Reason," "the Absolute," "Energy," are so many solving names. You can rest when you have them. You are at the end of your metaphysical quest.
>
> But if you follow the pragmatic method, you cannot look on any such word as closing your quest. You must bring out of each word its practical *cash-value*, set it at work within the stream of your experience. It appears less as a solution, then, than as a program for more work, and more particularly as an indication of the ways in which existing realities may be *changed*.
>
> (James 1987c, 509, emphasis added)

So, instead of the search for some idealized *truth* or basis of *reality*, James sought the "cash-value" of inquiry, *facts*, that would then lead to new facts and expanded understanding:

> *Theories thus become instruments, not answers to enigmas, in which we can rest.* We don't lie back upon them, we move forward, and, on occasion, make nature over again by their aid. Pragmatism unstiffens all our theories, limbers them up and sets each one at work . . .
>
> it stands for no particular results. It has no dogmas, and no doctrines save its method . . .
>
> No particular results then . . . but only an attitude of orientation, is what the pragmatic method means. *The attitude of looking away from first things, principles, "categories," supposed necessities; and of looking towards last things, fruits, consequences, facts.*
>
> (James 1987c, 509–10, emphasis in original)

And then in *The Meaning of Truth, A Sequel to Pragmatism*, published the same year he met Freud (1909) and already widely condemned (Taylor and Wozniak 1996b), James vigorously reasserts his rejection of idealized Truth in favor of knowledge-based in its pragmatic origins and uses:

> The pivotal part of my book named *Pragmatism* is its account of the relation called "truth" which may obtain between an idea (opinion, belief, statement, or what not) and its object. "Truth," I there say, "is a property of certain of our ideas. It means their agreement, as falsity means their disagreement, with reality . . ." The truth of an idea is not a stagnant property inherent in it. Truth *happens* to an idea. It *becomes* true, is *made* true by events. Its verity *is* in fact an event, a process, the process namely of its verifying itself, its veri*fication*. Its validity is the process of its valid*ation*. . . . Any idea that helps us to deal, whether practically or intellectually, with either the reality or its belongings, that doesn't entangle our progress in frustrations, that fits, in fact, and adapts our life to the reality's whole setting, will agree sufficiently to meet the requirement. It will be true of that reality.
>
> *The true*, to put it very briefly, *is only the expedient in the way of our thinking, just as the right is only the expedient in the way of our behaving*. Expedient in almost any fashion, and expedient in the long run and on the whole, of course; for what meets expediently all the experience in sight won't necessarily meet all farther experiences equally satisfactorily. Experience, as we know, has ways of *boiling* over, and making us correct our present formulas.
>
> (James 1987b, 823–4, emphasis in original)

James had made a radical proposal that challenged ordinary ways of thinking about *thinking* and, consequently, construing basic precepts about the world. I cannot imagine Freud endorsing such a view. For him, truth resided in the scientific philosophy in which he had forged his theory. Truth then was grounded in those positivist principles—objective empirical observations in which facts were derived and theories devised to test against nature, the "Standard Model" of science, if you will. And if James and Freud dove down to the foundations of their differing views concerning the application of such principles to a science of the mind, they would have quickly arrived at the dualist metaphysics James had dismissed. And there the conversation would sputter to an end.

As if we had not adequately established how James and Freud faced in opposite philosophical directions, we must still add the most important consequence of radical empiricism, which anticipated a major inflection in twentieth-century philosophy. Not the subject-object dualism that has so pervaded this narrative, but rather the most basic presupposition that has inspired philosophers for millennia—namely, explicating an underlying reality, obscure yet tantalizingly within our grasp. To comprehend the human world, philosophers have traditionally attempted to discern those underlying or overarching principles that order human understanding of reality. Accordingly, Freud is (ironically) a traditional metaphysician who, through psychoanalysis, claimed to have uncovered those submerged mysterious psychic forces that must be understood and then brought into alignment for emotional health. In this sense, his psychology was indeed a form of science, at least metaphysically, in the quest for the underlying "true" realty that lay below the surface of consciousness. And here we find the most radical separation of our protagonists.

Freud elaborated a metaphysics to reveal the psyche's hidden Reality, whereas James, as viewed through Wittgenstein's later philosophy, was an "anti-metaphysician," because for him, *nothing* is hidden:

> Philosophy simply puts everything before us, and neither explains nor deduces anything.—Since everything lies open to view there is nothing to explain. For what is hidden, for example, is of no interest to us. One might give the name "philosophy" to what is possible before discoveries and inventions.
> (Wittgenstein 1968, §126, 50e; see Edwards 1982; Rorty 1989; Tauber 2013a, 169–76).

Instead of traditional philosophy's ceaseless attempts to elucidate that which is hidden (the classic form of philosophical problems and subsequent inquiry), philosophers (and yes, scientists!) should seek clarity and perspicuity of *facts*—Clarity rather than Truth (Edwards 1982; 2004, 132). Or, as Wittgenstein famously said, "to shew the fly the way out of the fly-bottle" is to solve a philosophical problem (Wittgenstein 1968, §309, 103e). In sum,

> we must do away with all explanation, and description alone must take its place. And this description gets its light, that is to say its purpose—from the philosophical problems. . . . The problems are solved, not by giving new information, but by arranging what we have always known.
> (Wittgenstein 1968, §109, 47e)

And in this sense, James and Wittgenstein practiced philosophy as a therapeutic endeavor by showing how philosophy might break free of its traditional search for foundations and serve as a "therapeutic rather than constructive, edifying rather than systematic" function (Rorty 1979, 5; Peterman 1992).[16] Such clarity subordinates logic for practical instrumentality to allow "for improved belief" not some final Truth (Rorty 1991, 23). Although Freud would have dismissed that position as philosophical sophistry, the repercussions of that idea are difficult to overestimate.

Comment

James respected science, but he sought ways of balancing objective ways of thinking with personal ways of knowing. After all, the values through which one understands the world frames experience and are thus integral to the reality in which humans live. To fracture the objective/subjective balance governing that knowledge not only distorts understanding, but it also misconceives it. In his evaluation of that difficult balance, James understood that "reality outstrips the conceptual and the linguistic" (Dianda 2023, 65) and thus his emphasis on experience, the catch-all for that which remains unaccounted in the explicit but remains to frame that which we *know*. This so-called "humane" orientation pervaded James's thought and directed every aspect of his philosophy, perhaps most importantly, the meaning of truth and the authentication of the personal underlying it.

By appealing to "experience," James wanted to capture the moral-existential picture of human action and cognition in terms of individual experience and moral judgment. And that formulation drew from the reservoir of the personal (see Introduction, note #13).

> A philosophy whose principle is so incommensurate with our most intimate powers as to deny them all relevancy in universal affairs, as to annihilate their motives at one blow, will be even more unpopular than pessimism. Better face the enemy than the eternal Void! . . . Any philosophy which annihilates the validity of the reference by explaining away its object or translating them into terms of no emotional pertinency leaves the mind with little to care or act for.
>
> (James 1983, 941)

Here we face the crux of the Jamesian enterprise. How one appraises him—indeed, how one regards philosophy more generally—centers on judging how James placed *experience* in his philosophy. He bypassed classical empiricist efforts to build a psychological or linguistic/logical foundation for knowledge and instead endeavored to describe how the subject acts in the world, the relationships that mediate that intercourse, and the limits of analytics to capture "experience" (Dianda 2023, 232).

Despite his best efforts to deflect criticisms, James abandoned "pure experience" in his later works because of epistemological problems he could not resolve (Gale 1999). However, he would not discard his central thesis about the irreducible personal element that would not be ignored or discounted by science or philosophy. So, when facing the philosophical tribunal, he declared,

> I have finally found myself compelled to *give up the logic*, fairly, squarely, and irrevocably. It has an imperishable use in human life, but that use is not to make us theoretically acquainted with the essential nature of reality . . . Reality, life, experience, concreteness, immediacy, use what word you will, exceeds our logic, overflows and surrounds it . . . I prefer bluntly to call reality if not irrational then at least non-rational in its constitution,—and by reality here I mean reality where things happen, all temporal reality without exception.
>
> (James 1987d, 725–6, emphasis in original)

James goes on to explain:

> We are so subject to the philosophic tradition which treats *logos* or discursive thought generally as the sole avenue of truth, that to fall back on raw unverbalized life as more of a revealer, and to think of concepts as the merely practical things . . . comes very hard. It is putting off our proud maturity of mind and becoming again as foolish little children in the eyes of reason. But as difficult as such a revolution is, there is no other way, I believe, to the possession of reality.
>
> (James 1987d, 755)

And for James, that reality was fundamentally moral—human-valued, human-derived, human-constructed, and human-intended. On this view, *experience*, drawing from all the diverse sources of the personal, could stand only within a renewed humanism. He revitalized that mission and its further development. By valorizing and clarifying the structure of experience, despite its flawed discursive attempts, he sought to countermand the analytic imperative and thus save the personal.

That "pure experience" failed its metaphysical mission may be understood as either a relic of a misconceived project or that James had challenged philosophy to face its own limits with Logic retreating to cloister within its own fortress, for better and for worse. That theme of limits has had an illustrious history in the century that followed him, and it is in that array of ideas James holds *critical* authority.[17] No wonder Wittgenstein read him so carefully! (Goodman 2007). James's thought had other repercussive effects on twentieth-century philosophy, in which later pragmatists, Whitehead and process philosophers, phenomenologists, and moral philosophers of every school responded. Whitehead credited James as bringing about "the inauguration of a new stage in philosophy" by breaking Cartesian dualism and thereby inaugurating a philosophy of process (or "organism") that replaced the *thing-ness* inherent to the subject-object divide (Whitehead 1967, 143). With that endorsement, Whitehead placed James in the Pantheon with Plato, Aristotle, and Leibniz (Whitehead 1968, 2–3; Sinclair 2009).

Putting aside testimonials, it is fair to recognize that James's critique of positivism's epistemological claims inflected philosophy's arc by discarding the Enlightenment tradition that left neither Reason nor Truth standing as heretofore conceived. And with that epistemological turn, moral philosophy adjusted in tandem, because with James's pragmatism, truth, personal identity, ethics, and science lost foundational standing. Instead, he celebrated epistemological fluidity and valorized personal judgment directed by the intuition of one's own resourceful genius. Accordingly, James maintained that humans *choose* the construction of their realities—social and natural—that depend on composites of interpretations with different understandings of truth. And with that fundamental revamping, he reconfirmed the romantic primacy of subjectivity and the wide expanse of the personal in the celebration of human imagination and creativity against the objectification of the soul.

Notes

1 Decades after musing about mechanical models to describe psychic dynamics (see Chapter 1), Freud admitted circumspection about establishing cause in the mental domain, albeit he still held to a strict determinism:

> Our imperative need for cause and effect is satisfied when each process has *one* demonstrable cause. In reality, outside us this is hardly so; each event seems to be over-determined and turns out to be the effect of several converging causes. Intimidated by the countless complications of events research takes the part of one chain of events against another, stipulates contrasts that do not exist and that are created merely through tearing apart more comprehensive relations . . . I do not mean to say that the world is so complicated that every assertion must hit the truth somewhere. No, our thinking has preserved the liberty of inventing dependencies and connections that have no equivalent in reality. It obviously prizes this gift very highly, since it makes such ample use of it—inside as well as outside of science.
>
> (Freud 1939, 137, emphasis in original)

2 Note that Freudianism joins the same general promise of rationality that under-girds all modern political philosophies, from classical liberalism to the totali-tarian and all in between (Berlin 1958, 144).

3 As of 1994, over 400 types of psychotherapy were identified; as of this writing, over 500 (Garfield and Bergin 1994; Prochaska and Norcross 2024). Accurate statistics about incidence and effectiveness of therapies of those seeking psy-chotherapy ("talking cures") exclusive of medications are not available (due to the diversity of psychotherapies, the mixture of clinical settings, the criteria of improvement, and the confounding factor of various medications employed). What is clear, however, is that in the post-COVID era, a marked increase in Americans seeking mental health care has jumped from 13% in 2004 to 23% in 2022. In this cohort, about 40% receive psychotherapy ("talking cure") coun-seling either alone or in combination with medication (O'Connell-Domenech 2023). To what extent this increase is due to a higher incidence of mental dis-ease, more available health care resources, or greater cultural acceptance for seeking care is not clear.

4 Counting citations in professional psychological journals and introductory text-books, Freud is ranked first, while James does not make the top 25. However, when other criteria are included (i.e., a survey of professional psychologists and various professional rankings), Freud ranks #3 and James #14 (Haggbloom et al. 2002). Of course, such metrics are hardly the last word and must compete with testimonials based on different criteria. For instance, James holds a lofty position in psychology according to Edwin G. Boring, who considered him one of the "four great men" in the history of psychology, the others being Darwin, Helmholtz, and Freud (Boring 1950, 743).

5 Some have suggested that Freud's use of early nineteenth-century literary sources, his invocation of the mythologies of Oedipus, Moses, the primal father, and other poetic allusions suggest that some lingering Romanticism of his youth influenced his later thought that has tapped into a common under-standing of Western identity (Enckell 1981; Vermorel and Vermorel 1986; Merkur 1993).

6 *Gnothi seauton* literally translates to "know thy soul or psyche." Although there is a Greek pronoun for self in Plato, it is not used as a substantive; *psy-che* functions as the noun corresponding to our self (Griswold 1986). To know oneself is to know the psyche, which is best declared in its virtue and wisdom, *sophia*, upon which Socrates's entire ethic is erected. *Psyche*'s complex and laden meanings may be simplified as that which is capable of attaining wisdom or, in Socratic terms, as the true self:

> The living man *is* the *psyche*, and the body . . . is only the set of tools or instruments of which he makes use in order to live. . . . [L]ife can only be lived well if the *psyche* is in command of the body. It meant purely and sim-ply the intelligence, which in a properly ordered life is in complete control of the senses and emotions.
>
> (Guthrie 1971, 149–50, emphasis in original).

7 The simple mechanical models characterizing both physical and biological phenomena have proven inadequate to predict outcomes in complex systems

that exhibit varying degrees of predictability, including indeterminate causation. Complex behavior occurs in any system in which multiple interacting constituents follow dynamic mechanics. Such descriptions have become foundational in biology and serve as the theoretical framework for cognitive science. Indeed, recent evidence has characterized consciousness, from primitive to complex animals, as constituting the ability to make choices that fulfill the criteria of "free choice" (Mitchell 2023). And if one probes the dynamics of physics, indeterminism is embedded in the probabilistic mechanics of the quantum, which would have freed Freud from the Newtonian world of linear determinism. For Heisenberg's original reflections on how quantum physics altered basic Western metaphysics, see Heisenberg (1958a, 1958b); for how the probabilistic picture of causation may be regarded as a "metaphysics of uncertainty," see Tauber (2022, 124–37).

8 Emma Sutton (2023) portrays James as regarding himself an invalid throughout his life, and his responses to those challenges accounts for key elements of his philosophy. He broadly shared complaints about his persistent debilitating back pain, eye ailments, constipation, insomnia, headaches, and flu. His sufferings repeatedly drove him to European baths and desperate remedies including electrotherapy, lymph injections, testicular elixirs, and telepathic seances. Adding to this litany, serious depression, neurasthenia, and melancholia recurrently usurped his energies and compromised his well-being. Yet, as a philosopher, he suffered not in vain:

> James's melancholy opened up questions about the relationship between the mind and body; his pain was presented and probed as a form of metaphysical evil; the crippling nature of his back condition was positioned as an ethical threat to his ability to contribute to society; this combined burden of invalidism represented a moral embargo on fatherhood with its risk of passing on a sickly inheritance; and, throughout his life, he prized religious faith, first and foremost, as a stimulus or tonic for those struggling with illness and infirmity. Wherever you look, James's corpus is riddled with disease.
>
> (Sutton 2023, 5)

9 James suffered

> frequent psychological crises, sometimes almost suicidal in intensity, and early flirtation with nihilism . . . In fact, at the height of his fame in 1899–1902, James had a second major crisis, rivaling in severity the one he suffered as a young man in the late 1860s. It sent him into a psychological, physical, spiritual, even professional tailspin from which he perhaps never fully recovered before his death in 1910.
>
> (Jay 2005, 276)

10 James's attitude towards pragmatic justification and rationalization to serve just ends may be tracked to the Metaphysical Club discussions at Harvard during the 1870s (see Chapter 2, note #1), where his friend, Oliver Wendell Holmes Jr., later developed that same attitude and governing precept as a jurist both before and during his tenure as an Associate Justice of the U.S. Supreme Court (Menand 2001, 337–47).

11 The affective effects on judgment are well known, and one might well ask what the "fragility of pure reason'" portends for knowledge assessment (Solomon 2004; Johnson-Laird 2006, 72ff.). If reason is not self-inclusive, then its claims, even within its own province, are undermined (Fiumara 2001, 12; Tappolet 2016). The Kantian reliance on some notion of sacrosanct Reason has been supplemented by "emotional intelligence," which highlights that reasoning has several modes of analysis and that no strict line separates the emotional domain from logic. Indeed, emotions provide cognitive appraisals or value judgments that contribute to human reasoning (Matthews, Zeidner, and Roberts 2002). This cognitive theory of emotions has been most aptly applied to moral philosophy and has made strong claims (the literature on this topic is immense; see Solomon 1993, 2004, 2007; de Sousa 1997; Blackburn 1998; Nussbaum 2001; Goldie 2000, 2010; Prinz 2007; Ben-Ze'ev 2000; Tappolet 2016, 2022.)

12 While James's writing on ethics is sparce (he published only a single essay devoted to ethics, "The Moral Philosopher and the Moral Life" [1992j]), commentators have made a strong case that he was acutely self-reflective about his own ethical deliberations, the moral role of philosophy in the public domain, the ethics of belief, how pragmatism and utilitarianism conjoined, and how his own notions of truth effected moral discourses. Perhaps there is no single or sustained work because ethics permeates his thought (Marchetti 2015, 250; see also Jackman 2019).

13 Historical examples highlighting misapplication and distortion of scientific studies, e.g., Nazi racial science and Lysenko genetics (Joravsky 1986; Proctor 1988, 1991), reveal how scientific findings have been entwined in ideological commitments to promote political agendas (Tauber 2009a, 133ff.). Recent examples abound (e.g., Fraser 1995; Segerstrale 2000).

14 For how James's "humanistic principle" fits into his Romanticism, see Schulenberg 2022. Note that my discussion is not linked to Heidegger's general call for a new humanism based on facing Being (a revised spirituality [Heidegger 1962, 1993]), nor do I think that James would have regarded the "posthuman" effects of technological dominance of human interactions as a philosophical threat (e.g., Turkle 1985; Wolfe 2010; Ferrando 2020). Rather, he sought ways of balancing human need and human-centered values against the increasing dominance of the scientific perspective.

15 Dewey, following James, asserted that "mind is primarily a verb" (1980, 263). Dewey's point, directly built from James's own views, was that

> "mind" and "reality," like "stimulus" and "response," name nonexistent entities: They are abstractions from a single, indivisible process. It therefore makes little sense to talk about a "split" that needs to be overcome between the mind and the world as it does to talk about a "split" between the hand and the environment, or the spoon and the soup. "Things," he wrote ". . . are what they are experienced as, and thus knowledge is not a copy of something that exists independently of its being known; "*it is an instrument or organ of successful action*" [Dewey, *Ethics*, 1908]. "The chief service of pragmatism, as regards epistemology," Dewey wrote a friend in 1905, "will be . . . to give the *coup de grace to representationalism.*" (Menand 2001, 361, emphasis in original).

16 Although philosophy as therapy follows no formulae and certainly no prescription, since the 1990s philosophers have formalized their role as therapists in the United States and Western Europe. This professional venture has developed certification and practice guidelines (Marinoff 2001) and promoted efforts advocating philosophy's role in self-help therapies (e.g., Marinoff 2020); some even specifically invoke James as the orienting influence on their therapeutic approach (e.g., Kaag 2020; Beichman 2020).

17 Perhaps most notably, Wittgenstein followed James's overarching theme, i.e., ordinary experience serves to order human life and analytics obscure it (Goodman 1994, 2007; Still and Costall 1991, 20). Indeed, James clearly led Wittgenstein to the central theme of *Tractatus Logico-Philosophicus* (Wittgenstein 1974). As Wittgenstein insisted, the whole point of the book is to show that what is important cannot be expressed, and much of philosophy devoted to psychology, ethics, and aesthetics escapes analytics. Simply put, he was referring to subjective judgment, namely, all that which cannot be objectified or treated with the logic applied in scientific investigations (Tauber 2013a, 169–76).

Conclusion

Despite persistent misgivings about Freud's theory and therapeutic efficacy of psychoanalysis, *Interpretation of Dreams* (1900) marks a watershed in human self-appraisals and a new language for accommodating a novel depiction of the psyche. By showing that the "ego is not master in its own house," Freud claimed (and not unreasonably) that his findings were as disruptive to human standing as Copernicus dislodging the earth as the center of the universe and Darwin's dethroning human biological uniqueness (Freud 1917, 143). And as Freud portrayed the unconscious, he also devised a narrative, an elaborate myth, to translate the naturalism of his biological vision into humane terms. Placing inchoate organic forces into the human construct in which new coordinates of understanding might be achieved offered a novel view of human beings. In essence, he provided a translation *of* ourselves *to* us. Psychoanalysis appeared at an auspicious time. Similar jolts of the period included the re-discovery of Mendelian genetics in 1900, Planck's description of the quantum in the same year, and Einstein's presentation of relativity in 1905. These revolutionary scientific findings changed the very fabric of reality, and when coupled to the massive changes in social organization and technical advances of the period, modernism represented a collective response of relating that reconfigured reality into a human perspective with repercussive effects in the visual arts, music, and literature (Kern 1983; Golding 1988; Everdell 1997).

Both Freud and James justly hold premier positions in this revolution of thought and self-understanding that affected all sectors of culture (Posnock 1991, 1997; Richardson 2006; Gay 2008; Evans 2017; Friedl 2018). Their respective successes, at odds with each other and following several courses into the twentieth century, inflected Western consciousness. Of the myriad ways in which they might be placed in this context, perhaps most apt is Ross Posnock's general characterization of modernism as the "project to reunify human sensibility, dissociated by the hegemony of positivist

DOI: 10.4324/9781003565413-7

science" (Posnock 1991, 56). On this account, James and Freud clearly fall under the banner of modernism despite their radically different ways of being placed within that designation. Indeed, in the divergence of their views, we glimpse the extraordinary panorama of thought by which the modernists devised innovative ways of finding expression for conceiving a world turned upside down. In this milieu of artistic experimentation, revolutionary science, and cultural shifts accompanying the development of mass society, novel ways of characterizing agency emerged.

Freud responded to that challenge by tapping into a deep stratum of Western ideas about personal identity. Oedipus is our Ur-myth of the *who-am-I?* question. Freud gave a modern narrative of that enquiry based on a cardinal Enlightenment value: the power, indeed, sanctity of reason. Yet the authority of the narrative, the reason upon which it is based, the implicit objectivity marshalled for insight incorporates a deep irony, one that resonates with James's animosity to applying a rationalistic construct to the subjective. In a reversal of the usual interpretations of the Oedipus myth, Jean-Jacques Goux (1993) cogently argued that the turn from the oracle to find explanation and rational belief may well be the original case of Greek tragedy—not the march of indifferent fate, but rather the consequences of hubris—a misplaced reliance on human reason. James suffered no such illusions about authoritative analytics.

The timbre of James's thought originates in the romantic *Weltanschauung* of his Massachusetts ancestry. He (like his own father, Emerson, and Thoreau) sought ways of responding to the rise of scientific positivism, which had threatened the mystical intimacy and union that drew them so powerfully. Indeed, James's reaction to the "pernicious bifurcation between man and nature" became the underlying theme of his philosophy (Gale 1999, 220–2). He thus resisted mechanical philosophies throughout his career (e.g., James 1983, 1230, 1258) and lamented that science holds that "all the things and qualities men love . . . are but illusions of our fancy attached to accidental clouds of dust which will be dissipated by the eternal cosmic weather as carelessly as they were formed" (James 1983, 1260). In an address to the Society for Psychical Research in 1896, James declared that the "personal" and "romantic" view of life was incompatible with the mechanistic and materialist metaphysics of science:

> Science has come to be identified with a certain fixed general belief, the belief that the deeper order of Nature is mechanical exclusively, and that nonmechanical categories are irrational ways of conceiving and explaining even such a thing as human life. Now this mechanical rationalism, as one may call it, makes, if it becomes one's only way of thinking, a

violent breach with the ways of thinking that have until our own time played the greatest part in human history. Religious thinking, ethical thinking, poetical thinking, teleological, emotional, sentimental thinking, what one might call the personal view of life to distinguish it from the impersonal and mechanical, and the romantic view of life to distinguish it from the rationalistic view, have been and even still are, outside of well-drilled scientific circles, the dominant forms of thought. But for mechanical rationalism, personality is an insubstantial illusion; the chronic belief of mankind that events may happen for the sake of their personal significance is an abomination.

(James 1986b, 134–5)

Scientism cripples moral agency, for a philosophy devoid of human significance is "incommensurate with our most intimate powers" and thus unacceptable (Gale 1999, 221). In the same address, James then proclaimed his credo:

The only form of thing that we directly encounter, the only experience that we concretely have, is our own personal life. The only complete category of our thinking . . . is the category of personality, every other category being one of the abstract elements of that. And this systematic denial on Science's part of personality as a condition of events, this rigorous belief that in its own essential and innermost nature our world is a strictly impersonal world, may . . . prove to be the very defect that our descendants will be most surprised at in our own boasted Science, the omission that to their eyes will most tend to make *it* look perspectiveless and short.

(James 1986b, 136–7, emphasis in original)

This theme is reiterated in *Varieties of Religious Experience*, where James declares,

so long as we deal with the cosmic and the general [as does Science], we deal only with the symbols of reality, but *as soon as we deal with private and personal phenomena as such, we deal with realities in the completest sense of the term.*

(James 1987f, 446, emphasis in original)

And again, in concert with his forefathers, James reveals the heart not only of his philosophy, but the core of his temperament and its expression in that philosophy. He clearly elaborated how separating ideas from their psychological origins is to miss much of philosophy itself, for such introspective inquiry is constitutive to the basic precept of philosophy as self-knowledge and the basis of a moral life. Indeed, in asserting the primacy of his experience, more specifically the integrity of his moral individuality, James valorized the subjective:

Individuality is founded in feeling; and the recesses of feeling, the darker, blinder strata of character, are the only places in the world in which we catch real fact in the making, and directly perceive how events happen, and how work is actually done.

(James 1987f, 448)

In overcoming severe depression and asserting freedom of the will, James clearly exhibited this doctrine.

James's depressive episode and its willful resolution highlights a striking personality difference between our protagonists. Although James was introspective, he did not, like Freud, attempt to discern the underlying causes of his "melancholy," having considered it "untraceable" (Perry 1935, 514). Unlike Freud, who endeavored to dissect the underlying forces tormenting his patients, James pursued another tack. While psychoanalysis invokes science and rationality to overcome affliction, James chose his own will as an antidote. He accomplished his therapeutic goal by leaving cause in abeyance and constructed an ethics in which he could surmount his own profound psychological crisis. He drew from an ancient tradition that re-enacted a "love of wisdom" to heal, a wisdom that distinguished what he could *know* from what he must *believe*. The 1870 resolution dramatically illustrates how James understood the limits of philosophy and that, ultimately, the course of his thought and action were expressions of his own personality with the analytics added as so much spice to the meal.

Not only are the boundaries separating philosophy and psychology easily crossed, but they witness heavy traffic (Tauber 2022, 332–6). Of course, philosophy is not psychology, but each approach should take account of the other. Their strict division not only ignores the empirical evidence that psychology and cognitive science provide to philosophy (modes of reason, motivation, unconscious processes, etc.), but denies the voice of character that is so instrumental in every respect of a philosopher's labor—the choice of the problem, the way it is developed, and the conclusions drawn. For James, philosophy is an expression of what he called "temperament."[1]

The history of philosophy is to a great extent that of a certain clash of human temperaments. . . . Of whatever temperament a professional philosopher is, he tries, when philosophizing, to sink the fact of his temperament. Temperament is no conventionally recognized reason, so he urges impersonal reasons only for his conclusions. Yet his temperament really gives him a stronger bias than any of his more strictly objective premises. . . . Yet in the forum he can make no claim, on the bare ground of his temperament, to superior discernment or authority. There arises thus a certain insincerity in our philosophic discussions: the potentest of all our premises is never mentioned.

(James 1987b, 488–9)

For James, philosophy reflected the deepest "passional" commitment, and he fully acknowledged the central role of temperament in framing his philosophy (James 1986b, 136–7; 1987c, 488–9; 1987f, 446; see Fiumara 2001, 5; Tauber 2022, 332–6; Madelrieux 2022, 250). He did not dismiss the logic, argument, or analytic interpretation of philosophical discourse; rather, he acknowledged that underlying the most sophisticated presentations, the voice of character whispers loudly. He readily admitted that temperamental difference is at work in the choice of sides.

The rationalist mind, radically taken, is of a doctrinaire and authoritative complexion: the phrase "must be" is ever on its lips. The bellyband of its universe must be tight. A radical pragmatist on the other hand is a happy-go-lucky anarchistic sort of creature. If he had to live in a tub like Diogenes he wouldn't mind at all if the hoops were loose and the staves let in the sun.

(James 1987c, 600)

Moreover, he allotted temperament a larger epistemological standing:

Our passional nature not only lawfully may, but must, decide an option between propositions, whenever it is a genuine option that cannot by its nature be decided on intellectual grounds; for to say, under such circumstances, "Do not decide, but leave the question open," is itself a passional decision—just like deciding yes or no—and is attended with the same risk of losing the truth.

(James 1992h, 464, emphasis in original)

Emphasizing the role of the personal in his craft, James maintained that philosophy is

not a technical matter; it is our more or less dumb sense of what life honestly and deeply means. It is only partly got from books; it is our individual way of just seeing and feeling the total push and pressure of the cosmos.

(James 1987c, 487)

This view is vividly illustrated by his own biography.[2] James practiced philosophy as a form of therapy, both for himself and for a culture *dis*-eased. Indeed, the effort to understand his own mental life, from scientific reasoning to mystical and telepathic phenomena, marked James's full embrace of the subjective domain as only a true Romantic could.

Some might say that the introduction of the psychological breaks the bounds of philosophy. However, on James's view, the "temperament" orientation only broadens our comprehension by showing how a question is approached and developed as the outcome of the underlying disposition of the philosopher. Moreover, the rigid separation of the subjective from the analytical ignores how experience, judgment, and creative insight draws from the wellspring of the personal. To separate ideas from their psychological origins is to miss much of the philosophy itself.

Yet, this interplay is not often explored. The reticence may be explained because the topic falls through the cracks separating psychology and philosophy. It also violates the pride of analyticity. Philosophers generally like to think of themselves as driven by compelling arguments, and yet motivations (pertaining to what is addressed) and emotion (the timbre or tilt of the argument) clearly impact their writings. Perhaps official philosophy resists recognition of its dependence upon

resources that it draws from the mind's affective life. Certain areas of philosophy systematically tend to eschew a number of difficult questions on the grounds that they are peripheral or not quite to the point; obtruding emotional issues, in fact, are usually "described" as tangentially connected to truth claims, insufficiently clear, unfocused, inappropriately articulated, excessively controversial or sub-rational . . . . [S]ince the activity of separation and division is philosophically productive (as the proper "field," or Kantian island, is created by its exclusions), philosophy ultimately creates itself through what it represses.

(Fiumara 2001, 5)

Bottom line: the pursuit of knowledge is hardly a neutral pursuit.

Acknowledging the subjective as integral to philosophy's analytics (a view held, for example, by Hume, James, Nietzsche, Johann Fichte) does not disparage the logic, argument, or analytic interpretation of philosophical discourse, but rather admits that underlying the most sophisticated presentation, philosophy expresses the intimate voice of the philosopher. Emotional components derived from their intent and organized by personality are inextricable from the philosophical questions asked and the answers found. Simply, to separate ideas from their psychological origins is to miss much of philosophy itself. Accordingly, acknowledging temperament becomes a philosophical exercise, inasmuch as such inquiry is constitutive to the basic precept of philosophy as self-knowledge and the basis of a moral life (R. A. Putnam 2017). This attitude is at the heart of James's own pluralism.

By enlisting in the ancient practice of philosophy as a *way of life*, James offers a rich "case report" of philosophy at work (Hadot 1995, 266–7; Flanagan 1997, 47). He found his own equilibrium through philosophy, both in discourse and in practice. While his temperament might account for the optimism of "Be not afraid of life. Believe that life *is* worth living, and your belief will help create the fact" (James 1992h, 503), the ways in which he overcame the despair and melancholy that contested his pronouncement was through philosophical exercise. When he exhausted all arguments, and none prevailed, he *chose* to believe in free will, his temperament directing that decision. James's self-therapy is a striking story of philosophy facing its limits and how, in the end, temperament adjudicates philosophical dilemmas.

In contrast, Freud deliberately, perhaps too evidently, rejected philosophy. His dismissal rested upon his diagnosis of three weaknesses: (1) philosophy represents an encompassing mode of knowledge (or perhaps a metaphysics) that cannot respond to new empirical findings; (2) beyond its blindness to empiricism (viz, science), philosophy's logic is closed and limited; and (3) philosophers elevate nonscientific forms of knowledge to an epistemological level that is rightly reserved for positivist findings. That this characterization distorts "philosophy" requires little comment, other than to note the irony that Freud accepted his own positivism without the same critical appraisal that he applied to what he called "speculative philosophy" (Tauber 2010, xii–xviii). He thus avoided exploring the logic of his own science and its presumptive claims on knowledge; and finally, he seemingly ignored the metaphysical foundations of his own efforts to devise an encompassing philosophy of human nature based upon the presumed "certainties" of other empirically based positivist successes (Tauber 2010, xiii).[3]

Freud presumed a privileged perspective in respect to the non-empirical speculations of philosophers by holding the high-ground of what he considered empirical evidence that critics have rightly disputed since he announced his theory.[4] Freud pursued a science of causes that provided a compelling narrative but lacked grounding in objective principles. Although he was well aware of the precarious status of his "science of the mind," he nevertheless insisted on the centrality of unconsciousness and thereby discarded those philosophies based on consciousness. And that rejection extended to all of philosophy. As late as his *New Introductory Lectures* of 1933, he sounded his repeated refrain about "philosophers" and his own philosophy: "It goes astray in its method of over-estimating the epistemological value of our logical operations and by accepting other sources of knowledge such as intuition" (Freud 1933, 160–1). As if science advanced by logic alone! His anathema for philosophy never lifted, and even in Freud's most speculative essays, he maintained that his critical views of religion, social organization, the future of civilization, the character of art, and so on, were rightful extrapolations of his clinical findings, and thus they assumed a different veracity than those methods or interpretations that could not claim the same scientific authority for their respective approaches. Indeed, he seemed most comfortable in his proselytizing polemics when he donned the authenticating scientific cloak (Tauber 2010, 25).

While Freud heralded the positivist virtues of his theory, his philosophical inclinations could not be repressed. He knew philosophy and drew from that tradition as he built his theory, consciously or not (Tauber 2010, 24ff.). Certainly, by 1913, when Freud began to shift his thinking about the ego's structure, his writings assumed a distinctive new character under the guise of a "metapsychology." Although he continued to espouse positivist ideals to develop the science of psychoanalysis, he acknowledged that he had returned "after making a lifelong detour through the natural sciences, medicine, and psychotherapy . . . to the cultural problems which had fascinated me long before, when I was a youth scarcely old enough for thinking" (Freud 1935, 72).

Note that, although Freud retreated from orthodox philosophy for science, that abandonment was to a particular brand of philosophizing. "Philosophy" for him represented the lingering influence of idealism and more generally what he called "speculative" and "totalizing" philosophies. His aversion to philosophy's confusion and critical faults led him to focus on an epistemology more to his liking, for legitimization, first as a scientist and then for the social approbation that would accompany any success in that sphere (Gay 1988). As he later explained, "in my youth I felt an overpowering need to understand something of the riddles of the world in which we live and perhaps even to contribute something to their solution" (Freud 1927b, 253). Most immediately, that meant research in a neuroanatomy laboratory; but underlying that work, Freud held to a much broader agenda and had much grander ambitions.

While the extent to which Freud held to his earliest interests cannot be resolved, one might fairly conclude that he went through several stages and seemed ever conscious of his earliest intellectual roots that had framed the discarded philosophy he had studied in his youth and the philosophy of mind he hoped to create.[5] Perhaps Thomas Mann, on the occasion of Freud's eightieth birthday, spoke most clearly about Freud's relationship to philosophy, one marked by a strange misunderstanding.

> [Freud] does not esteem philosophy very highly. His scientific exactitude does not permit him to regard it as a science. He reproaches it with imagining that it can present a continuous and consistent picture of the world; with overestimating the objective value of logical operations; with believing in intuitions as a source of knowledge and with indulging in . . . the magic of words and the influence of thought upon reality. But would philosophy really be thinking too highly of itself on these assumptions? Has the world ever been changed by anything save by thought and its magic vehicle the Word? I believe in actual fact philosophy ranks before and above the natural sciences and that all method and exactness serve its intuitions and its intellectual and historical will. . . . One might strain the point and say that science has never made a discovery without being authorized and encouraged thereto by philosophy.
>
> (Mann 1947, 419).

Mann pierces Freud's defenses and points out that while "scientific freedom from assumptions is or should be a *moral* fact" (Mann 1947 [1936], 419, emphasis added), not even the most fervent positivists can assume such innocence. Indeed, Freud himself must have recognized that edict but did not critically incorporate it into his condemnation. More to the point, Freud's rejection of philosophy appears to have offered him a release from a deeper critical assessment of his own scientific philosophy and its application to subjective states.

When Binswanger first presented Freud with his phenomenological perspective on the mind in 1917, Freud reportedly replied, "What are you going to do without the unconscious, or rather, how will you manage without the unconscious? Has the philosophical devil got you in its claws after all? Reassure me" (Binswanger 1957, 64, quoted by Frie 2004, 31).[6] Perhaps apocryphal, Freud's response not only captures his own aversion to philosophy (and the criticism based on such a perspective), but it also ironically forecasts the fate of the "science of the unconscious." Freud's inability to subject his theory to a self-critical philosophical assessment of his presuppositions proved the Achilles Heel of his grand venture . . . at least as a *scientific* enterprise (Grünbaum 1984; Eysenck 1985; Webster 1995; Macmillan 1997; Cioffi

1998; Crews 2017). Indeed, he never relinquished his hostility towards philosophy, and he based that animosity on the narrow understanding of empiricism he promoted and the positivism that supported it.

Eventually, however, Freud himself became more circumspect about his science when he acknowledged the distinction between his empirical observations and the interpretations he attached to them (Fulgencio 2005; Tauber 2010, 67, 81–2). Shortly after the meeting with Binswanger, he mused,

> It may be asked whether and how far I myself am convinced of the truth of the hypotheses that have been set out in these pages. My answer would be that I am not convinced myself and that I do not seek to persuade other people to believe in them. Or, more precisely, that I do not know how far I believe them.
>
> (Freud 1920, 59, emphasis added)

Whether Freud is referring strictly to the meta-psychological argument or to the more basic underlying theory upon which it is based remains unclear. However, putting aside the disingenuous denial of polemic intent, his tentativeness seems apparent, and one wonders what shifted the bravado of his earlier defenses to such self-reflection.

I suggest that Freud was aware by this point that he could not establish a *science* of the unconscious as some separate entity or faculty of the mind. By inferential reasoning, he was convinced of his own conclusions, but convictions are not easily translated into proof (Rubovits-Seitz 1998; Tauber 2010, 63–5). Although he claimed empirical support, psychic causality was not established in terms he had originally hoped.[7] And by 1920 Freud suggested that biology might "blow away the whole of our *artificial* structure of hypotheses" (Freud 1920, 60, emphasis added), but even in his last testament he re-iterated the basic outline of his findings and their empirical basis as a first attempt to establish the laws governing the psychic dynamics (Freud 1940, 144, 158–9, 196–7). In other words, the quest (and expectation) of establishing psychic *laws* remained unrestrained.

James too was an empiricist, a radical one at that, but freed of a restrictive, pre-determined criteria of truth. His "open" epistemological architecture built from a pragmatic pluralism. So, while Freud proceeded as a scientist to depict the psyche, James chose to characterize the mind from another perspective, one that required a different methodology derived from a different metaphysics. As an early phenomenologist, he sought in his "radical empiricism" to present the flow of the mental without artificially breaking the continuous "stream of consciousness" into "bits" that results from a secondary reconstruction of consciousness. Whereas Freud's view of philosophy left no quarter for its consideration, James became a philosopher in the sense Wittgenstein would later advocate (Goodman 1994, 2007). By abjuring analytical solutions for "nonsense," he would bring "words back from their metaphysical to their everyday use" (Wittgenstein 1968, §116, 48e) and with that move, advocacy for a pragmatic understanding of truth. The critical step in changing that misapplied metaphysical language was to reformulate the dualism of an ego representing the world and oneself to oneself in a Cartesian theater. In James's "turn," he corrected "modernity's mistake," or what he called the "psychologist's fallacy," by characterizing experience as *experience*, unmediated or processed by retrospective self-reflection.

Of the many who have attacked the presumptions of dualist philosophies, James stands as a key figure for replacing positivist conceptions of the mental, and with that reform, the metaphysics of the subject and moral agency. Whereas Freud and James had embarked on seemingly similar pathways, James had transfigured his early hopes for a scientific psychology into a contextualist and multidimensional account of psychic life. His pluralism coupled to pragmatism effectively sheds Freudian scientism and in so doing provides a very different sort of Wittgensteinian "philosophical therapy," one perhaps better attuned to our current appreciation of human experience and the voice of the human soul.

The Freud-James confrontation provides another example of how metaphysics frames epistemology, and as exemplified by Freud, how a scientific view of the world has percolated into the ways in which we think of ourselves in the most intimate terms. Freud is, at best, a "compromised" humanist: if freedom of the will is asserted, then his scientific claims are threatened, most importantly, the determinism he had so carefully explicated and woven into his theory would be sacrificed. So, if James and Freud addressed the looming question that has been rigorously debated over the past two centuries—namely, "can science save us?"—Freud would have affirmed its promise, because for him, humankind's only hope, in principle, is the quiet voice of the intellect, and science instantiated its best exercise (Freud 1923a, 53). To what extent the intellect would be successful is another question, but with all accounts settled, he rested humankind's salvation in the Chapel of Science. James adamantly opposed such a role for science. Indeed, for him, the materialistic philosophies had corrupted the sanctity of the personal and thus science had become deleterious to humanism.

Heidegger, Husserl, Max Weber, and many others would have charged Freud and his positivist allies of making a Faustian pack with dire consequences (e.g., M. Weber 1946; Husserl 1970; Bambach 1995; Toulmin

2001; Beiser 2014, 13–16; Heidegger 2017). However, given James's pluralism, I imagine he would have smiled at such a resignation and redirected the question to ask, what can science offer, and what must it leave to other ways of thinking (Tauber 2009a)? That retort would fit his epistemological eclecticism and expansive worldview in which different kinds of knowledge find their legitimate place in human experience. Freud, in advocating the panacea of science, would have missed James's message: The translations of experience that science provides imposes a deforming structure on the *personal*, where human-centered interest organizes reality, a reality mediated by human categories in which meaning may—nay, must—be found (Flanagan 2007). James falls naturally into this humanist orbit, freed from the scientist view of the mind in which Freud was entrapped.

So, we conclude: on what basis would our protagonists have discussed psychology or even philosophy? Freud had put thought, feelings, memories, and motivations under the scalpel of what he thought was objective scrutiny, while James had even jettisoned *logic* as a casualty of his understanding of pure experience and thus forsook analytics, altogether. Considering their stark philosophical differences, we can suspend the fantasy of a Freud-James dialogue. Because their metaphysics radically conflicted, they shared no common views about reality, truth, or personal identity. Given their disparate views on almost everything, why argue or even debate? They were civil gentlemen, so they probably gossiped about their colleagues or commented on the weather during their short walk to the train that late summer afternoon in Worcester. In a deeper exchange, neither would have been convinced by the other. After all, how often does a Paul on his way to Damascus see Reality turned utterly upside down?

Notes

1 Stéphane Madelrieux distinguishes three meanings of "temperament" as used by James: (1) *romantic expressivism*, the expression of a unique, individual character; (2) *scientific* ethologism, in which the choice of a philosophy depends on an individual's constitutional temperament and vital need; and (3) *logico-ethical dispositionalism*, in which philosophical doctrines embody and exhibit general dispositions of mind and intellectual/moral attitudes. She selects the last as superior, because: (1) it merges the expressivist thesis (without its subjectivism) and the ethologist thesis (without its reductionism); and (2) because it forms an image of philosophy more in tune with pragmatism (Madelrieux 2022, 250). Here I cite "temperament" as it generally supports the melding of psychology and philosophy (Leary 2022) and, in the case of James, the underlying role of psychology in formulating his criteria of truth (Cormier 2022; Gunnarsson 2022).

2 Nietzsche joined James in tracking the source of philosophical machinations to the philosopher's underlying character:

> I have gradually come to realize what every great philosophy so far has been: a confession of faith on the part of its author, and a type of involuntary and unself-conscious memoir; in short, that the moral (or immoral) intentions in every philosophy constitute the true living seed from which the whole plant has always grown.

(Nietzsche 2002, 8)

Despite this agreement, little else connected Nietzsche and James; the German reminded the American ("half the time") "of the sick shrieking" of a "dying rat" (James 1987f, 42).

3 Another underlying reason for Freud's animus was his association of philosophy with religion, which encompasses different, but related criticisms. See Gay (1987); Capps (2001); Hewitt (2014).

4 According to Freud:

> It is true that philosophy has repeatedly dealt with the problem of the unconscious, but with few exceptions, philosophers have taken up one or other of the two following positions. Either their unconscious has been something mystical, something intangible and indemonstrable, whose relation to the mind has remained obscure, or they have identified the mental with the conscious and have proceeded to infer from this definition that what is unconscious cannot be mental or a subject for psychology. These opinions must be put down to the fact that philosophers have formed their judgment on the unconscious without being acquainted with the phenomena of unconscious mental activity, and therefore without any suspicion of how far unconscious phenomena resemble conscious ones or of the respects in which they differ from them.

(Freud (1913b, 178)

5 Ambivalence marks Freud's relationship to philosophy. In a letter written to Wilhelm Fliess on New Year's Day, 1896, Freud admits to a powerful philosophical inclination:

> I see how, via the detour of medical practice, you are reaching your first ideal of understanding human beings as a physiologist, just as I most secretly nourish the hope of arriving, via these same paths, at my initial goal of philosophy. For that is what I wanted originally, when it was not yet at all clear to me to what end I was in the world.

(Freud 1985, 159)

6 Binswanger attempted to apply Heidegger's philosophy to psychoanalysis, and instead of looking for causes or basic drives as Freudian psychoanalysis does, he sought to uncover why such causes and drives have their effects (Needleman 1967, 139).

7 The most trenchant point was made by Wittgenstein, who drew the critical distinction that *reasons* are not *causes*, and while Freud had elaborated a

systematic reasoned account of psychic events, he had not established causation and thus failed to establish a sound basis for psychoanalysis as a scientific venture (Bouveresse 1995; Beale and Kidd 2017). Wittgenstein's telling critique of psychoanalysis did not argue that self-composed stories were "wrong," but they could not be "true" in any objective sense. A Wittgensteinian-inspired psychoanalysis would offer insight through "perspicuous presentations," whereby interpretations are not confused as establishing scientific causes of unconscious forces, but rather provide insight into the reasons psychic events appear as they do, and the influence antecedents might have on behavior and affect (Edwards 1982). Accordingly, those reasons may become more accessible and thereby enrich interpretations by allowing them to "speak" for themselves, i.e., to become manifest. Thus, Wittgenstein critiqued Freud's model of the mind for (1) confusing "reasons" for "causes"; and (2) the subject-object dualism of introspection and the distortions imposed by such fabricated "private language" representations, a cognitive model contrived from a misapplied Cartesian epistemology (Tauber 2010, chapter 2). His conception of language without appeal to inner mental states had broad repercussions for rejecting representationalism and largely defined Wittgenstein's dismissal of "private language" and the philosophical foundations upon which such a psychology was based (Tauber 2013a, 179–85).

Bibliography

Adorno, T. W. 1973. *Negative Dialectics*. New York: Seabury Press.

Allen, B. 2023. *Living in Time. The Philosophy of Henri Bergson*. Oxford: Oxford University Press.

Ameriks, K. and Sturma, D. (eds.) 1995. *The Modern Subject: Conceptions of the Self in Classical German Philosophy*. Albany: State University of New York Press.

Armour-Garb, B. P. and Beall, J. C. (eds.) 2005. *Deflationary Truth*. Chicago: Open Court.

Askay, R. and Farquhar, J. 2006. *Apprehending the Inaccessible: Freudian Psychoanalysis and Existential Phenomenology*. Evanston, IL: Northwestern University Press.

Auxier, R. E. and Hahn, L. E. (eds.) 2010. *The Philosophy of Richard Rorty*. La Salle, IL: Open Court.

Balog, K. 2016. "The stone: 'Son of Saul,' Kierkegaard and the holocaust." *New York Times*, February 28. https://philarchive.org/rec/BALSOS-8

Bambach, C. R. 1995. *Heidegger, Dilthey, and the Crisis of Historicism*. Ithaca, NY: Cornell University Press.

Banks, E. C. 2014. *The Realistic Empiricism of Mach, James, and Russell: Neutral Monism Reconceived*. Cambridge: Cambridge University Press.

Barratt, B. B. 1993. *Psychoanalysis and the Postmodern Impulse: Knowing and Being Since Freud's Psychology*. Baltimore: Johns Hopkins University Press.

Barzun, J. 1992. "William James: The mind as artist." In *A Century of Psychology as Science*, S. Koch and D. E. Leary (eds.). Washington, DC: American Psychological Association, 904–10.

Beale, J. and Kidd, I. J. (eds.) 2017. *Wittgenstein and Scientism*. London: Routledge.

Bedau, M. A. and Humphreys, P. (eds.) 2008. *Emergence: Contemporary Readings in Science and Philosophy*. Cambridge, MA: MIT Press.

Beichman, J. 2020. "Pluralistic therapy and William James's a pluralistic universe." https://pluralisticpractice.com/main-blog/practice/pluralistic-therapy-and-william-jamess-a-pluralistic-universe/

Beiser, F. 2002. *German Idealism: The Struggle Against Subjectivism*. Cambridge, MA: Harvard University Press.

Beiser, F. 2014. *The Genesis of Neo-Kantianism: 1796–1880*. Oxford: Oxford University Press.

Bell, J. 2014. "Taking a wrench to reality." *The New York Review of Books* 61: 23–5.

Ben Jacob, E., Shapira, Y. and Tauber, A. I. 2005. "Seeking the foundations of cognition in bacteria: From Schrödinger's negative entropy to functional information." *Physica A* 359: 495–524.

Ben Jacob, E., Shapira, Y. and Tauber, A. I. 2011. "Smart bacteria." In *Chimera and Consciousness: Evolution of the Sensory Self*, L. Margulis, C. A. Asikainen and W. E. Krumbein (eds.). Cambridge, MA: MIT Press, 55–62.

Benjamin, J. 2017. *Beyond Doer and Done to: Recognition Theory, Intersubjectivity, and the Third*. London: Routledge.

Ben-Ze'ev, A. 2000. *The Subtlety of Emotions*. Cambridge, MA: MIT Press.

Bergson, H. 1911a. *Creative Evolution*, A. Mitchell (trans.) New York, NY: Henry Holt.

Bergson, A. 1911b. *Matter and Memory*, N. M. Paul and W. S. Palmer (trans.). London: Allen & Unwin.

Bergson, H. 1946. *The Creative Mind. An Introduction to Metaphysics*, M. L. Andison (trans.). New York, NY: Philosophical Library.

Berlin, I. 1958. *Two Concepts of Liberty*. Oxford: Oxford University Press.

Berlin, I. 1999. *The Roots of Romanticism*. Princeton, NJ: Princeton University Press.

Berman, M. 1982. *All That Is Solid Melts into Air: The Experience of Modernity*. New York: Penguin.

Bermúdez, J. L. 2003. *Thinking Without Words*. New York: Oxford University Press.

Bermúdez, J. L. and Cahen, H. 2020. "Nonconceptual mental content." In *The Stanford Encyclopedia of Philosophy*, E. N. Zalta (ed.). https://plato.stanford.edu/archives/sum2020/entries/content-nonconceptual/

Bernstein, R. J. 2010. *The Pragmatic Turn*. Malden, MA: Polity Press.

Binswanger, L. 1957. *Freud: Reminiscences of a Friendship*, N. Guterman (trans.). New York: Grune and Stratton.

Bjork, D. W. 1983. *The Compromised Scientist: William James in the Development of American Psychology*. New York: Columbia University Press.

Bjork, D. W. 1988. *William James: The Center of His Vision*. Washington, DC: American Psychological Association.

Blackburn, S. 1998. *Ruling Passions*. Oxford: Oxford University Press.

Boeree, C. G. 2000. "Wilhelm Wundt and William James." https://webspace.ship.edu/cgboer/wundtjames.html

Boothby, R. 2001. *Freud as Philosopher: Metapsychology After Lacan*. New York: Routledge.

Borch-Jacobsen, M. 1988. *The Freudian Subject*, F. Roustang (trans.). Stanford: Stanford University Press.

Bordogna, F. 2007. "Inner division and uncertain contours: William James and the politics of the modern self." *British Journal for the History of Science* 40: 505–36.

Bordogna, F. 2008. *William James at the Boundaries: Philosophy, Science, and the Geography of Knowledge.* Chicago: University of Chicago Press.

Boring, E. G. 1950. *A History of Experimental Psychology, 2nd ed.* New York: Appleton Century-Crofts.

Bouveresse, J. 1995. *Wittgenstein Reads Freud: The Myth of the Unconscious,* C. Cosman (trans.). Princeton, NJ: Princeton University Press.

Brandom, R. B. (ed.) 2000. *Rorty and His Critics.* Malden, MA: Blackwell.

Braver, L. 2012. *Groundless Grounds: A Study of Heidegger and Wittgenstein.* Cambridge, MA: MIT Press.

Brentano, F. 1973. *Psychology from an Empiricist Point of View,* A. C. Rancurello, D. B. Terrell and L. McAlister (trans.). London: Routledge.

Breuer, J. and Freud, S. 1895. "Studies on hysteria." In *The Standard Edition of the Complete Psychological Works of Sigmund Freud, Vol. 2,* J. Strachey (ed. and trans.). London: Hogarth Press and The Institute of Psycho-Analysis, 3–305.

Breuer, J. and Freud, S. 1955 [1893]. "On the psychical mechanism of hysterical phenomena: Preliminary communication." In *The Standard Edition of the Complete Psychological Works of Sigmund Freud, Vol. 2,* J. Strachey (ed. and trans.). London: Hogarth Press and The Institute of Psycho-Analysis, 3–17.

Bromberg, P. M. 2009. "Truth, human relatedness, and the analytic process: An interpersonal/relational perspective." *International Journal of Psychoanalysis* 90: 347–61.

Brown, N. O. 1959. *Life Against Death: The Psychological Meaning of History.* Middletown, CT: Wesleyan University Press.

Bucci, W. 1997. *Psychoanalysis and Cognitive Science: A Multiple Code Theory.* New York: Guilford Press.

Buss, D. M. 2019. *Evolutionary Psychology: The New Science of the Mind, 6th ed.* New York: Routledge.

Calcaterra, R. M. 2022. "The legacy of James within Putnam's philosophy." In *The Jamesian Mind,* S. Marchetti (ed.). London: Routledge, 459–70.

Calkins, M. W. 1900. "Psychology as science of selves." *The Philosophical Review* 9: 490–501.

Calkins, M. W. 1930. "Autobiography of Mary Whiton Calkins." In *History of Psychology in Autobiography, Vol. 1,* C. Murchison (ed.). Worcester, MA: Clark University Press, 31–61. https://psychclassics.yorku.ca/Calkins/murchison.htm#f18

Campbell, J. K. 2017. *Experiencing William James: Belief in a Pluralistic World.* Charlottesville: University of Virginia Press.

Campbell, J. K., O'Rourke, M. and Slater, M. H. (eds.) 2011. *Carving Nature at Its Joints: Natural Kinds in Metaphysics and Science.* Cambridge, MA: MIT Press.

Capek, M. 1971. *Bergson and Modern Physics.* Dordrecht: Reidel.

Capps, D. (ed.) 2001. *Freud and Freudians on Religion: A Reader.* New Haven, CT: Yale University Press.

Cardinal, R. 1997. "Romantic travel." In *Rewriting the Self: Histories from the Renaissance to the Present,* R. Porter (ed.). London: Routledge, 135–55.

Carruthers, P. 2011. *The Opacity of Mind: An Integrative Theory of Self-Knowledge.* Oxford: Oxford University Press.

Cassam, Q. (ed.) 1994. *Self-Knowledge.* Oxford: Oxford University Press.

Cavell, M. 1993. *The Psychoanalytic Mind: From Freud to Philosophy.* Cambridge, MA: Harvard University Press.

Cavell, M. 2006. *Becoming a Subject: Reflections on Philosophy and Psychoanalysis.* Oxford: Clarendon Press.

Cavell, S. 1976. "The availability of Wittgenstein's later philosophy." In *Must We Mean What We Say?* Cambridge: Cambridge University Press, 44–72.

Chalmers, D. 1995. "Facing up to the problem of consciousness." *Journal of Consciousness Studies* 2: 200–19.

Chiesa, L. 2007. *Subjectivity and Otherness: A Philosophical Reading of Lacan.* Cambridge, MA: MIT Press.

Cioffi, F. 1998. *Freud and the Question of Pseudoscience.* Peru, IL: Open Court.

Civitarese, G., Katz, S. M. and Tubert-Oklander, J. (eds). 2015. "Postmodernism and psychoanalysis." *Psychoanalytic Inquiry* 35: 559–662.

Clarke, J. M. 1894. "Hysteria and neurasthenia. I: Papers on the theory of hysteria and neurasthenia." *Brain* 17: 120–45. https://doi-org.ezproxy.bu.edu/10.1093/brain/17.1.120

Colapietro, V. 2022. "James's rejection of the unconscious: A fallacious disavowal?" In *The Jamesian Mind*, S. Marchetti (ed.). London: Routledge, 109–20.

Colebrook, C. 2005. *Philosophy and Post-Structuralsit Theory: From Kant to Deleuze.* Edinburgh: Edinburgh University Press.

Coleridge, S. T. 1983 [1817]. *Biographia Literaria, Vol. 2*, J. Engell and W. J. Bate (eds.). Princeton, NJ: Princeton University Press, 25–6.

Cooper, W. 2002. *The Unity of William James's Thought.* Nashville, TN: Vanderbilt University Press.

Cormier, H. 2022. "William James's psychology of truth." In *The Jamesian Mind*, S. Marchetti (ed.). London: Routledge, 285–91.

Crews, F. 1995. *The Memory Wars: Freud's Legacy in Dispute.* New York: New York Review of Books.

Crews, F. 2017. *Freud: The Making of an Illusion.* New York: Henry Holt.

Crosby, A. W. 1997. *The Measure of Reality: Quantification and Western Society, 1250–1600.* Cambridge: Cambridge University Press.

Crosby, D. A. and Viney, W. 1992. "Toward a psychology that is radically empirical: Capturing the version of William James." In *Reinterpreting the Legacy of William James*, M. E. Donnelly (ed.). Washington, DC: American Psychological Association, 101–17.

D'Agostino, A., Mancini, M. and Monti, M. R. 2019. "Phenomenology in psychoanalysis: Still and open debate?" *Psychopathology* 52, no. 2: 104–9.

Damasio, A. 1999. *The Feeling of What Happens: Body and Emotion in the Making of Consciousness.* New York: Houghton Mifflin Harcourt.

Daston, L. and Galison, P. 2011. *Objectivity.* Brooklyn: Zone Books.

Daston, L. and Lunbeck, E. (eds.) 2011. *Histories of Scientific Observation.* Chicago: University of Chicago Press.

Davis, P. 2022. *William James: My Reading*. Oxford: Oxford University Press.

Decker, H. S. 1977. *Freud in Germany: Revolution and Reaction in Science, 1893–1907*. New York: International Universities Press.

Deigh, J. 2010. "Concepts of emotions in modern philosophy and psychology." In *The Oxford Handbook of the Emotions*, P. Goldie (ed.). Oxford: Oxford University Press, 17–40.

De Kesel, M. 2009. *Eros and Ethics: Reading Lacan's Seminar VII*, S. Jöttkandt (trans.). Albany: State University of New York Press.

Deleuze, G. 1988. *Bergsonism*, H. Tomlinson and B. Habberjam (trans.). New York: Zone Books.

Deleuze, G. and Guattari, F. 1977. *Anti-Oedipus: Capitalism and Schizophrenia*, R. Hurley, M. Seem and H. R. Lane (trans.). New York: Penguin.

De Man, P. 1993. "The Gauss seminar of 1967." In *Romanticism and Contemporary Criticism, the Gauss Seminar and Other Papers*, E. S. Burt, K. Newmark and A. Warminski (eds.). Baltimore: Johns Hopkins University Press, 3–122.

Dennett, D. 1991. *Consciousness Explained*. Boston: Little, Brown.

Dennett, D. 1996. *Darwin's Dangerous Idea: Evolution and the Meanings of Life*. New York: Simon and Schuster.

Descartes, R. 1985 [1637]. "Discourse on method." In *The Philosophical Works of Descartes, Vol. 1*, J. Cottingham, R. Stoothoff and D. Murdoch (trans.). Cambridge: Cambridge University Press.

de Sousa, R. 1997. *The Rationality of Emotion*. Cambridge, MA: MIT Press.

Dewey, J. 1931. "Philosophy and civilization." In *Philosophy and Civilization*. New York: Capricorn Books, 3–12.

Dewey, J. 1940. "The vanishing subject in the psychology of James." *Journal of Philosophy* 37: 589–99.

Dewey, J. 1980. *Art as Experience*. New York: Berkeley Publishing Group.

Dewey, J. 1984 [1929]. *The Quest for Certainty: A Study of the Relation of Knowledge and Action*. Carbondale, IL: Southern Illinois University Press.

Dewey, J. 2002 [1922]. *Human Nature and Conduct: An Introduction to Social Psychology*. Amherst, NY: Prometheus Books.

Dianda, A. 2023. *The Varieties of Experience: William James After the Linguistic Turn*. Cambridge, MA: Harvard University Press.

Diggins, J. P. 1994. *The Promise of Pragmatism: Modernism and the Crisis of Knowledge and Authority*. Chicago: University of Chicago Press.

Dijksterhuis, A. and Nordgren, L. F. 2006. "A theory of unconscious thought." *Perspectives on Psychological Science* 1: 95–109.

Dilman, I. 1984. *Freud and the Mind*. Oxford: Blackwell.

Draenos, S. 1982. *Freud's Odyssey: Psychoanalysis and the End of Metaphysics*. New Haven, CT: Yale University Press.

Dreyfus, H. L. 1992. *What Computers Still Can't Do: A Critique of Artificial Intelligence, Rev ed*. Cambridge, MA: MIT Press.

Edie, J. M. 1987. *William James and Phenomenology*. Bloomington: Indiana University Press.

Edwards, J. C. 1982. *Ethics Without Philosophy: Wittgenstein and the Moral Life*. Tampa, FL: University Press of Florida.

Edwards, J. C. 2004. "From myth to metaphysics: Freud and Wittgenstein as philosophical thinkers." In *Psychoanalysis at the Limit. Epistemology, Mind, and the Question of Science*, J. Mills (ed.). Albany, NY: State University of New York Press, 117–37.

Egginton, W. 2007. *The Philosopher's Desire: Psychoanalysis, Interpretation, and Truth*. Stanford: Stanford University Press.

Ellenberger, H. F. 1970. *The Discovery of the Unconscious: The History and Evolution of Dynamic Psychiatry*. New York: Basic Books.

Elliott, A. (ed.) 1999. *Freud 2000*. New York: Routledge.

Elliott, A. and Spezzano, C. 2019. *Psychoanalysis at Its Limits: Navigating the Postmodern Turn*. New York: Routledge.

Emerson, R. W. 1971. "Nature." In *The Collected Works of Ralph Waldo Emerson, Vol. 1, Nature, Addresses, and Lectures*. Cambridge, MA: Harvard University Press, 7–45.

Emerson, R. W. 1983. "Experience." In *The Collected Works of Ralph Waldo Emerson, Vol. 3, Essays: Second Series*. Cambridge, MA: Harvard University Press, 25–49.

Enckell, M. 1981. "Freud and Romanticism." *The Scandinavian Psychoanalytic Review* 4: 177–92.

Eriksson, J. 2010. "Freud and philosophy." *Scandinavian Psychoanalytic Review* 33: 142–48.

Eriksson, J. 2012. "Freud's metapsychology—the formal a priori of psychoanalytic experience." *Scandinavian Psychoanalytic Review* 35: 16–29.

Evans, D. A. 2017. *Understanding James, Understanding Modernism*. New York and London: Bloomsbury Academic.

Evans, G. 1982. *The Varieties of Reference*. Oxford: Oxford University Press.

Evans, R. B. and Koelsch, W. A. 1985. "Psychoanalysis arrives in America: The 1909 psychology conference at Clark University." *American Psychologist* 40: 942–8.

Everdell, W. R. 1997. *The First Moderns*. Chicago: University of Chicago Press.

Eysenck, H. J. 1985. *The Decline and Fall of the Freudian Empire*. New York: Viking.

Fairfield, S., Layton, L. and Stack, C. 2002. *Bringing the Plague: Toward a Postmodern Psychoanalysis*. New York: Other Press.

Fedorenko, E., Piantadosi, S. T. and Gibson, E. A. F. 2024. "Language is primarily a tool for communication rather than thought." *Nature* 630: 575–86. https://doi.org/10.1038/s41586-024-07522-w

Feinberg, T. E. and Mallatt, J. M. 2016. *The Ancient Origins of Consciousness: How the Brain Created Experience*. Cambridge, MA: MIT Press.

Ferrando, F. 2020. *Philosophical Posthumanism*. London: Bloomsbury Academic.

Fink, B. 1995. *The Lacanian Subject: Between Language and Jouissance*. Princeton, NJ: Princeton University Press.

Fisch, M. and Bebaji, Y. 2011. *The View from Within: Normativity and the Limits of Self-Criticism*. Notre Dame: University of Notre Dame Press.

Fiumara, G. C. 2001. *The Mind's Affective Life: A Psychoanalytical Inquiry*. Philadelphia: Taylor & Francis.

Flanagan, O. 1997. "Consciousness as a pragmatist views it." In *The Cambridge Companion to William James*, R. A. Putnam (ed.). Cambridge: Cambridge University Press, 25–48.

Flanagan, O. 2007. *The Really Hard Problem: Meaning in a Material World*. Cambridge, MA: MIT Press.

Fodor, J. A. 1980. *The Language of Thought*. Cambridge, MA: Harvard University Press.

Fodor, J. A. 1981. *Representations*. Cambridge, MA: MIT Press.

Fontinell, E. 1986. *Self, God, and Immortality: A Jamesian Investigation*. Philadelphia: Temple University Press.

Ford, M. P. 1982. *William James's Philosophy: A New Perspective*. Amherst, MA: University of Massachusetts Press.

Foucault, M. 1980. *Power/Knowledge*, C. Gordon (ed.). New York: Pantheon.

Fox Keller, E. 1994. "The paradox of scientific subjectivity." In *Re-Thinking Objectivity*, A. Megill (ed.). Durham, NC: Duke University Press, 313–31.

Fraser, S. 1995. *The Bell Curve Wars: Race, Intelligence, and the Future of America*. New York: Basic Books.

Freud, A. 1936. *Das Ich und die Abwehrmechanisme*. Vienna: Internationaler Psychoanalytischer Verlag.

Freud, A. 1966 [1937]. *The Ego and the Mechanisms of Defense*, C. Baines (trans.). New York: International Universities Press.

Freud, S. 1953 [1891]. *On Aphasia: A Critical Study*. New York: International Universities Press.

Freud, S. 1953–74 [1895]. "Project for a scientific psychology." In *The Standard Edition of the Complete Psychological Works of Sigmund Freud*, J. Strachey (ed. and trans.) in collaboration with A. Freud, assisted by A. Strachey and A. Tyson, Reprint. 1955. London: Hogarth Press and The Institute of Psycho-Analysis, 1: 295–397.

Freud, S. 1900. "Interpretation of dreams." In *The Standard Edition of the Complete Psychological Works of Sigmund Freud, Vol. 4–5*, J. Strachey (ed. and trans.). London: Hogarth Press and The Institute of Psycho-Analysis.

Freud, S. 1901. "The psychopathology of everyday life." In *The Standard Edition of the Complete Psychological Works of Sigmund Freud, Vol. 6*, J. Strachey (ed. and trans.). London: Hogarth Press and The Institute of Psycho-Analysis.

Freud, S. 1909. "Analysis of a phobia in a five-year-old boy." In *The Standard Edition of the Complete Psychological Works of Sigmund Freud, Vol. 10*, J. Strachey (ed. and trans.). London: Hogarth Press and The Institute of Psycho-Analysis, 5–149.

Freud, S. 1910. "Five lectures on psycho-analysis." In *The Standard Edition of the Complete Psychological Works of Sigmund Freud, Vol. 11*, J. Strachey (ed. and trans.). London: Hogarth Press and The Institute of Psycho-Analysis, 3–55.

Freud, S. 1912. "Recommendations to physicians practicing psycho-analysis." In *The Standard Edition of the Complete Psychological Works of Sigmund Freud, Vol. 12*, J. Strachey (ed. and trans.). London: Hogarth Press and The Institute of Psycho-Analysis, 111–20.

Freud, S. 1913a. "Totem and taboo." In *The Standard Edition of the Complete Psychological Works of Sigmund Freud, Vol. 13*, J. Strachey (ed. and trans.). London: Hogarth Press and The Institute of Psycho-Analysis, 1–161.

Freud, S. 1913b. "The claims of psycho-analysis to scientific interest." In *The Standard Edition of the Complete Psychological Works of Sigmund Freud, Vol. 13*, J. Strachey (ed. and trans.). London: Hogarth Press and The Institute of Psycho-Analysis, 165–90.

Freud, S. 1914. "The Moses of Michelangelo." In *The Standard Edition of the Complete Psychological Works of Sigmund Freud, Vol. 13*, J. Strachey (ed. and trans.). London: Hogarth Press and The Institute of Psycho-Analysis, 211–36.

Freud, S. 1915a. "Repression." In *The Standard Edition of the Complete Psychological Works of Sigmund Freud, Vol. 14*, J. Strachey (ed. and trans.). London: Hogarth Press and The Institute of Psycho-Analysis, 141–58.

Freud, S. 1915b. "The unconscious." In *The Standard Edition of the Complete Psychological Works of Sigmund Freud, Vol. 14*, J. Strachey (ed. and trans.). London: Hogarth Press and The Institute of Psycho-Analysis, 166–215.

Freud, S. 1916. "Introductory lectures on psycho-analysis." In *The Standard Edition of the Complete Psychological Works of Sigmund Freud, Vol. 15–16*, J. Strachey (ed. and trans.). London: Hogarth Press and The Institute of Psycho-Analysis.

Freud, S. 1917. "A difficulty in the path of psycho-analysis." In *The Standard Edition of the Complete Psychological Works of Sigmund Freud, Vol. 17*, J. Strachey (ed. and trans.). London: Hogarth Press and The Institute of Psycho-Analysis, 137–44.

Freud, S. 1919. "The uncanny." In *The Standard Edition of the Complete Psychological Works of Sigmund Freud, Vol. 17*, J. Strachey (ed. and trans.). London: Hogarth Press and The Institute of Psycho-Analysis, 219–52.

Freud, S. 1920. "Beyond the pleasure principle." In *The Standard Edition of the Complete Psychological Works of Sigmund Freud, Vol. 18*, J. Strachey (ed. and trans.). London: Hogarth Press and The Institute of Psycho-Analysis, 7–64.

Freud, S. 1923a. "The ego and the id." In *The Standard Edition of the Complete Psychological Works of Sigmund Freud, Vol. 19*, J. Strachey (ed. and trans.). London: Hogarth Press and The Institute of Psycho-Analysis, 12–66.

Freud, S. 1923b. "Two encyclopedia articles." In *The Standard Edition of the Complete Psychological Works of Sigmund Freud, Vol. 18*, J. Strachey (ed. and trans.). London: Hogarth Press and The Institute of Psycho-Analysis, 235–59.

Freud, S. 1925a. "An autobiographical study." In *The Standard Edition of the Complete Psychological Works of Sigmund Freud, Vol. 20*, J. Strachey (ed. and trans.). London: Hogarth Press and The Institute of Psycho-Analysis, 7–74.

Freud, S. 1925b. "Resistances to psychoanalysis." In *The Standard Edition of the Complete Psychological Works of Sigmund Freud, Vol. 19*, J. Strachey (ed. and trans.). London: Hogarth Press and The Institute of Psycho-Analysis, 213–22.

Freud, S. 1926. "Psycho-analysis." In *The Standard Edition of the Complete Psychological Works of Sigmund Freud, Vol. 20*, J. Strachey (ed. and trans.). London: Hogarth Press and The Institute of Psycho-Analysis, 263–70.

Freud, S. 1927a. "The future of an illusion." In *The Standard Edition of the Complete Psychological Works of Sigmund Freud, Vol. 21*, J. Strachey (ed. and trans.). London: Hogarth Press and The Institute of Psycho-Analysis, 5–56.

Freud, S. 1927b. "Postscript to the question of lay analysis." In *The Standard Edition of the Complete Psychological Works of Sigmund Freud, Vol. 20*, J. Strachey (ed. and trans.). London: Hogarth Press and The Institute of Psycho-Analysis, 251–8.

Freud, S. 1930. "Civilization and its discontents." In *The Standard Edition of the Complete Psychological Works of Sigmund Freud*, Vol. 17, Bilingual ed., J. Strachey (ed. and trans.). London: Hogarth Press and The Institute of Psycho-Analysis. www.freud2lacan.com/docs/Civilization_and_Its_Discontents.pdf

Freud, S. 1932. "Why war?" In *The Standard Edition of the Complete Psychological Works of Sigmund Freud, Vol. 21*, J. Strachey (ed. and trans.). London: Hogarth Press and The Institute of Psycho-Analysis, 203–15.

Freud, S. 1933. "New introductory lectures on psycho-analysis." In *The Standard Edition of the Complete Psychological Works of Sigmund Freud, Vol. 22*, J. Strachey (ed. and trans.). London: Hogarth Press and The Institute of Psycho-Analysis.

Freud, S. 1935. "An autobiographical study, postscript." In *The Standard Edition of the Complete Psychological Works of Sigmund Freud, Vol. 20*, J. Strachey (ed. and trans.). London: Hogarth Press and The Institute of Psycho-Analysis, 71–4.

Freud, S. 1937. "Constructions in analysis." In *The Standard Edition of the Complete Psychological Works of Sigmund Freud, Vol. 23*, J. Strachey (ed. and trans.). London: Hogarth Press and The Institute of Psycho-Analysis, 255–70.

Freud, S. 1939. "Moses and monotheism: Three essays." In *The Standard Edition of the Complete Psychological Works of Sigmund Freud, Vol. 23*, J. Strachey (ed. and trans.). London: Hogarth Press and The Institute of Psycho-Analysis, 7–137.

Freud, S. 1940. "An outline of psycho-analysis." In *The Standard Edition of the Complete Psychological Works of Sigmund Freud, Vol. 23*, J. Strachey (ed. and trans.). London: Hogarth Press and The Institute of Psycho-Analysis.

Freud, S. 1985. *The Complete Letters of Sigmund Freud to Wilhelm Fliess 1887–1904*, J. M. Masson (trans. and ed.). Cambridge, MA: Harvard University Press.

Freud, S. 2003. "Screen memories." In *The Uncanny*, A. Philips (ed.) and D. McLintock (trans.). London: Penguin Books.

Frie, R. 2004. "Formulating unconscious experience from Freud to Binswanger and Sullivan." In *Psychoanalysis at the Limit: Epistemology, Mind, and the Question of Science*, J. Mills (ed.). Albany: State University of New York Press, 31–45.

Friedl, H. 2018. *Thinking in Search of a Language: Essays on American Intellect and Intuition*. New York and London: Bloomsbury Academic.

Fulgencio, L. 2005. "Freud's metapsychological speculations." *International Journal of Psycho-Analysis* 86: 99–123.

Galaty, D. H. 1974. "The philosophical basis for mid-nineteenth-century German reductionism." *Journal of the History of Medicine and Allied Sciences* 29: 295–316.

Gale, R. M. 1999. *The Divided Self of William James*. Cambridge: Cambridge University Press.

Garfield, S. and Bergin, A. 1994. "Introduction and historical overview." In *Handbook of Psychotherapy and Behaviour Change*, A. Bergin and S. Garfield (eds.). Chichester: Wiley, 3–18.

Gavin, W. J. 1992. *William James and the Reinstatement of the Vague*. Philadelphia: Temple University Press.

Gay, P. 1987. *A Godless Jew: Freud, Atheism, and the Making of Psychoanalysis*. New Haven, CT: Yale University Press.

Gay, P. 1988. *Freud: A Life for Our Time*. New York: Norton.

Gay, P. 2008. *Modernism: The Lure of Heresy. From Baudelaire to Beckett and Beyond*. New York: W. W. Norton.

Gertler, B. 2011. *Self-Knowledge*. London: Routledge.

Gilman, S. L. 1991. "Reading Freud in English: Problems, paradoxes, and a solution." *International Review of Psycho-Analysis* 18: 331–44.

Gilovich, T., Griffin, D. and Kahneman, D. 2002. *Heuristics and Biases: The Psychology of Intuitive Judgment*. Cambridge: Cambridge University Press.

Goldie, P. 2000. *The Emotions: A Philosophical Exploration*. Oxford: Clarendon Press.

Goldie, P. (ed.) 2010. *The Oxford Handbook of Philosophy of Emotion*. Oxford: Oxford University Press.

Golding, J. 1988. *Cubism: A History and an Analysis 1907–1914, 3rd ed.* Cambridge, MA: Harvard University Press.

Goldsmith, J. A. and Laks, B. 2019. *Battle in the Mind Fields*. Chicago: University of Chicago Press.

Goodman, R. B. 1990. *American Philosophy and the Romantic Tradition*. Cambridge: Cambridge University Press.

Goodman, R. B. 1994. "What Wittgenstein learned from William James." *History of Philosophy Quarterly* 11: 339–54.

Goodman, R. B. 2007. *Wittgenstein and William James*. Cambridge: Cambridge University Press.

Goux, J. J. 1993. *Oedipus, Philosopher*. Stanford: Stanford University Press.

Greenberg, V. D. 1997. *Freud and His Aphasia Book: Language and the Sources of Psychoanalysis*. Ithaca, NY: Cornell University Press.

Griswold, C. L. 1986. *Self-Knowledge in Plato's Phaedrus*. New Haven, CT: Yale University Press.

Groddeck, G. 1976. *The Book of the It*. New York: International Universities Press.

Grünbaum, A. 1984. *The Foundations of Psychoanalysis: A Philosophical Critique*. Berkeley: University of California Press.

Guerlac, S. 2006. *Thinking in Time: An Introduction to Henri Bergson*. Ithaca, NY: Cornell University Press.

Gunnarsson, L. 2022. "Emotion, experience, and philosophical truth in early James." In *The Jamesian Mind*, S. Marchetti (ed.). London: Routledge, 262–73.

Guthrie, W. K. C. 1971. *Socrates*. Cambridge: Cambridge University Press.

Hadot, P. 1995. *Philosophy as a Way of Life*, A. I. Davidson (ed.) and M. Chase (trans.). Oxford: Blackwell.

Haggbloom, S. J., Warnick, R., Warnick, J. E., Jones, V. K., Yarbrough, G. L., Russell, T. M., Borecky, C. M., McGahhey, R., Powell, J. L. III, Beavers, J. and Monte, E. 2002. "The 100 most eminent psychologists of the 20th century." *Review of General Psychology* 6: 139–51.

Hale, N. G. 1971. *Freud and the Americans: The Beginnings of Psychoanalysis in the United States, 1876–1917*. Oxford: Oxford University Press.

Halliwell, M. 1999. *Romantic Science and the Experience of the Self: Transatlantic Crosscurrents from William James to Oliver Sacks*. Aldershot: Ashgate.

Hanna, R. 2006. *Rationality and Logic*. Cambridge, MA: MIT Press.

Harper, R. S. 1950. "The first psychological laboratory." *Isis* 41: 158–61.

Harris, J. C. 2010. "Clark university vicennial conference on psychology and pedagogy." *Archives of General Psychiatry* 67, no. 3: 218–19. https://doi.org/10.1001/archgenpsychiatry.2010.16

Hawkins, S. 2018. "Invisible terminology, visible translations: The new penguin Freud translations and the case against standardized terminology." *The Translator* 24: 233–48. https://doi.org/10.1080/13556509.2018.1503525

Hayles, N. K. 2017. *Unthought: The Power of the Cognitive Nonconscious*. Chicago: University of Chicago Press.

Heidegger, M. 1962. *Being and Time*, J. Macquarrie and E. Robinson (trans.). New York: Harper & Row.

Heidegger, M. 1977a [1954]. "The age of the world picture." In *The Question Concerning Technology and Other Essays*, W. Lovitt (trans.). New York: Harper Torchbooks, 115–54.

Heidegger, M. 1977b [1954]. "Science and reflection." In *The Question Concerning Technology and other Essays*, W. Lovitt (trans.). New York: Harper Torchbooks, 155–82.

Heidegger, M. 1993. "Letter on humanism." In *Martin Heidegger: Basic Writings*, D. F. Krell (ed.). New York: HarperCollins, 213–65.

Heidegger, M. 2017 [1976]. "Only a God can save us." In *Heidegger: The Man and the Thinker*, T. Sheehan (ed.) and W. Richardson (trans.). Oxfordshire: Routledge, 45–67. www.ditext.com/heidegger/interview.html

Heisenberg, W. 1958a. "The Copenhagen interpretation of quantum theory." In *Physics and Philosophy: The Revolution in Modern Science*. New York: Harper & Row, 44–58.

Heisenberg, W. 1958b. "The development of philosophical ideas since Descartes in comparison with the new situation in quantum theory." In *Physics and Philosophy: The Revolution in Modern Science*. New York: Harper & Row, 76–92. Reprinted in Tauber 1997b.

Henry, M. 1993. *The Genealogy of Psychoanalysis*, D. Brick (trans.). Stanford: Stanford University Press.

Herring, E. 2024. *Herald of a Restless World. How Henri Bergson Brought Philosophy to the People*. New York, NY: Basic Books.

Hewitt, M. A. 2014. *Freud on Religion*. London: Routledge.

Hickman, L. A. 2007. *Pragmatism as Post-Postmodernism: Lessons from John Dewey*. New York: Fordham University Press.

Hoffman, I. Z. 1998. *Ritual and Spontaneity in the Psychoanalytic Process: A Dialectical—Constructivist View*. Hillsdale, NJ: The Analytic Press.

Horkheimer, M. and Adorno, T. W. 1993 [1947]. *Dialectic of Enlightenment*. New York: Continuum.

Horwich, P. 2005. *From a Deflationary Point of View*. Oxford: Clarendon Press.

Hume, D. 1978 [1739]. *Treatise of Human Nature*, L. A. Selby-Bigge and P. H. Nidditch (eds.). Oxford: Oxford University Press.

Humphreys, P. 2019. *Emergence*. Oxford: Oxford University Press.

Hunter, J. D. and Nedelisky, P. 2018. *Science and the Good: The Tragic Quest for the Foundations of Morality*. New Haven, CT: Yale University Press.

Husserl, E. 1970 [1935]. *The Crisis of European Sciences and Transcendental Phenomenology*, D. Carr (trans.). Evanston, IL: Northwestern University Press.

Huxley, T. H. 1894. "Evolution and ethics—prolegomena." In *Evolution & Ethics and Other Essays, Vol. XI: Collected Essays*. http://aleph0.clarku.edu/huxley/CE9/E-EProl.html

Inukai, Y. 2012. "James's answer to Hume: The empirical basis of the unified self." *British Journal for the History of Science* 20: 363–89.

Israel, J. 2001. *The Radical Enlightenment*. Oxford: Oxford University Press.

Jackman, H. 2019. "William James on moral philosophy and its regulative ideals." *William James Studies* 15: 1–25.

James, W. 1920. *The Letters of William James*, H. James (ed.). Boston: Atlantic Monthly Press.

James, W. 1976 [1912]. *The Works of William James: Essays in Radical Empiricism*, F. B. Bowers and K. Skrupsekelis (eds.). Cambridge, MA: Harvard University Press.

James, W. 1978. "'Experience': From Baldwin's *Dictionary*." In *Essays in Philosophy*, F. H. Burkhardt, F. Bowers and I. K. Skrupsekelis (eds.). Cambridge, MA: Harvard University Press.

James, W. 1977 [1905]. "The notion of consciousness." In *The Writings of William James, Essays in Radical Empiricism*, J. J. McDermott (ed.). Chicago: University of Chicago Press, 184–94.

James, W. 1979. *The Works of William James: Some Problems of Philosophy*, F. H. Burkhardt, F. Bowers and I. K. Skrupskelis (eds.). Cambridge, MA: Harvard University Press.

James, W. 1983. *Principles of Psychology*. Cambridge, MA: Harvard University Press. Reprint of James, W. 1890. *Principles of Psychology, 2 Vols.* New York: Henry Holt.

James, W. 1986a. *William James: Selected Unpublished Correspondence*, F. J. D. Scott (ed.). Columbus: Ohio State University Press.

James, W. 1986b. *The Works of William James: Essays in Psychical Research*, R. A. McDermott (ed.). Cambridge, MA: Harvard University Press.

James, W. 1987a [1904]. "Does consciousness exist?" In *William James: Writings 1902–1910*, B. Kuklick (ed.). New York: Library of America, 1141–58.

James, W. 1987b [1909]. "The meaning of truth." In *William James: Writings 1902–1910*, B. Kuklick (ed.). New York: Library of America, 822–978.

James, W. 1987c [1907]. "Pragmatism: A new name for some old ways of thinking." In *William James: Writings 1902–1910*, B. Kuklick (ed.). New York: Library of America, 479–624.

James, W. 1987d [1909]. "The pluralistic universe." In *William James: Writings 1902–1910*, B. Kuklick (ed.). New York: Library of America, 627–819.

James, W. 1987e [1910]. "Some problems of philosophy." In *William James: Writings 1902–1910*, B. Kuklick (ed.). New York: Library of America, 981–1106.

James, W. 1987f [1902]. "Varieties of religious experience." In *William James: Writings 1902–1910*, B. Kuklick (ed.). New York: Library of America, 1–478.

James, W. 1987g [1905]. "The thing and its relations." In *William James: Writings 1902–1910*, B. Kuklick (ed.). New York: Library of America, 782–96.

James, W. 1987h [1905]. "The experience of activity." In *William James: Writings 1902–1910*, B. Kuklick (ed.). New York: Library of America, 797–812.

James, W. 1987i [1904]. "A world of pure experience." In *William James: Writings 1902–1910*, B. Kuklick (ed.). New York: Library of America, 1159–82.

James, W. 1992a [1895]. "The knowing of things together." In *William James, Writings 1879–1899*, G. E. Myers (ed.). New York: Library of America, 1057–76.

James, W. 1992b [1884]. "On some omissions of introspective psychology." In *William James, Writings 1879–1899*, G. E. Myers (ed.). New York: Library of America, 986–1020.

James, W. 1992c [1899]. "Stream of consciousness (chapter two, *Talks to Teachers and Students*." In *William James, Writings 1879–1899*, G. E. Myers (ed.). New York: Library of America, 722–25.

James, W. 1992d [1892]. "Psychology: The briefer course. In *William James, Writings 1879–1899*, G. E. Myers (ed.). New York: Library of America, 1–443.

James, W. 1992e [1896]. "The sentiment of rationality." In *William James, Writings 1879–1899*, G. E. Myers (ed.). New York: Library of America, 504–39.

James, W. 1992f [1879]. "The sentiment of rationality." In *William James, Writings 1879–1899*, G. E. Myers (ed.). New York: Library of America, 950–85.

James, W. 1992g [1889]. "The psychology of belief." In *William James, Writings 1879–1899*, G. E. Myers (ed.). New York: Library of America, 1021–56.

James, W. 1992h [1896]. "The will to believe." In *William James, Writings 1879–1899*, G. E. Myers (ed.). New York: Library of America, 445–704.

James, W. 1992i [1899]. "Talks to teachers on psychology; and to students on some of life's ideals." In *William James, Writings 1879–1899*, G. E. Myers (ed.). New York: Library of America, 707–880.

James, W. 1992j [1891]. "The moral philosopher and the moral life." In *William James, Writings 1879–1899*, G. E. Myers (ed.). New York: Library of America, 595–617.

James, W. 1996. *The Correspondence of William James, Vol. II, April 1905– March 1908*, I. K. Skrupskelis and E. M. Berkeley (eds.). Charlotte, VA: University of Virginia Press.

Janack, M. 2012. *What We Mean by Experience*. Stanford: Stanford University Press.

Jay, M. 2005. *Songs of Experience: Modern American and European Variations on a Universal Theme*. Berkeley: University of California Press.

Johnson-Laird, P. N. 2006. *How We Reason*. Oxford: Oxford University Press.

Jones, E. 1955. *The Life and Work of Sigmund Freud: Vol. 2. Years of Maturity. 1901–1919*. New York: Basic Books.

Jopling, D. A. 2000. *Self-Knowledge and the Self*. New York: Routledge.

Joravsky, D. 1986. *The Lysenko Affair*. Chicago: University of Chicago Press.

Joyce, R. 2005. *The Evolution of Morality*. Cambridge, MA: MIT Press.

Kaag, J. 2020. *Sick Souls, Healthy Minds: How William James Can Save Your Life*. Princeton, NJ: Princeton University Press.

Kahneman, D. and Tversky, A. (eds.) 2000. *Choices, Values, and Frames*. Cambridge: Cambridge University Press.

Kant, I. 1987 [1790]. *Critique of Judgment*, W. S. Pluhar (trans.). Indianapolis, IN: Hackett Publishing.

Kant, I. 1996 [1798]. *Anthropology from a Pragmatic Point of View*, V. L. Dowdell (trans.). Carbondale, IL: Southern Illinois University Press.

Kant, I. 1998 [1787]. *Critique of Pure Reason*, P. Guyer and A. W. Wood (eds.) and A. W. Wood (trans.). Cambridge: Cambridge University Press.

Kant, I. 2006 [1798]. *Anthropology from a Pragmatic Point of View*, R. B. Louden (ed. and trans.). Cambridge: Cambridge University Press.

Kern, S. 1983. *The Culture of Time and Space: 1880–1918*. Cambridge, MA: Harvard University Press.

Kierkegaard, S. 1941 [1846]. *Concluding Unscientific Postscript*, D. F. Swenson and W. Lowrie (trans.). Princeton, NJ: Princeton University Press.

Kierkegaard, S. 1980 [1849]. *The Sickness Unto Death*, H. V. Hong and E. H. Hong (trans.). Princeton, NJ: Princeton University Press.

Kitcher, P. 1992. *Freud's Dream: A Complete Interdisciplinary Science of the Mind*. Cambridge, MA: MIT Press.

Klein, A. 2020. "The death of consciousness? James's case against psychological unobservables." *Journal of the History of Philosophy* 58: 293–323.

Klemm, D. E. and Zoller, G. (eds.) 1997. *Figuring the Self: Subject, Absolute, and Others in Classical German Philosophy*. Albany: State University of New York Press.

Knapp, K. D. 2017. *William James: Psychical Research and the Challenge of Modernity*. Chapel Hill: University of North Carolina Press.

Kobrin, N. 1993. "Freud's concept of autonomy and Strachey's translation: A piece of the puzzle of the Freudian self." *Annual of Psychoanalysis* 21: 201–23.

Koch, S. and Leary, D. E. (eds.) 1992. *A Century of Psychology as Science*. Washington, DC: American Psychological Association.

Koelsch, W. A. 1970. "Freud discovers America." *The Virginia Quarterly Review* 46, no. 1. www.vqronline.org/articles/2015/07/freud-discovers-america

Kohut, H. 1977. *The Restoration of the Self*. New York: International Universities Press.

Kriegel, U. 2009. *Subjective Consciousness: A Self-Representational Theory*. Oxford: Oxford University Press.

Kurchuck, S. 2021. *The Relational Revolution in Psychoanalysis and Psychotherapy*. London: Karnac Books.

Kusch, M. 2005. *Psychological Knowledge: A Sociological History and Philosophy*. Oxfordshire: Routledge.

Kusch, M. 2011. "Psychologism." In *The Stanford Encyclopedia of Philosophy*, E. N. Zalta (ed.). http://plato.stanford.edu/entries/psychologism/

Lacan, J. 1991. *The Ego in Freud's Theory and in the Technique of Psychoanalysis, 1954–1955: The Seminar of Jacques Lacan Book II*, J.-A. Miller (ed.) and S. Tomaselli (trans.). New York: W. W. Norton.

Lacan, J. 2006. *Écrits: The First Complete Edition in English*, B. Fink (trans.). New York: W. W. Norton.

Lacey, A. R. 1989. *Bergson*. New York: Routledge.

Laplanche, J. and Pontalis, J. B. 1973. *The Language of Psychoanalysis*, D. Nicholson-Smith (trans.). New York, NY: W. W. Norton.

Lear, J. 1990. *Love and Its Place in Nature: A Philosophical Interpretation of Freudian Psychoanalysis*. New York: Farrar, Straus, and Giroux.

Leary, D. E. 2018. *The Routledge Guidebook to William James's Principles of Psychology*. London: Routledge.

Leary, D. E. 2022. "The psychological roots of William James's thought." In *The Jamesian Mind*, S. Marchetti (ed.). London: Routledge, 35–48.

Lenharo, M. 2024. "Do insects have an inner life? Animal consciousness needs a rethink." *Nature*. https://doi.org/10.1038/d41586-024-01144-y

Lepore, J. 2011. "Twilight." *The New Yorker*, March 6; Print March 14, 2011. www.newyorker.com/magazine/2011/03/14/twilight-jill-lepore

Levin, A. 2009. "Clark notes centenary of historic Freud visit." *Psychiatric News*. https://doi.org/10.1176/pn.44.17.0004

Levine, H. B., Reed, G. S. and Scarfone, D. (eds.) 2013. *Unrepresented States and the Construction of Meaning: Clinical and Theoretical Contributions*. London: Karnac Books.

Li, J. 2024. *The Self in the West and East Asia. Being and Becoming*. Cambridge: Polity Press.

Lindley, R. 1986. *Autonomy*. London: Palgrave Macmillan.

Linschoten, J. 1968. *On the Way Towards a Phenomenological Psychology: The Psychology of William James.* Pittsburgh: Duquesne University Press.

Lipton, P. 1991. *Inference to the Best Explanation, 2nd ed.* London: Routledge.

Loftus, E. and Ketchum, K. 1994. *The Myth of Repressed Memory: False Memories and Allegations of Sexual Abuse.* New York: St. Martin's Press.

Longuenesse, B. 2017. *I, Me, Mine: Back to Kant, and Back Again.* New York: Oxford University Press.

Lycan, W. G. and Prinz, J. J. (eds.) 2008. *Mind and Cognition: An Anthology, 3rd ed.* Malden, MA: Blackwell.

Mach, E. 1914. *Analysis of Sensations,* C. M. Williams and S. Waterlow (trans.). Chicago: University of Chicago Press.

MacIntyre, A. 1958. *The Unconscious.* London: Routledge and Kegan Paul.

MacIntyre, A. 2007. *After Virtue.* Notre Dame, IN: University of Notre Dame Press.

Macmillan, M. 1997. *Freud Evaluated: The Completed Arc.* Cambridge, MA: MIT Press.

Madden, E. H. 1963. *Chauncey Wright and the Foundations of Pragmatism.* Seattle: University of Washington Press.

Madelrieux, S. 2022. "Pragmatism as a temper: William James and the idea of philosophy." In *The Jamesian Mind,* S. Marchetti (ed.). London: Routledge, 249–61.

Magri, T. 2022. "The self in James's *Principles.*" In *The Jamesian Mind,* S. Marchetti (ed.). London: Routledge, 79–92.

Makari, G. 1994. "In the eye of the beholder: Helmholtzian perception and the origins of Freud's 1900 theory of transference." *Journal of the American Psychoanalytic Association* 42: 549–80.

Mandler, G. 2006. *A History of Modern Experimental Psychology: From James and Wundt to Cognitive Science.* Cambridge, MA: MIT Press.

Mann, T. 1947 [1936]. "Freud and the future." In *Essays of Three Decades,* H. T. Lowe-Porter (trans.). New York: Alfred A. Knopf, 411–28.

Marchetti, S. 2015. *Ethics and Philosophical Critique in William James.* London: Palgrave Macmillan.

Marcuse, H. 1955. *Eros and Civilization: A Philosophical Inquiry into Freud.* Boston: Beacon Press.

Marinoff, L. 2001. *Philosophical Practice.* San Diego: Academic Press.

Marinoff, L. 2020. *Therapy for the Sane: How Philosophy Can Change Your Life.* Cardiff, CA: Waterside Productions.

Matthews, G., Zeidner, M. and Roberts, R. D. (eds.) 2002. *Emotional Intelligence: Science and Myth.* Cambridge, MA: MIT Press.

Mauss, M. 1985. "A category of the person: Anthropology, philosophy, history, the notion of self." In *The Category of the Person: Anthropology, Philosophy, History,* M. Carrithers, S. Collins and S. Lukes (eds.). Cambridge: Cambridge University Press, 1–25.

McDermott, J. J. 1967. "Introduction: Person, process and the risk of belief." In *The Writings of William James: A Comprehensive Edition*, J. J. McDermott (ed.). New York: Random House, 7–42.

McDermott, J. J. 1976. "Introduction." In *The Works of William James: Essays in Radical Empiricism*, F. B. Bowers and K. Skrupsekelis (eds.). Cambridge, MA: Harvard University Press, xi–xlviii.

McFarland, T. 1969. *Coleridge and the Pantheist Tradition*. Oxford: Clarendon Press.

McIntosh, D. 1986. "The ego and the self in the thought of Sigmund Freud." *International Journal of Psycho-Analysis* 67: 429–48.

Megill, A. (ed.) 1994. *Rethinking Objectivity*. Durham, NC: Duke University Press.

Menand, L. 2001. *The Metaphysical Club: A Story of Ideas in America*. New York: Farrar, Straus and Giroux.

Mercier, P. 2008. *Night Train to Lisbon*, B. Harshav (trans.). New York: Grove Press.

Merkur, D. 1993. "Mythology into metapsychology: Freud's misappropriation of Romanticism." In *The Psychoanalytic Study of Society, Vol. 18*, L. B. Boyer, R. M. Boyer and S. M. Sonnenberg (eds.). Hillsdale, NJ: Analytic Press, 345–60.

Merleau-Ponty, M. 1982–1983. "Phenomenology and psychoanalysis: Preface to Hesnard's *L'Oeuvre de Freud*." *Review of Existential Psychology & Psychiatry* 18: 67–72.

Merz, J. T. 1965 [1896]. *A History of European Thought in the Nineteenth Century, Vols. 1–4*. New York: Dover.

Meyer-Palmedo, I. 2014. "Introduction." In *Correspondence 1904–1938: Sigmund Freud and Anna Freud*, I. Meyer-Palmedo (ed.) and N. Somers (trans.). Cambridge: Polity Press, 1–18.

Mills, J. 2002. *The Unconscious Abyss: Hegel's Anticipation of Psychoanalysis*. Albany: State University of New York Press.

Misak, C. 2013. *The American Pragmatists*. Oxford: Oxford University Press.

Mitchell, K. J. 2023. *Free Agents. How Evolution Gave Us Free Will*. Princeton, NJ: Princeton University Press.

Mitchell, S. A. 1993. *Hope and Dread in Psychoanalysis*. New York: Basic Books.

Moran, F. 1993. *Subject and Agency in Psychoanalysis*. New York: New York University Press.

Morris, B. 1994. *Anthropology of the Self: The Individual in Cultural Perspective*. London: Pluto Press.

Mullarkey, J. 2000. *Bergson and Philosophy*. Notre Dame, IN: Notre Dame University Press.

Myers, G. E. 1986. *William James: His Life and Thought*. New Haven, CT: Yale University Press.

Myers, G. E. 1990. "James and Freud." *The Journal of Philosophy* 87: 593–9.

Nagel, T. 1986. *View from Nowhere*. New York: Oxford University Press.

Natsoulas, T. 1984. "Freud and consciousness. I: Intrinsic consciousness." *Psychoanalysis and Contemporary Thought* 7: 195–232.

Natsoulas, T. 1985. "Freud and consciousness. II: Derived consciousness." *Psychoanalysis and Contemporary Thought* 8: 183–220.

Needleman, J. 1967. "Introduction." In *Being-in-the-World: Selected Papers of Ludwig Binswanger*, J. Needleman (trans.). New York: Harper Torchbooks, 1–144.

Neill, C. 2011. *Lacanian Ethics and the Assumption of Subjectivity*. Houndmills: Palgrave Macmillan.

Neiman, S. 1994. *The Unity of Reason: Rereading Kant*. New York: Oxford University Press.

Newell, A., Shaw, J. C. and Simon, H. 1958. "Elements of a human problem solving." *Psychological Review* 65: 151–66.

Nicholson, D. J. and Dupré, J. (eds.) 2018. *Everything Flows: Towards a Processual Philosophy of Biology*. Oxford: Oxford University Press.

Nietzsche, F. 1982. *Daybreak*, R. J. Hollingdale (trans.). Cambridge: Cambridge University Press.

Nietzsche, F. 2002. *Beyond Good and Evil*, J. Norman (trans.). Cambridge: Cambridge University Press.

Nietzsche, F. 2005. *The Anti-Christ, Ecce Homo, Twilight of the Idols*, A. Ridley (ed.) and J. Norman (trans.). Cambridge: Cambridge University Press.

Nietzsche, F. 2006. *Thus Spoke Zarathustra: A Book for All and None*, A. Del Cro and R. B. Pippin (eds.) and A. Del Caro (trans.). Cambridge: Cambridge University Press.

Nisbett, R. E. 2003. *The Geography of Thought: How Asians and Westerners Think Differently*. New York: Free Press.

Nissim-Sabat, M. 1986. "Psychoanalysis and phenomenology: A new synthesis." *Psychoanalytic Review* 73: 273–99.

Nussbaum, M. C. 2001. *Upheavals of Thought: The Intelligence of Emotions*. Cambridge: Cambridge University Press.

O'Connell-Domenech, A. 2023. "Why more Americans are going to therapy." *The Hill*. https://thehill.com/policy/healthcare/3975996-why-more-americans-are-going-to-therapy/

Ogden, T. H. 1992. "The dialectically constituted/decentered subject of psychoanalysis. 1: The Freudian subject." *International Journal of Psychoanalysis* 73: 517–26.

Pawelski, J. O. 2007. *The Dynamic Individualism of William James*. Albany: State University of New York Press.

Peirce, C. S. 1992. "Evolutionary love." In *The Essential Peirce, Selected Philosophical Writings, Vol. 1 (1867–1893)*, N. Houser and C. Kloesel (eds.). Bloomington, IN: Indiana University Press, 352–71.

Perlow, M. 1995. *Understanding Mental Objects*. London: Routledge.

Perry, R. B. 1935. *The Thought and Character of William James*. Boston: Little Brown and Co.

Peterman, J. F. 1992. *Philosophy as Therapy: An Interpretation and Defense of Wittgenstein's Later Philosophical Project*. Albany: State University of New York Press.

Pinkard, T. 2002. *German Philosophy 1760–1860: The Legacy of Idealism*. Cambridge: Cambridge University Press.

Poggi, C. 1992. "Braque's early Papiers Collés: The certainties of Faux Bois." In *Picasso and Braque: A Symposium*, L. Zelevansky (ed.). New York: Museum of Modern Art, 129–49.

Polanyi, M. 1962. *Personal Knowledge: Towards a Post-critical Philosophy, Corrected ed.* Chicago: University of Chicago Press.

Poovey, M. 1998. *A History of the Modern Fact: Problems of Knowledge in the Sciences of Wealth and Society, 2nd ed.* Chicago, IL: University of Chicago Press.

Posnock, R. 1991. *The Trial of Curiosity: Henry James, William James, and the Challenge of Modernity*. Oxford: Oxford University Press.

Posnock, R. 1997. "The influence of William James on American culture." In *The Cambridge Companion to William James*, R. A. Putnam (ed.). Cambridge: Cambridge University Press, 322–42.

Prinz, J. J. 2007. *The Emotional Construction of Morals*. Oxford: Oxford University Press.

Prinz, W. 2012. *Open Minds: The Social Making of Agency and Intentionality.* Cambridge, MA: MIT Press.

Prochaska, J. O. and Norcross, J. C. 2024. *Systems of Psychotherapy: A Transtheoretical Analysis, 10th ed.* Oxford: Oxford University Press.

Prochnik, G. 2006. *Putnam Camp: Sigmund Freud, James Jackson Putnam and the Purpose of American Psychology*. New York: Other Press.

Proctor, R. N. 1988. *Racial Hygiene: Medicine Under the Nazis*. Cambridge, MA: Harvard University Press.

Proctor, R. N. 1991. *Value-Free Science? Purity and Power in Modern Knowledge.* Cambridge, MA: Harvard University Press.

Putnam, H. 1981. *Reason, Truth, and History*. Cambridge: Cambridge University Press.

Putnam, H. 1982. "Beyond the fact/value dichotomy." *Critica* 14: 3–12. Reprinted in *Realism with a Human Face*, J. Conant (ed.). Cambridge: Harvard University Press, 1990, 135–41.

Putnam, H. 1988. *Representation and Reality*. Cambridge, MA: MIT Press.

Putnam, H. 1990a. "William James's ideas." In *Realism with a Human Face*, J. Conant (ed.). Cambridge, MA: Harvard University Press, 217–31.

Putnam, H. 1990b. "James's theory of perception." In *Realism with a Human Face*, J. Conant (ed.). Cambridge, MA: Harvard University Press, 232–51.

Putnam, H. 1990c. "Realism with a human face." In *Realism with a Human Face*, J. Conant (ed.). Cambridge, MA: Harvard University Press, 3–29.

Putnam, H. 1994. "Sense, nonsense, and the senses: An inquiry into the powers of the human mind." *The Journal of Philosophy* 91: 445–517.

Putnam, H. 1997. "James's theory of truth." In *The Cambridge Companion to William James*, R. A. Putnam (ed.). Cambridge: Cambridge University Press, 166–85.

Putnam, H. 2002. *The Collapse of the Fact/Value Dichotomy and Other Essays*. Cambridge, MA: Harvard University Press.

Putnam, H. 2004. *Ethics Without Ontology*. Cambridge, MA: Harvard University Press.

Putnam, H. 2005. "James on Truth (Again)." In *William James and the Varieties of Religious Experience: A Centenary Celebration*, J. R. Carrette (ed.). London: Routledge, 172–82.

Putnam, H. 2012. "On not writing off scientific realism." In *Philosophy in an Age of Science: Physics, Mathematics, and Skepticism*, M. De Caro and D. Macarthur (eds.). Cambridge, MA: Harvard University Press, 91–108.

Putnam, H. 2015. "Intellectual autobiography." In *The Philosophy of Hilary Putnam*, R. E. Auxier, D. R. Anderson and L. E. Hahn (eds.). Chicago: Open Court, 3–110.

Putnam, H. 2017. "Rorty's vision: Philosophical courage and social hope." In *Pragmatism as a Way of Life: The Lasting Legacy of William James and John Dewey*, D. Macarthur (ed.). Cambridge, MA: Harvard University Press, 87–107. (Originally published, "Democracy without foundations." *Ethics* 110: 388–404.

Putnam, H. and Putnam, R. A. 1996. "What the spilled beans can spell: The difficult and deep realism of William James." *Times Literary Supplement* 14–15, June 21.

Putnam, H. and Putnam, R. A. 2017. *Pragmatism as a Way of Life: The Lasting Legacy of William James and John Dewey*, D. Macarthur (ed.). Cambridge, MA: Harvard University Press.

Putnam, R. A. 2017. "The moral impulse." In *Pragmatism as a Way of Life: The Lasting Legacy of William James and John Dewey*, D. Macarthur (ed.). Cambridge, MA: Harvard University Press, 349–59.

Ramsey, W. M. 2007. *Representation Reconsidered*. Cambridge: Cambridge University Press.

Reber, A. S. and Allen, R. (eds.) 2022. *The Cognitive Unconscious: The First Half Century*. Oxford: Oxford University Press.

Reé, J. 2019. *Witcraft: The Invention of Philosophy in English*. New Haven, CT: Yale University Press.

Reed, E. S. 1997. *From Soul to Mind: The Emergence of Psychology from Erasmus Darwin to William James*. New Haven, CT: Yale University Press.

Reeder, J. 2002. *Reflecting Psychoanalysis: Narrative and Resolve in the Psychoanalytic Experience*. London: Karnac Books.

Reeder, J. 2008. "The enigmatic 'nature of the subject': With philosophy at the interface of psychoanalysis and society." *Scandinavian Psychoanalytic Review* 31: 114–21.

Reeder, J. 2012. "The empty core: Metapsychological reflections upon the lost object, an ethical order, and the inevitable void at the center of our existence." *Scandinavian Psychoanalytic Review* 35: 35–44.

Reiss, T. J. 2002. *Against Autonomy. Global Dialectics of Cultural Exchange*. Stanford: Stanford University Press.

Richardson, R. D. 2006. *William James: In the Maelstrom of American Modernism*. Boston: Houghton Mifflin.

Ricoeur, P. 1970. *Freud and Philosophy: An Essay on Interpretation*. New Haven, CT: Yale University Press.

Rieff, P. 1959. *Freud: The Mind of the Moralist*. New York: Viking Press.

Rochefort, P.-Y. 2021. "Did Putnam really abandon internal realism in the 1990s?" *European Journal of Pragmatism and American Philosophy* XIII, no. 1. https://doi.org/10.4000/ejpap.2515

Rogozinski, J. 2010. *The Ego and the Flesh: An Introduction to Egoanalysis*, R. Vallier (trans.). Stanford: Stanford University Press.

Roland, A. 1988. *In Search of Self in India and Japan: Toward a Cross-Cultural Psychology.* Princeton, NJ: Princeton University Press.

Rorty, R. 1979. *Philosophy and the Mirror of Nature.* Princeton, NJ: Princeton University Press.

Rorty, R. 1980. "Pragmatism, relativism, and irrationalism." *Proceeds and Address of the American Philosophical Association* 50: 719–38.

Rorty, R. 1982. *Consequences of Pragmatism (Essays: 1972–1980).* Minneapolis: University of Minnesota Press.

Rorty, R. 1989. "The contingency of language." In *Contingency, Irony, and Solidarity.* Cambridge: Cambridge University Press, 3–22.

Rorty, R. 1991. "Solidarity or objectivity." In *Objectivity, Relativism, and Truth.* Cambridge: Cambridge University Press, 21–34.

Rorty, R. 1998. *Philosophical Papers, Vol. 3: Truth and Progress.* Cambridge: Cambridge University Press.

Rorty, R. 1999. "Religious faith, responsibility, and romance." In *Philosophy and Social Hope.* New York: Penguin Press, 148–67.

Rorty, R. 2002. "Worlds or words apart? The consequences of pragmatism for literary studies: An interview with Richard Rorty." *Philosophy and Literature* 26: 369–96.

Rorty, R. 2007. "Pragmatism and Romanticism." In *Philosophy as Cultural Politics: Philosophical Papers, Vol. 4.* Cambridge: Cambridge University Press, 105–19.

Rosenzweig, S. 1994. *The Historic Expedition to America (1909): Freud, Jung, and Hall the Kingmaker.* St. Louis, MO: Rana House.

Rothenberg, M. A. 2010. *The Excessive Subject: A New Theory of Social Change.* Cambridge: Polity Press.

Rovane, C. 2022. "James on personal identity." In *The Jamesian Mind*, S. Marchetti (ed.). London: Routledge, 93–108.

Rubovits-Seitz, P. F. D. 1998. *Depth-Psychological Understanding: The Methodologic Grounding of Clinical Interpretations.* London: Routledge.

Rubovits-Seitz, P. F. D. 2001. *The Interpretive Process in Clinical Practice: Progressive Communication of Latent Meanings.* Lanham, MD: Jason Aronson.

Rudnytsky, P. L. 1987. *Freud and Oedipus.* New York: Columbia University Press.

Ryan, F., Butler, B. E. and Good, J. A. 2019. *The Real Metaphysical Club: The Philosophers and Debates and Selected Writings from 1870 to 1885.* Albany: State University of New York Press.

Ryan, J. 1991. *The Vanishing Subject: Early Psychology and Literary Modernism.* Chicago: University of Chicago Press.

Sacks, O. 2000. "The other road: Freud as neurologist." In *Freud, Conflict and Culture: Essays on His Life, Work, and Legacy*, M. S. Roth (ed.). New York: Viking, 221–34.

Sandler, J., Holder, A., Dare, C. and Dreher, A. U. 1997. *Freud's Models of the Mind: An Introduction*. London: Karnac Books.

Sartre, J.-P. 1957. *The Transcendence of the Ego: An Existentialist Theory of Consciousness*, F. Williams and R. Kirkpatrick (trans.). New York: Hill and Wang.

Schacht, R. 1970. *Alienation*. Garden City, NY: Doubleday and Co.

Schmidgen, H. 2014. *The Helmholtz Curves: Tracing Lost Time*, N. F. Schott (trans). New York: Fordham University Press.

Schneider, K. J. and Krug, O. T. (eds.) 2017. *Existential-Humanistic Therapy, 2nd ed*. Washington, DC: American Psychological Association.

Schroeder, M. 2008. *Slaves of the Passions*. Oxford: Oxford University Press.

Schulenberg, U. 2015. *Romanticism and Pragmatism: Richard Rorty and the Idea of a Poeticized Culture*. Basingstoke: Palgrave Macmillan.

Schulenberg, U. 2022. "William James, Romanticism, and the 'humanistic principle'." In *The Jamesian Mind*, S. Marchetti (ed.). London: Routledge, 365–74.

Scott, W. T. and Moleski, M. X. 2005. *Michael Polanyi: Scientist and Philosopher*. Oxford: Oxford University Press.

Scott-Bauman, A. 2009. *Ricoeur and the Hermeneutics of Suspicion*. London: Continuum.

Searle, J. 1992. *The Rediscovery of the Mind*. Cambridge, MA: MIT Press.

Segerstrale, U. 2000. *Defenders of the Truth: The Sociobiology Debate*. New York: Oxford University Press.

Seigel, J. 2005. *The Idea of the Self: Thought and Experience in Western Europe Since the Seventeenth Century*. Cambridge: Cambridge University Press.

Seigfried, C. H. 1984. "Extending the Darwinian model." *Idealistic Studies* 14, no. 3: 259–72. https://doi.org/10.5840/idstudies198414331

Seigfried, C. H. 1990. *William James's Radical Reconstruction of Philosophy*. Albany: State University of New York Press.

Sellars, W. 1997. *Empiricism and the Philosophy of Mind*. Cambridge, MA: Harvard University Press.

Shakow, D. and Rapaport, D. 1964. "The influence of Freud on American psychology." In *Psychological Issues, Vol. iv*, Monograph 13. New York: International Universities Press.

Shanon, B. 1993. *The Representational and the Presentational: An Essay on Cognition and the Study of Mind*. London: Harvester Wheatsheaf.

Shaw, J. 2017. *The Memory Illusion: Remembering, Forgetting, and the Science of False Memory*. New York: Random House.

Sherratt, Y. 2002. *Adorno's Positive Dialectic*. Cambridge: Cambridge University Press.

Shoemaker, S. 1984. "Personal identity: A materialist account." In *Personal Identity*, S. Shoemaker and R. Swinburne (eds.). Oxford: Basil Blackwell, 67–132.

Sinatora, F. and Mezzalira, S. 2021. "Freud's concept of 'trieb': A psychoanalytic account of its antinomic nature." *International Journal of Psychoanalysis and Education: Subject, Action, and Society (SAS)* 1: 54–69. https://doi.org/10.32111/SAS.2021.1.2.3

Sinclair, S. 2009. "William James as American Plato?" *William James Studies* 4: 111–29.

Sio, U. N. and Ormerod, T. C. 2009. "Does incubation enhance problem solving? A meta-analytic review." *Psychological Bulletin* 135: 94–120.

Skrupskelis, I. K. 1988. "Introduction." In *The Works of William James: Manuscript Essays and Notes*, F. H. Burkhardt, F. B. Bowers and K. Skrupsekelis (eds.). Cambridge, MA: Harvard University Press, xiii–xlviii.

Smith, D. L. 1999. *Freud's Philosophy of the Unconscious*. Dordrecht, The Netherlands: Kluwer Academic Publishers.

Smith, D. L. 2004. "Freud and Searle on the ontology of the unconscious." In *Psychoanalysis at the Limit: Epistemology, Mind, and the Question of Science*, J. Mills (ed.). Albany: State University of New York Press, 73–90.

Smith, J. E. 1970. *Themes in American Philosophy*. New York: Harper & Row.

Smith, R. 1997a. *The Norton History of the Human Sciences*. New York: W. W. Norton.

Smith, R. 1997b. "Self-reflection and the self." In *Rewriting the Self: Histories from the Renaissance to the Present*, R. Porter (ed.). London: Routledge, 49–57.

Smithies, D. and Stoljar, D. (eds.) 2012. *Introspection and Consciousness*. Oxford: Oxford University Press.

Smocovitis, V. B. 1996. *Unifying Biology: The Evolutionary Synthesis and Evolutionary Biology*. Princeton, NJ: Princeton University Press.

Solomon, R. C. 1993. *The Passions: Emotions and the Meaning of Life*. Indianapolis: Hackett.

Solomon, R. C. 2004. *Thinking About Feeling: Contemporary Philosophers on Emotions*. New York: Oxford University Press.

Solomon, R. C. 2007. *True to Our Feelings: What Our Emotions Are Really Telling Us*. Oxford: Oxford University Press.

Sprigge, T. L. S. 1993. *James & Bradley: American Truth and British Reality*. Chicago: Open Coiourt.

Starobinski, J. 1988. *Jean-Jacques Rousseau: Transparency and Obstruction*, A. Goldhammer (trans.). Chicago: University of Chicago Press.

Stern, D. B. 1983. "Unformulated experience: From familiar chaos to creative disorder." *Contemporary Psychoanalysis* 19: 71–99.

Stern, D. B. 1990. "Courting surprise: Unbidden perceptions in clinical practice." *Contemporary Psychoanalysis* 26: 452–78.

Stern, D. B. 1992. "Commentary on constructivism in clinical psychoanalysis." *Psychoanalytic Dialogues* 2: 331–63.

Stern, D. B. 1997. *Unformulated Experience: From Dissociation to Imagination in Psychoanalysis*. New York: Routledge.

Stern, D. B. 2010. *Partners in Thought: Working with Unformulated Experience, Dissociation, and Enactment.* London: Routledge.

Stern, D. B. 2015. *Relational Freedom: Emergent Properties of the Interpersonal Field.* New York: Routledge.

Stern, D. B. 2019. *The Infinity of the Unsaid: Unformulated Experience, Language, and the Nonverbal.* New York Routledge.

Stern, D. N. 1985. *The Interpersonal World of the Infant: A View from Psychoanalysis and Developmental Psychology.* New York: Basic Books.

Stern, D. N., Sander, L. W., Nahum, J. P., Harrison, A. M., Lyons-Ruth, K., Morgan, A. C., Bruschweilerstern, N. and Tronick, E. Z. 1998. "Non-interpretive mechanisms in psychoanalytic therapy: The 'something more' than interpretation." *International Journal of Psycho-Analysis* 79: 903–21.

Stern, W. 1914. *Psychologie der frühen Kindheit bis zum sechsten Lebensjahr* (*The Psychology of Early Childhood Up to the Sixth Year of Age*). Leipzig: Quelle & Meyer.

Still, A. 1991. "Mechanism and Romanticism: A selective history." In *Against Cognitivism: Alternative Foundations for Cognitive Psychology*, A. Still and A. Costall (eds.). New York: Harvester Wheatsheaf, 7–26.

Still, A. and Costall, A. (eds.) 1991. *Against Cognitivism: Alternative Foundations for Cognitive Psychology.* New York: Harvester Wheatsheaf.

Stone, A. A. 1983. "A brief note on Kant and free association." *International Review of Psycho-Analysis* 10: 445.

Sulloway, F. J. 1979. *Freud, Biologist of the Mind.* New York: Basic Books.

Sutton, E. K. 2023. *William James, MD: Philosopher, Psychologist.* Chicago: University of Chicago Press.

Tappolet, C. 2016. *Emotions, Values, and Agency.* Oxford: Oxford University Press.

Tappolet, C. 2022. *Philosophy of Emotion: A Contemporary Introduction.* London: Routledge.

Tauber, A. I. 1993. "Goethe's philosophy of science: Modern resonances." *Perspectives in Biology and Medicine* 36: 244–57.

Tauber, A. I. 1994. *The Immune Self: Theory or Metaphor?* Cambridge: Cambridge University Press.

Tauber, A. I. (ed.) 1996. *The Elusive Synthesis: Aesthetics and Science.* Dordrecht: Kluwer Academic Publishers.

Tauber, A. I. 2001. *Henry David Thoreau and the Moral Agency of Knowing.* Berkeley and Los Angeles: University of California Press.

Tauber, A. I. 2005. *Patient Autonomy and the Ethics of Responsibility.* Cambridge, MA: MIT Press.

Tauber, A. I. 2006. "The reflexive project: Reconstructing the moral agent." *History of the Human Sciences* 18: 49–75.

Tauber, A. I. 2009a. *Science and the Quest for Meaning.* Waco, TX: Baylor University Press.

Tauber, A. I. 2009b. "Freud's dreams of reason: The Kantian structure of psychoanalysis." *History of the Human Sciences* 22: 1–29.

Tauber, A. I. 2009c. "Freud's philosophical path: From a science of the mind to a philosophy of human being." *The Scandinavian Psychoanalytic Review* 32: 32–43.

Tauber, A. I. 2010. *Freud, the Reluctant Philosopher*. Princeton, NJ: Princeton University Press.

Tauber, A. I. 2012a. "Thoreau's moral-epistemology and its contemporary relevance." In *Thoreau's Importance for Philosophy*, R. A. Furtak, J. Ellsworth and J. D. Reid (eds.). New York: Fordham University Press, 127–42.

Tauber, A. I. 2012b. "Freud's social theory: Modernist and postmodernist revisions." *History of the Human Sciences* 25: 41–70.

Tauber, A. I. 2013a. *Requiem for the Ego: Freud and the Origins of Postmodernism*. Stanford: Stanford University Press.

Tauber, A. I. 2013b. "Freud without Oedipus: The cognitive unconscious." *Philosophy, Psychiatry, & Psychology* 20: 231–41.

Tauber, A. I. 2014. "The rational unconscious: The Freudian mind reconsidered." *Philosophy, Psychiatry, & Psychology* 20: 255–9.

Tauber, A. I. 2015. "The other within: Freud's representation of the mind." In *Psychology and the Other*, D. Goodman and M. Freeman (eds.). Oxford: Oxford University Press, 71–93.

Tauber, A. I. 2017. *Immunity, the Evolution of an Idea*. New York: Oxford University Press.

Tauber, A. I. 2022. *The Triumph of Uncertainty: Science and Self in the Postmodern Age*. Vienna: Central European University Press. https://ceupress.com/sites/ceupress.ceu.edu/files/9789633865828.pdf

Tauber, A. I. 2023. "The psychoanalytic *das Ich*: Lost in translation." In *The Routledge Handbook of Psychoanalysis and Philosophy*, A. Govrin and T. Caspi (eds.). New York, NY and Abingdon, Oxon: Routledge, 359–73.

Tauber, A. I. 2025. "Freud and the problem of moral agency." In *Sigmund Freud as a Critical Social Theorist: Psychoanalysis and the Neurotic in Contemporary Society*, D. J. Byrd and S. J. Miri (eds.). Chicago, IL: Haymarket, 321–49.

Taylor, C. 1976. "Responsibility for self." In *The Identities of Persons*, A. O. Rorty (ed.). Berkeley: University of California Press, 281–99.

Taylor, C. 1989. *Sources of the Self*. Cambridge, MA: Harvard University Press.

Taylor, C. 2016. *The Language Animal: The Full Shape of the Human Linguistic Capacity*. Cambridge, MA: Harvard University Press.

Taylor, E. 1983. *William James on Exceptional Mental States: The 1896 Lowell Lectures*. New York: Scribner.

Taylor, E. 1996. *William James on Consciousness Beyond the Margin*. Princeton, NJ: Princeton University Press.

Taylor, E. 1999. "William James and Sigmund Freud: 'The future of psychology belongs to your work'." *Psychological Science* 10: 465–9.

Taylor, E. and Wozniak, R. 1996a. "Introduction." In *Pure Experience: The Response to William James*, E. Taylor and R. Wozniak (eds.). Bristol: Thommes, ix–xxxii. https://psychclassics.yorku.ca/James/TaylorWoz.htm

Taylor, E. and Wozniak, R. (eds.) 1996b. *Pure Experience: The Response to William James*. Bristol: Thommes.

Taylor, M. C. 1980. *Journeys to Selfhood: Hegel and Kierkegaard*. Berkeley: University of California Press.

Thiel, U. 2011. *The Early Modern Subject: Self-Consciousness and Personal Identity from Descartes to Hume*. Oxford: Oxford University Press.

Thoreau, H. D. 1962 [1906]. *The Journal of Henry David Thoreau*, B. Torrey and F. H. Allen (eds.). New York: Dover Books.

Toulmin, S. 2001. *Return to Reason*. Cambridge, MA: Harvard University Press.

Toulmin, S. and Leary, D. E. 1992. "The cult of empiricism in psychology, and beyond." In *A Century of Psychology as Science*, S. Koch and D. E. Leary (eds.). Washington, DC: American Psychological Association, 594–617.

Touraine, A. 1995. *Critique of Modernity*, D. Macey (trans.). Oxford: Blackwell.

Trilling, L. 1965. *Beyond Culture: Essays on Literature and Culture*. New York: Viking.

Tugendhat, E. 1986. *Self-Consciousness and Self-Determination*, P. Stern (trans.). Cambridge, MA: MIT Press.

Turkle, S. 1985. *The Second Self: Computers and the Human Spirit*. New York: Simon and Schuster.

Van Leer, D. 1986. *Emerson's Epistemology: The Argument of the Essays*. Cambridge: Cambridge University Press.

Varga, S. and Guignon, C. 2017. "Authenticity." In *The Stanford Encyclopedia of Philosophy, Fall ed.*, E. N. Zalta (ed.). https://plato.stanford.edu/archives/fall2017/entries/authenticity

Vermorel, M. and Vermorel, H. 1986. "Was Freud a romantic?" *International Review of Psycho-Analysis* 13: 15–37.

Vygotsky, L. 1986 [1934]. *Thought and Language, Revised ed.*, A. Kozulin (ed. and trans.). Cambridge, MA: MIT Press.

Weber, E. T. 2012. "James's critiques of the Freudian unconscious—the Freudian unconscious." *William James Studies* 9: 94–119.

Weber, M. 1946 [1919]. "Science as a vocation." In *From Max Weber: Essays in Sociology*, H. H. Gerth and C. W. Mills (eds. and trans.). New York: Oxford University Press, 137–56.

Webster, R. 1995. *Why Freud Was Wrong: Sin, Science, and Psychoanalysis*. New York: Basic Books.

Weinberger, J. 2000. "William James and the unconscious: Redressing a century-old misunderstanding." *Psychological Science* 11: 439–45.

Weiner, P. 1949. *Evolution and the Founders of Pragmatism*. Cambridge, MA: Harvard University Press.

Wheeler, K. M. 1993. *Romanticism, Pragmatism, and Deconstruction*. Oxford: Blackwell.

Whewell, W. 1840. *Philosophy of the Inductive Sciences*. London: J. W. Parker.

Whitebook, J. 1995. *Perversion and Utopia: A Study in Psychoanalysis and Critical Theory*. Cambridge, MA: MIT Press.

Whitehead, A. N. 1925. *Science and the Modern World*. New York, NY: Macmillan.

Whitehead, A. N. 1929. *Process and Reality*. New York, NY: Macmillan.

Whitehead, A. N. 1968 [1938]. *Modes of Thought*. New York: Free Press.

Whyte, L. L. 1978. *The Unconscious Before Freud*. London: Julian Friedman Publishers.

Wilkinson, S. T. 2024. *Purpose: What Evolution and Human Nature Imply About the Meaning of Our Existence*. Cambridge: Pegasus Books.

Wilshire, B. 1979. *William James and Phenomenology: A Study of "The Principles of Psychology"*. New York: AMS Press.

Wilshire, B. 1997. "The breathtaking intimacy of the material world: William James's last thoughts." In *The Cambridge Companion to William James*, R. A. Putnam (ed.). Cambridge: Cambridge University Press, 103–24.

Wilson, E. 1987. "Did Strachey invent Freud?" *International Review of Psycho-Analysis* 14: 299–315.

Wilson, E. O. 1998. *Consilience: The Unity of Knowledge*. New York: Knopf.

Wilson, T. D. 2002. *Strangers to Ourselves: Discovering the Adaptive Unconscious*. Cambridge, MA: Harvard University Press.

Wittgenstein, L. 1960. *The Blue and Brown Books: Preliminary Studies for the "Philosophical Investigations"*. New York: Harper & Row.

Wittgenstein, L. 1968. *Philosophical Investigations, 3rd ed.*, G. E. M. Anscombe (trans.). New York: Palgrave Macmillan.

Wittgenstein, L. 1979. *Notebooks 1914–1916, 2nd ed.*, G. H. von Wright and G. E. M. Anscombe (eds.) and G. E. M. Anscombe (trans.). Chicago: University of Chicago Press.

Wittgenstein, L. 1974 [1922]. *Tractatus Logico-Philosophicus*, D. F. Pears and B. F. McGuinness (trans.). New York: Routledge.

Wolfe, C. 2010. *What Is Posthumanism?* Minneapolis: University of Minnesota Press.

Woodward, W. R. 1983. "Introduction." In *The Works of William James: Essays in Psychology*, F. H. Burkhardt, F. Bowers and I. K. Skrupskelis (eds.). Cambridge, MA: Harvard University Press, xi–xxxiv.

Yeung, A. W. K. 2021. "Is the influence of Freud declining in psychology and psychiatry? A bibliometric analysis." *Frontiers in Psychology*. https://doi.org/10.3389/fpsyg.2021.631516

Zammito, J. H. 2004. *A Nice Derangement of Epistemes: Post-Positivism in the Study of Science from Quine to Latour*. Chicago: University of Chicago Press.

Zaner, R. M. 1975. "Context and reflexivity: The genealogy of self." In *Evaluation and Explanation in the Biomedical Sciences*, H. T. Engelhardt, Jr. and S. F. Spicker (eds.). Dordrecht: Reidel, 153–74.

Zarbo, C., Tasca, G. A., Cattafi, F. and Compare, A. 2015. "Integrative psychotherapy works." *Frontiers in Psychology*. https://doi.org/10.3389/fpsyg.2015.02021

Index